The Stranger's Welcome

MICHIGAN MONOGRAPHS IN CLASSICAL ANTIQUITY

The Stranger's Welcome

Oral Theory and the Aesthetics of the Homeric Hospitality Scene

STEVE REECE

Ann Arbor

THE UNIVERSITY OF MICHIGAN PRESS

A CIP catalogue record for this book is available from the British Library.

Library of Congress Cataloging-in-Publication Data

Reece, Steve, 1959–
    The stranger's welcome : oral theory and the aesthetics of the
Homeric hospitality scene / Steve Reece.
        p.   cm. — (Michigan monographs in classical antiquity)
    Includes bibliographical references and index.
    ISBN 0-472-10386-5 (alk. paper)
    1. Homer—Criticism and interpretation. 2. Epic poetry, Greek—
History and criticism. 3. Hospitality in literature. 4. Outsiders
in literature. 5. Oral-formulaic analysis. 6. Oral tradition—
Greece. 7. Aesthetics, Ancient.   I. Title.   II. Series.
PA4037.R375   1993
883'.01—dc20   92-32698
                                                                   CIP

74420

Acknowledgments

The modern teacher, like the ancient Homeric bard, is, even in this highly literate age, a receptacle and guardian of a rich oral tradition. And like the ancient bard, the modern teacher passes this tradition on to the next generation, and it in turn to the next. I have been particularly fortunate in having a succession of teachers who generously and skillfully passed this tradition on to me, and to them I dedicate this work. To Walter Defner, Frank Austel, Ann Wigglesworth, Howard Blair, Allen Mawhinney, Gordon Clark, Robert Ball, Dennis Ellsworth, Robert Littman, Alfred Burns, Paul Roth, Mortimer Chambers, Ingred Rowland, Peter Colaclidès, Andrew Szegedy-Maszak, Steven Lattimore, Philip Levine, Cynthia Shelmerdine, Oliver Taplin, David Blank, Martin West, Walter Burkert, Sander Goldberg, Jaan Puhvel, Michael Haslam, Ann Bergren, and Richard Janko.

I wish to acknowledge a special debt to John Lenz, Delores Lunceford, Donald Ward, Joseph Nagy, Jaan Puhvel, Ann Bergren, John Foley, Mark Edwards, and Richard Janko, whose careful and informed reading of my manuscript during various stages of its evolution did much to improve the final product.

Contents

Introduction

This is a book about the rituals of hospitality (ξενία, *xenia*) in Homer. But it is only secondarily so; it could just as well be about sacrifice, assembly, arming, or any of a number of frequently recurring actions in Homer. This book is primarily about how oral poetry works; it is an attempt to define the aesthetics of oral poetry on its own terms.

The specific objects of analysis are the conventional elements in Homeric hospitality scenes, on the level of the formulaic diction of which each verse is composed, on the level of the rigidly constructed type-scenes through which frequently recurring activities are described, and on the level of the larger and more flexible patterns in which the story as a whole is narrated. Of course conventional elements are not a feature of oral poetry exclusively; every art form relies to some degree on a conventional background to inform each particular instance. But Homeric poetry, because of the fundamentally oral nature of its composition, performance, and transmission, is exceptionally rich in conventional elements: the poet relied on preformulated diction in his composition of the very demanding dactylic hexameter verse, on conventional sequences of details and events in his framing of scenes, and on inherited patterns in his building of the overall narrative structure.

Only by becoming immersed in these conventions can we as a modern audience, oriented more toward written literature than oral performance, approach the experience of Homer's contemporary audience and respond intuitively to the poet's employment and transformation of these traditional elements. Formulaic phrases, type-scenes, and repeated themes and narrative patterns are much more than convenient verse-fillers, generic descriptions, and mnemonic devices designed to assist an extemporaneously composing oral poet. These conventional elements, inherited from a long and rich tradition, are dynamic ingredients of oral poetry that have accrued deep and significant meaning over time through their accumulated use in various contexts, and in each particular instance, they call these associative meanings to mind for a well-informed audience. In a sense, then, this book is an attempt to bridge the gap, widened by time and culture and language, between us and Homer's contemporary audience.

Today we rarely hear Homer's poetry performed aloud. Instead, usually in our solitude, we scan with our eyes a printed text that is but a transcription of what was once a live public performance. When we read these texts, we confront a language that is very foreign to us, with little feeling for the nuances of the diction. Moreover, we read from eclectic editions of the Homeric texts that cannot claim to replicate with any verisimilitude the words of the original performances.

Our experience, then, is a very detached and artificial one. But, ironically, it has been not through attempts to reenact oral performances but through tedious scholarly research of an even more artificial kind that we have come to a greater appreciation of the oral nature of the Homeric poems. On the level of the individual verse, we owe a great debt to Milman Parry and his successors for their contributions to our understanding of the nature of Homeric diction and the mechanisms of oral verse composition.[1] On the level of the larger building blocks of Homeric poetry—the type-scenes, the larger motifs and themes, and the narrative patterns that arch over the epic whole, all of which are as formulaic and typical as Homeric diction—we owe an equally great debt to the earliest scholar of Homeric type-scenes, Walter Arend, who did much more than plot their recurring elements on grids; he showed how these elements were adapted by the poet to fit their particular contexts through elaboration, curtailment, negation, and omission.[2]

My debt to Parry, Arend, and their successors will be apparent in my analysis of Homeric hospitality scenes. In particular I should mention Albert Lord, who showed that the practice of resorting to such type-scenes, or "themes" as he called them, was not unique to Homer but a characteristic of many unrelated traditions of oral poetry;[3] Bernard Fenik, whose two monographs on typical elements in the *Iliad* and the *Odyssey* have become in many ways models for my work on typical

1. Parry 1971.
2. Arend 1933.
3. Lord 1960.

elements in Homeric hospitality scenes;[4] and Mark Edwards, whose perceptive observations on typical elements, both on the level of diction and on the level of broader themes and story patterns, and whose ability to articulate these observations into a constructive theory of oral poetics have been an inspiration for my work.[5]

In the chapters that follow, all Greek quotations of Homer are from the Oxford Classical Texts of T.W. Allen and D.B. Monro; quotations of the Odyssean scholia are from the editions of A. Ludwich (for *Od.* 1.1–309) and G. Dindorf (for the rest of the *Odyssey*); quotations of Eustathius' commentary on the *Odyssey* are from the edition of G. Stallbaum. All translations are my own and are intended for clarity rather than for any poetic value. Parenthetical citations are to the *Odyssey* unless otherwise indicated. As a practical matter, I cite, and even quote, verses of dubious authenticity, identifying such verses as possible interpolations by placing them in brackets.

---

4. Fenik 1968, 1974.

5. Edwards 1975, 1980, 1987a, 1987b.

For a bibliography on type-scenes, one may presently consult Hainsworth 1969, under "Theme." An updated and expanded bibliography by M.W. Edwards will soon appear in the journal *Oral Tradition*.

Chapter 1

The Conventions of the Homeric Hospitality Scene

Ζεὺς δ' ἐπιτιμήτωρ ἱκετάων τε ξείνων τε,
ξείνιος, ὃς ξείνοισιν ἅμ' αἰδοίοισιν ὀπηδεῖ.

[Zeus is the protector of suppliants and guests,
Zeus Xeinios, who attends to revered guests.]
—(*Od.* 9.270–71)

In the hospitality scene, I include everything that occurs from the moment
a visitor approaches someone's house until the moment he departs. As
such, it is really a composite of many smaller type-scenes, including,
among others, arrival, reception, seating, feasting, identification, bed-
ding down, bathing, gift giving, and departure, all composed in highly
formulaic diction and arranged in a relatively fixed order. I count eighteen
such hospitality scenes in the verses that have come down to us under
the name "Homer": twelve in the *Odyssey* (Athena-Mentes in Ithaca,
Telemachus in Pylos, Telemachus in Sparta, Hermes and Calypso, Odys-
seus and the Phaeacians, Odysseus and Polyphemus, Odysseus and Aeo-
lus, Odysseus and the Laestrygonians, Odysseus and Circe, Odysseus
and Eumaeus, Telemachus and Eumaeus, Odysseus' homecoming); four
in the *Iliad* (the embassy to Achilles, Nestor and Odysseus in Phthia,
Thetis and Hephaestus, Priam and Achilles); and two in the *Hymns*
(Demeter in the home of Celeos, Aphrodite and Anchises). In addition
to these, a few minor hospitality scenes scattered throughout Homer are
considered in this study (e.g., *Od.* 3.488–90; 15.186–88; *Il.* 6.171–77),
but since they are too short to contribute much of importance to my
analysis, I give them less formal treatment.

Some of the scenes that I have included in my analysis could just as
well, perhaps better, be categorized as messenger scenes (Athena-Mentes
in Ithaca, Hermes and Calypso, the embassy to Achilles) or supplication

5

scenes (Odysseus and the Phaeacians, Odysseus and Polyphemus, Priam and Achilles). Many conventional elements, such as arrival, seating, feasting, sacrifice, and libation, are not tied exclusively to the hospitality scene; they are more fluid and can be found attached to various kinds of scenes. I include messenger and supplication scenes in my treatment of hospitality scenes because conventional elements of hospitality intrude and even become pervasive in each of them (see Appendix). In the embassy to Achilles (*Il.* 9.185–668), for example, the messenger scene is transformed into a scene of hospitality when Achilles rises from his seat, greets the visitors as friends, leads them in, and serves them a feast. Similarly, when Priam approaches Achilles as a suppliant in order to ransom the body of his son (*Il.* 24.334–694), Achilles first pushes him away from his knees and then takes him by the hand, offers him a seat, serves him a meal, and even provides him a bed in the portico. The shifts on a formal level from messenger or supplication scene to hospitality scene mirror the activity on the contextual level of Achilles' generous elevation of messengers and suppliants to the status of revered guests.

As a tool for defining the conventional background against which each individual instance of hospitality may be viewed, I have constructed a grid of thirty-eight elements that occur repeatedly in the eighteen hospitality scenes under consideration:

I. Maiden at the well/Youth on the road
II. Arrival at the destination
III. Description of the surroundings
    a. Of the residence
    b. Of (the activities of) the person sought
    c. Of (the activities of) the others
IV. Dog at the door
V. Waiting at the threshold
VI. Supplication
VII. Reception
    a. Host catches sight of the visitor
    b. Host hesitates to offer hospitality
    c. Host rises from his seat
    d. Host approaches the visitor
    e. Host attends to the visitor's horses
    f. Host takes the visitor by the hand

       g. Host bids the visitor welcome

       h. Host takes the visitor's spear

       i. Host leads the visitor in

VIII. Seat

  IX. Feast

       a. Preparation

       b. Consumption

       c. Conclusion

   X. After-dinner drink

  XI. Identification

       a. Host questions the visitor

       b. Visitor reveals his identity

  XII. Exchange of information

 XIII. Entertainment

 XIV. Visitor pronounces a blessing on the host

  XV. Visitor shares in a libation or sacrifice

 XVI. Visitor asks to be allowed to sleep

XVII. Bed

XVIII. Bath

 XIX. Host detains the visitor

  XX. Guest-gifts

 XXI. Departure meal

 XXII. Departure libation

XXIII. Farewell blessing

XXIV. Departure omen and interpretation

 XXV. Escort to visitor's next destination

This grid is of course a highly artificial abstraction, a mechanical device by which the modern reader may by conscious effort shed some light on the backdrop of inherited conventions. Homer's audience needed no such explicit analysis; Homer himself did not consciously rely on it as a pattern for the composition of his hospitality scenes. The grid is merely descriptive, not prescriptive; in practice Homer shows great flexibility in his narration of these scenes, from the three-verse description of Diocles' hospitality toward Telemachus and Pisistratus in Pherae (3.488–90) to the multi-book description of the Phaeacians' hospitality toward Odysseus in Scheria (5.388–13.187). No hospitality scene in Homer contains every element on this grid; in fact, no hospitality scene in Homer is exactly identical to any other. Yet many of these elements on the grid are to be found in each hospitality scene, and perhaps more important, the sequence into which these elements fall seems to underlie every scene. This grid, then, reveals the "syntax" of the standard Homeric hospitality scene and provides us, an audience unfamiliar with the linguistic, poetic, and mythic acculturation of Homer's contemporary audience, with a device by which to elucidate and appreciate the operation of Homer's individual work against its backdrop of inherited conventions.[1]

Homer's audience was well versed in the conventions of epic poetry, and Homer relied on this familiarity in order to communicate with them. Such a familiarity is essential in order for an audience to appreciate the nuances and connotations of the formulaic diction; recognize significant sequences and patterns in their various combinations; detect allusions, irony, parody, humor, and foreshadowing; and, in general, distinguish between what is deliberately conventional and generic and what is innovative and unique. It is precisely this tension, between the conventional and the innovative, between the generic and the context-specific, between the background of tradition and the foreground of a particular performance, that defines the aesthetics of Homeric poetry.

The main barrier to our appreciation of the artistry of Homer is our ignorance, as a modern audience, of the backdrop of conventions against which he is working; because of our lack of proper experience with other performances, we are simply not well educated enough in the oral poetic tradition to be an effective audience. The Homeric scholar, then, must overcome, and help others overcome, the wide gap that separates us linguistically and culturally from Homer's audience, using lexica and concordances, charts of formulaic phrases, parallel verses, and scenes, comparative collections of myths and folktales, and a thorough immersion in the diction and narrative patterns of the epic poetry that has survived from this period, including the Homeric Hymns, the epic frag-

---

1. Almost all the conventional elements occur at least twice in Homer, most of them several times. But a simple enumeration of occurrences should not be the only criterion for judging conventionality. A conventional element may happen to occur only once in the surviving Homeric corpus. The motif of hospitality extended to horses (VIIe), for example, occurs only once in Homer (*Od.* 4.39–42), but this is because visitors arrive by horse and chariot only once in the surviving corpus. There is no reason to think that this scene was unique in epic verse; similar scenes of "horse hospitality" occur in the *Iliad,* although not in hospitality scenes (*Il.* 8.432–35; 13.34–38). And there is no reason to doubt that the motif would prove to be a regular element of hospitality scenes if more epic poetry had survived. All this also holds true for the motif of the departure omen and interpretation (XXIV), which happens to occur only once in surviving hospitality scenes (*Od.* 15.160–81).

ments, and Hesiod, while always keeping in mind the salutary caution that this is but a small portion of the corpus of epic poetry with which Homer's audience was familiar. In this admittedly artificial and pedantic way, we may learn to share, albeit obscurely, in that tacit and subliminal level of communication between Homer and his contemporary audience, and we may thereby aspire to become, even in this highly literate age, a reasonably competent audience.[2]

The conventions of the Homeric hospitality scene are described and schematized in this introductory chapter. Chapters 2–8 each analyze how an individual hospitality scene from the *Odyssey* functions against the background of these conventions; hence, the perspective is largely diachronic. These analyses reveal many artistic, yet seldom appreciated, transformations of conventional elements in the major hospitality scenes of the *Odyssey,* some of which are of great importance to the underlying themes of the epic whole. Finally, chapter 9 examines how the scenes of hospitality in the *Odyssey* interact with one another within the bounds of this individual epic, anticipating, echoing, and variously informing one another; hence, the perspective is largely synchronic.

The terms *synchronic* and *diachronic* were first coined to describe the opposition between the static and evolutionary aspects of linguistics,[3] but insofar as the formulae, the type-scenes, and the larger narrative patterns of Greek epic poetry function as the diction, the grammar, and the syntax of the oral poet, the terms are equally useful for describing the opposition and balance between a performance of Homer when viewed as a particular event and that same performance when viewed against its traditional background. These viewpoints do not exclude each other; they are simply different perspectives on the same material: the diachronic perspective, for example, sees motifs repeated within an epic as independent allomorphs of a common ancestor, while the synchronic perspective observes how these same repeated motifs interact with each other within the epic—an epic that presumably reflects, however dimly, a particular historic performance before a live audience. While the two perspectives cannot be separated, and while indeed they complement

---

2. On the challenge inherent in an oral tradition for a literate audience, see Foley 1987, 185–212. Foley has maintained a fine balance in articulating a common aesthetic for various traditions of oral poetry while still appreciating the significant generic differences between these traditions; cf. Foley 1986, 1988, 1990.

3. De Saussure 1959, 79–100.

each other and depend upon each other for meaning, my emphasis in chapters 2–8 is primarily diachronic; in chapter 9, primarily synchronic.[4]

The scene of Athena's visit to Ithaca (see chap. 2), in its simplest form merely a messenger scene, is molded into the framework of a theoxeny, in which a divinity comes to earth to test the hospitality of mortals and is rejected by some, usually the rich and greedy, and hospitably received by others, usually the impoverished but generous. This framework of a theoxeny increases the suspense surrounding the reception of Athena in Ithaca, and it serves to accentuate the contrast between Telemachus' generous hospitality and the suitors' blatant disregard for the stranger, a theme more fully developed later in the epic, upon Odysseus' return. This contrast is articulated at every level of Homer's diction, from the short formulaic phrases to the larger elements of the conventional type-scene. Thus the poet draws the contrast between Telemachus and the suitors on the level of form as well as content.

Consideration of the hospitality that Telemachus receives from Nestor in Pylos (chap. 3) and Menelaus in Sparta (chap. 4) reveals an underlying flaw in these otherwise proper, indeed paradigmatic, hosts: both Nestor and Menelaus are overzealous in their hospitality, detaining Telemachus and thus threatening to become obstacles to his return home (νόστος). This threat of obstruction ties the experience of Telemachus thematically to that of his father: both son and father must sagaciously extricate themselves from the hands of overbearing hosts who have become obstacles to their homecomings (νόστοι).

Close attention to the deviations of the Phaeacians from the usual conventions of hospitality (chap. 5) reveals a curious ambivalence toward visitors. Scheria is not simply a realm of safety and hospitality for Odysseus; it poses obstacles to his return similar to those that he has recently confronted during his wanderings, and it poses dangers similar to those that he will soon confront in Ithaca. The ambiguity of the Phaeacians' hospitality thus connects this episode thematically both to what precedes and to what will follow.

An analysis of Polyphemus' treatment of Odysseus and his men as guests against the backdrop of conventional elements of hospitality (chap. 6) accentuates the cynical parody that colors this episode. Perhaps most memorable are Polyphemus' perversions of the rituals of feasting (IX)—rather than offering a feast to his guests, he makes a feast of

---

4. With good results, Foley (1990, esp. 1–19, 235–39, 386–87) applies the terms *synchronic* and *diachronic* to various comparative oral traditions.

them—and of gift giving (XX)—his gift to Odysseus is his offer to eat him last. But the Cyclops also perverts some of the less conspicuous conventional elements of hospitality: the formal request for a guest's identity (XIa), the departure libation (XXII), the farewell blessing upon departure (XXIII), and the offer of escort to the guest's next destination (XXV), all of which add to the parody of the scene.

Eumaeus' hospitality toward the disguised Odysseus (see chap. 7) follows the pattern of the conventional hospitality scene and includes almost all the conventional elements. Slight innovations in the details of these elements emphasize the highly proper, exceptionally generous, and intensely personal nature of Eumaeus' hospitality: he assures his guest that he will not interrogate him until after he has eaten (XIa); he offers the portion of honor, the chine, to his guest (IX); he provides his guest a bed by the hearth, while he himself sleeps outside (XVII); he gives his guest a goatskin from his own bed as a seat (VIII), his own cup to drink from (X), and his own cloak as a blanket (XVII). Yet in order to accommodate the uniquely humble and unheroic setting of this scene—a swineherd's hut rather than a king's palace—the poet has modified much of the inherited diction of the conventional hospitality scene. Remarkably, it is precisely at these points of modification that a high concentration of late linguistic forms can be detected, revealing the secondary and derivative nature of this scene. In the absence of inherited, preformulated diction in which to describe the humble hospitality of a swineherd, Homer relied more than usual on his own linguistic vernacular. This raises the possibility that such tales of swineherd hospitality, though undoubtedly a staple of popular folktale from the earliest times, were not part of the epic tradition passed down to Homer through the medium of dactylic hexameter verse.

The final hospitality scene of the *Odyssey,* Odysseus' homecoming and reception by the suitors (see chap. 8), is also structured architecturally upon the conventional scene of hospitality. But in almost every instance, the suitors invert the conventional elements of the proper hospitality scene: they turn the very implements of hospitality—footstools (VIII) and the contents of the meat basket (IX)—into weapons to hurl at the guest, and they offer the guest "escort" (XXV) not to his desired destination but as a slave to the wicked king Echetus. The suitors' many breaches of convention on the level of form mirror their actual breaches of conduct in the topsy-turvy world of Ithaca, where host and guest have virtually exchanged positions.

Descriptive Synopses of Conventions of Hospitality

The following detailed descriptions of each of the thirty-eight conventional elements that make up the Homeric hospitality scene, both in their standard forms and in their various transformations, were elicited largely from the eighteen scenes of hospitality under consideration. A schema of each of these eighteen scenes of hospitality may be seen in synoptic form in the Appendix.

I. Maiden at the Well/Youth on the Road

Four times in the *Odyssey*, a newly arrived stranger encounters at a fountain, well, or river a young maiden who is kind to him and directs him to the city or palace. The various occurrences of this motif seem to inform one another, and in this case, the earlier occurrences seem to provide the pattern—on a linguistic level the diction, grammar, and syntax—in a standard form whereby later transformations of the motif may be appreciated for their emotional and aesthetic value. First, the shipwrecked Odysseus meets Nausicaa washing clothes at a river; in this very elaborate version of the motif, the princess assists him and directs him to her father's palace (6.110–322). Second, in a shorter doublet of this episode that occurs soon thereafter, Odysseus approaches the city and meets Athena, who, disguised as a young girl carrying a water jar, directs him to Alcinous' palace (7.18–81). Third, in a less auspicious version of the motif, Odysseus' men meet with the daughter of the Laestrygonian king, who is drawing water at a spring; she too directs the men to her father's palace, but with a less fortunate outcome (10.103–11). And fourth, Eumaeus tells a tale about how Phoenician traders met a Sidonian slave girl from his father's house washing clothes at the beach; an erotic encounter with one of the men leads to her aiding them in looting the palace and kidnapping Eumaeus (15.415–84). A version of this motif also occurs in the *Hymn to Demeter* (98–183): Demeter encounters the daughters of Celeos by the spring Parthenion, where they have come to draw water, and is led by them to the palace.[5]

This motif must have had its basis in historical reality; the town well was one of the few places in archaic Greece where a young man might encounter an unmarried maiden. It is often the site of abduction, both in

---

5. On the traditional nature of this scene, see Richardson 1974, 179–80, 339–43.

Greek myth and in art. But the motif is not restricted to the Greek world; it is a universal tale that knows no geographical bounds.[6]

Four times in the *Odyssey*, there occurs a male counterpart to this motif, in which a young man, twice the son of a king, gives aid to a newly arrived stranger and directs him to the palace. Hermes, likening himself to a young man, meets Odysseus on his way to Circe's palace and instructs him about how to conduct himself there (10.274–306). Athena, in the form of a young man, is the first to meet the newly arrived Odysseus on Ithaca, and she instructs him about how to regain his wife and palace, advising him to go first to the hut of the swineherd Eumaeus (13.221–440). The son of Pheidon, king of the Thesprotians, comes to the aid of the shipwrecked Odysseus and leads him to his father's palace (14.314–20). In a rather contorted version of this motif, the abusive goatherd Melanthius encounters Odysseus en route to his palace at the spring of the nymphs, but instead of directing him to the palace, he warns him to stay away (17.204–53). A version of this motif also occurs in the *Iliad* (24.334–467), where Hermes, in the form of a young man, meets Priam, who is on his way to recover Hector's body, and escorts him to Achilles' camp.

II. Arrival at the Destination

A hospitality scene is initiated by the arrival of a visitor at his destination. Whether this destination is an island, a harbor, a city, a palace, or even a cave, the visitor's arrival is almost always signified by a form of the verb ἱκνέομαι: ἵκετο (5.57, etc.), ἵκοντο (3.388, etc.), ἷξον (3.5, etc.), ἱκόμεσθα (10.13, etc.), ἷξε (*Il.* 6.172), ἱκέσθην (*Il.* 9.185), ἵκανεν (*H.Aphr.* 68), ἀφίκετο (5.55, etc.), ἀφίκοντο (*Il.* 24.448), ἀφικόμεθα (9.181, etc.), ἀφίκανε (*H.Aphr.* 75). Rarely a form of εἶμι (ἤϊεν 5.57; ἤϊα 10.309; ἴε 7.82), ἔρχομαι (ἐρχομένῳ 17.261; ἦλθε [*Il.*18.381]; ἤλθομεν 10.87), or βαίνω (βῆν 10.60; προσέβη 14.1) is used; κίεν (*Il.* 24.471), ἐδύσετο (17.336), and εὗρον (10.210) each occur once.

IIIa–c. Description of the Surroundings

Upon a visitor's arrival at his destination there is almost always a description of the physical residence and of the activities of the inhabitants, or at least of their appearance.

---

6. Thompson 1955–58, N715.1. For occurrences in the Old Testament—Rebekah (Gen. 24:10–61), Rachel (Gen. 29:1–20), Zipporah (Exod. 2:15b–21)—see Alter 1981, 51–62.

a. Of the Residence

Often the sight of the residence inspires awe in the visitor, as do Menelaus' and Alcinous' palaces and Calypso's and Polyphemus' caves: ἰδόντες θαύμαζον (4.43–44); τάρπησαν ὁρώμενοι ὀφθαλμοῖσιν (4.47); σέβας μ' ἔχει εἰσορόωντα (4.75); θηήσαιτο ἰδὼν καὶ τερφθείη φρεσὶν ᾗσιν (5.74); στὰς θηεῖτο (5.75, 7.133); θηήσατο θυμῷ (5.76, 7.134). Whether the residence is a swineherd's hut, a god's palace, or a warrior's tent, it is typically described in a syntactic structure in which a series of adjectives describing the building is followed by a relative clause acknowledging the builder (14.5–10; *Il.* 18.369–71; 24.448–50; cf. *Od.* 24.205–7).

b-c. Of (the Activities of) the Person Sought and Others

The visitor commonly "catches sight"—εὗρε, εὗρον, εὕρομεν (1.106; 4.3; 7.136; 9.217; 10.113; 14.5; *Il.* 9.186; 11.771; 18.372; 24.473; *H.Aphr.* 76), alternatively τέτμεν (5.58), ἔτετμεν (5.81), ἐκίχανον (10.60), ἄκουον (10.221), γιγνώσκω (17.269)—of the inhabitant(s), who is usually involved in the activities of the banquet: sacrifice, libation, feast preparation, eating and drinking, lyre and song. An account of the inhabitant(s) is often given, even when he is not home: Odysseus is down at the shore weeping (5.81–84), Polyphemus is out herding cattle (9.216–17), Eumaeus' fellow workers are attending to the pigs (14.24–28; 16.3), and Anchises' companions are grazing the cows (*H.Aphr.* 78–80). A particularly striking example of Homer's tendency to adhere to the conventional schema is his substitution, in the face of Polyphemus' absence from his cave upon Odysseus' arrival, of a description not of what Polyphemus is doing but of what he usually does, and his further substitution, in view of the absence of companions, of a remark on the Cyclops' notorious isolation from society (9.187–92).

IV. Dog at the Door

Often a newly arrived stranger confronts a guard dog at the door. This motif occurs five times in the *Odyssey* in a variety of forms, the unique properties of each occurrence providing a special aura and significance to the respective scene. The immortal gold and silver dogs, the work of Hephaestus, that guard the palace of the Phaeacian king Alcinous, hint at the supernatural qualities of the inhabitants and contribute to the extravagant splendor of the palace, which inspires the newly arrived Odysseus with awe (7.91–94). The eerie reception of Odysseus' men by the enchanted wolves and mountain lions surrounding Circe's palace, which fawn on the men and wag their tails at them like dogs greeting their master, foreshadows the danger of enchantment that awaits them in the palace (10.212–19). The four dogs of Eumaeus, which, like wild beasts (14.21), attack Odysseus and force him to sit helplessly on the ground, even as he arrives "at his own steading" (ᾧ πὰρ σταθμῷ 14.32), presage his treatment at the hands of the suitors in his own home and symbolize the initial helplessness of the returned master (14.21–22, 29–32).[7] Later, upon the arrival of Telemachus, these same dogs do not bark but with fawning and tail-wagging welcome a master whom they recognize (16.4–10). Then, in a rather humorous finale to this series, these same dogs, upon the arrival of Athena, cower, with a whimper, to the other side of the steading (16.162–63). The culmination of this progression of receptions of strangers by dogs at the door is Odysseus' reception by his old dog Argus (17.291–327). It is a powerful scene. The old, flea-bitten dog, neglected by the household, lying in dung outside the door, is a sympathetic representation of his master: Odysseus too will be abused and neglected.[8]

V. Waiting at the Threshold

The area in front of the doorway (ἐν προθύροισι, εἰνὶ θύρῃσι, πὰρ σταθμῷ), and specifically the threshold (οὐδός) itself, has both a symbolic and practical function in Homeric hospitality scenes, as it no doubt did in the historic society that underlies the epics. It is the physical boundary between the worlds of the outsider and insider, and by crossing this physical boundary, the visitor places himself under the protection of the master of the house. Typically the visitor remains at the doorway for some time, waiting for the master to notice him and either offer hospitality or send him elsewhere.[9] If the visitor is a social equal, coming

---

7. Note that Odysseus himself later addresses the suitors as "dogs" (ὢ κύνες 22.35)

8. Edwards (1987a, 76–77; 1987b, 54), in his discussion of expansions and transformations of type-scenes, attributes this varied usage of a common motif to the original genius of the poet; I agree. For a fuller exposition of the thematic relationship between dog, house, and master in the *Odyssey,* see Beck 1991.

9. No visitor in Homer is actually sent away, but Eteoneus raises the possibility of sending Telemachus and Pisistratus to someone else for hospitality upon their arrival in Sparta (4.28–29).

as a messenger (ἄγγελος) or a guest (ξεῖνος), he stands at the doorway: στῆ... ἐπὶ προθύροις... οὐδοῦ ἐπ᾽ αὐλείου (1.103-4); ἐν προθύροισι δόμων... στῆσαν (4.20-22); ἔνθα στάς (5.75); ἱσταμένῳ, πρὶν χάλκεον οὐδὸν ἱκέσθαι (7.83); ἔνθα στάς... ὑπὲρ οὐδὸν ἐβήσετο δώματος εἴσω (7.133-35); ἔσταν δ᾽ ἐν προθύροισι (10.220); ἔστην δ᾽ εἰνὶ θύρῃσι... ἔνθα στάς (10.310-11); ἔστη ἐνὶ προθύροισι (16.12); στήτην ἐρχομένω (17.261); στὰν δὲ πρόσθ᾽ αὐτοῖο (*Il.* 9.193); στῆμεν ἐνὶ προθύροισι (*Il.* 11.777); ἐπ᾽ οὐδὸν ἔβη ποσί (*H.Dem.* 188); στῆ δ᾽ αὐτοῦ προπάροιθε (*H.Aphr.* 81). If the visitor is a social inferior, coming as a beggar (πτωχός) or a suppliant (ἱκέτης), he sits at the doorway in a posture that symbolizes submission and helplessness: παρὰ σταθμοῖσιν ἐπ᾽ οὐδοῦ ἑζόμεθ᾽ (10.62-63); ἕζετο... ἔνθα κεν ᾦ πὰρ σταθμῷ (14.31-32); ἷζε δ᾽ ἐπὶ μελίνου οὐδοῦ ἔντοσθε θυράων, κλινάμενος σταθμῷ (17.339-40).

By modifying and adapting this conventional element of waiting at the threshold, Homer sometimes emphasizes the setting of a particular scene. Odysseus and his men disregard the sanctity of the threshold by entering Polyphemus' cave uninvited (9.216-18); appropriately Polyphemus places a huge rock on this very threshold (9.240-43), as though to make inaccessible what had previously been too accessible. The goddess Demeter's presence at the doorway of Celeos' palace takes on the form of a divine epiphany, as she fills the doorway with her greatness and radiance (*H.Dem.* 188-89). Upon his homecoming, Odysseus not only waits at the threshold of his own palace but maintains a permanent position there (17.339-41; 20.257-59); his ambiguous status—whether master or beggar, insider or outsider—is thus visualized by his position in this liminal space.

VI. Supplication

In three hospitality scenes—Odysseus and the Phaeacians, Odysseus and Polyphemus, Priam and Achilles—the visitor is in such dire straits that he initially approaches his host not as a guest but as a suppliant, assuming the standard position of the suppliant by prostrating himself and clasping the knees of his host, a type of physical contact that entailed a powerful ritual sanctity: ἀμφὶ δ᾽ ἄρ᾽ Ἀρήτης βάλε γούνασι χεῖρας (7.141); σά τε γούναθ᾽ ἱκάνω (7.147); τὰ σὰ γοῦνα ἱκόμεθ᾽ (9.266-67); χερσὶν Ἀχιλλῆος λάβε γούνατα (*Il.* 24.478).[10] Both Alcinous and Achilles gen-

---

10. The full range of physical gesture in a proper supplication—prostration, clasping

erously elevate their suppliants to the level of guests by taking them by the hand and lifting them up (χειρὸς ἑλὼν... ὦρσεν 7.168–69; χειρὸς ἀνίστη *Il.* 24.515; cf. *Od.* 14.319), seating them on a seat of honor (ἐπὶ θρόνου εἷσε 7.169; ἕζευ ἐπὶ θρόνου *Il.* 24.522), and thereafter treating them in a manner appropriate to guests rather than suppliants. Polyphemus, who does not care for Zeus (9.272–78), the "protector of suppliants and guests" (ἐπιτιμήτωρ ἱκετάων τε ξείνων τε 9.270), shows no such consideration.

VIIa–i. Reception

A host's reception of a visitor follows a conventional sequence: the host catches sight of the visitor, hesitates at first to offer hospitality, then rises from his seat, approaches him, attends to his horses, takes him by the hand, bids him welcome, relieves him of his spear, and leads him into the house. As usual Homer shows great flexibility: no hospitality scene includes the entire range of elements, some hospitality scenes contain none of them, and some elements occur only once or twice. But the elements that do occur generally follow this sequence.

a. Host Catches Sight of the Visitor

It is often the youngest son of the master of the house who first notices a visitor and rises to greet him: Telemachus in Ithaca (1.113; 17.328), Pisistratus in Pylos (3.36), Achilles in Phthia (*Il.* 11.777). The actual sighting of the visitor is usually signified by a form of the verb ὁράω: πολὺ πρῶτος ἴδε (1.113), εἴσιδ' (1.118), ἴδον (3.34; 14.29), ἴδετο (4.22), ἰδοῦσα (5.78), ἰδόντες, θαύμαζον δ' ὁρόωντες (7.144–45), ἴδε (*Il.* 9.195; 18.382), θάμβησεν ἰδών (*Il.* 24.483), ὁρόων (*H.Aphr.* 84); occasionally it is signified by ταφών (16.12; *Il.* 9.193; 11.777).

Homer often manipulates this conventional element with great artistic effect. While Telemachus is "by far the first to notice" (πολὺ πρῶτος ἴδε 1.113) Athena-Mentes standing at the door, the suitors remain oblivious to her presence; this contrast draws attention to the wide gulf that separates the proper and improper hosts. In Sparta, not the host but

---

(even kissing) the knees, and taking hold of the chin—can best be seen in Thetis' supplication of Zeus (*Il.* 1.498–527; 8.370–72). On the physical gestures of supplication, and on the relationship between suppliancy in Greek literature and its reality as a historical institution, see Gould 1973.

the official herald of the palace notices Telemachus and Pisistratus at the door (4.22–23); this herald embodies the extravagant, but somewhat impersonal, hospitality that awaits these guests in Sparta. At Eumaeus' hut, not Eumaeus but the dogs first notice the visitor (ἴδον 14.29); the danger they pose to Odysseus foreshadows the danger he will soon face from the "dogs" (ὦ κύνες) in his own palace, as Odysseus himself calls the suitors (22.35). The description of Metaneira's first sight of Demeter at the door is expanded to include the great fear that overcomes her (H.Dem. 190); this anticipates the divine epiphany of the goddess.

b. Host Hesitates to Offer Hospitality

Telemachus, a paradigm of a proper host, is anxious that his guest not suffer the indignity of waiting for a long time at the door (νεμεσσήθη δ' ἐνὶ θυμῷ ξεῖνον δηθὰ θύρῃσιν ἐφεστάμεν 1.119–20). But this is exactly what happens in two other hospitality scenes. In Sparta, Menelaus' herald Eteoneus sees Telemachus and Pisistratus at the door, but instead of hastening to them and leading them in, he goes to consult with Menelaus as to whether they should offer the visitors hospitality or send them elsewhere. Menelaus angrily rebukes him and orders him to lead the visitors in (4.24–36). Similarly, in Scheria, Alcinous and Arete fail to respond to their suppliant Odysseus, who is sitting in the ashes of the hearth, until the old hero Echeneus, "after some time" (ὀψέ 7.155), reprimands them for their inhospitality and bids them to provide a seat and a meal and to offer a libation to Zeus, who looks after suppliants (7.153–66).

The immediate context of both these scenes provides sufficient excuse for hesitation: the Spartans are in the middle of a wedding celebration; the Phaeacians are simply incapacitated by their surprise at the sudden appearance of a stranger in their midst. Outside the immediate context, too, there appears to be some motive for hesitation: the Spartans' hospitality had previously been violated by their most notorious guest, Paris, who had seized his host's wife;[11] the Phaeacians had been fated to suffer punishment at the hands of Poseidon for their hospitable provision of an escort for strangers (13.170–83). But the Spartans' and Phaeacians' ambivalence toward strangers, and the Phaeacians' reputed intolerance of foreigners generally (7.32–33), is perhaps also a reflection of the basic

---

11. This is the explanation given by the scholiast to 4.26.

ambivalence of archaic Greek society toward strangers, a dubious class who could prove to be either friendly or hostile. This ambivalence is encapsulated in the term ξεῖνος, which has a broad semantic range, from "a guest-friend from a foreign country, who is to be treated with all the respect of an 'insider'" (a φίλος), to "a potentially hostile stranger, who is outside one's own social group" (a non-φίλος).[12]

c. Host Rises from his Seat

When a host catches sight of a visitor at the door, he rises from his seat in order to welcome him; the verb is usually ἀνόρουσε (16.12; Il. 9.193; 11.777), alternatively ἀνέστη (Il. 9.195). In two instances, the hosts appear to yield their own seats to visitors, Metaneira out of fear of the goddess Demeter (εἶξε δέ οἱ κλισμοῖο H.Dem. 191), Achilles out of respect for the aged Priam (ἀπὸ θρόνου ὦρτο Il. 24.515; cf. Il. 24.522, 553, 597).[13]

d. Host Approaches the Visitor

Since it is improper to let a visitor linger at the door, a proper host approaches him quickly: βῆ δ᾽ ἰθὺς προθύροιο (1.119); μεγάροιο διέσσυτο (4.37); αἶψ᾽ ἐξελθοῦσα (10.230, 312); ὦκα ... ἔσσυτ᾽ ἀνὰ πρόθυρον (14.33-34).

e. Host Attends to the Visitor's Horses

In Homeric hospitality scenes, there is only one occurrence of hospitality being extended to horses—Menelaus' generous accommodation of Telemachus' and Pisistratus' horses in Sparta (4.39-42). But this element should not be regarded as unconventional; its uniqueness is due simply to the rarity of arrivals by chariot in Homeric hospitality scenes. Comparable scenes of attending to horses, although not in hospitality scenes, are fairly common in the Iliad (cf. especially 8.432-35; 13.34-38; also 5.368-69, 775-77; 8.49-50, 440-41).

---

12. On the semantic range of ξεῖνος, see H. Kakridis 1963, 87-105. A similar ambivalence toward strangers is reflected in the etymologically related Latin hostis and hospes. On this ambivalence in an Indo-European context, see Benveniste 1969, 65-101.

13. R.M. Frazer (1971) notes the delicate point of etiquette involved in Achilles giving up his royal θρόνος to Priam and taking a lesser κλισμός for himself.

f. Host Takes the Visitor by the Hand

A host first makes physical contact with a visitor by grasping (αἱρέω) one or both of his hands—only the right hand is specified, never the left: χεῖρ᾽ ἕλε δεξιτερήν (1.121); ἀμφοτέρων ἕλε χεῖρα (3.37); χειρὸς ἑλών (7.168; *Il.* 11.778); ἐν τ᾽ ἄρα οἱ φῦ χειρί (*Il.* 18.384, 423).

Homer manipulates this conventional element in several scenes. Eumaeus, in his joy at seeing his master Telemachus, "kisses both his hands" (κύσσε... χεῖρας τ᾽ ἀμφοτέρας 16.15–16). Achilles, after pushing Priam away from his knees (*Il.* 24.508), "lifts him up by the hand" (χειρὸς ἀνίστη *Il.* 24.515), signifying by this gesture his elevation of Priam's status from suppliant to guest (cf. *Od.* 14.319). Anchises "seizes Aphrodite by the hand" (λάβε χεῖρα *H.Aphr.* 155), a gesture evocative of a seduction scene, in which a man is leading a maiden to bed.

g. Host Bids the Visitor Welcome

Sometimes a host greets a visitor with a formal welcoming speech. The content of the speech varies, but it is usually introduced with the greeting χαῖρε followed by a vocative: χαῖρε ξεῖνε (1.123), χαίρετον (4.60; *Il.* 9.197), χαῖρε γύναι (*H.Dem.* 213), χαῖρε ἄνασσ᾽ (*H.Aphr.* 92).

h. Host Takes the Visitor's Spear

In two hospitality scenes, Athena-Mentes in Ithaca and Telemachus and Eumaeus, the host relieves the visitor of his spear before he enters the house: ἐδέξατο χάλκεον ἔγχος (1.121; 16.40; cf. 15.282). This gesture perhaps had its origin in the historic society underlying the epics, where it served the practical function of disarming a potentially dangerous stranger. In the hospitality scene in Ithaca, this element is elaborated to emphasize Telemachus' generous and personal hospitality toward Athena-Mentes: he places her spear in his father's own spear stand (1.127–29).

i. Host Leads the Visitor In

Finally a host leads (ἄγω, ἡγέομαι) a visitor into the house, and the visitor follows (ἕπομαι): ἡγεῖθ᾽, ἡ δ᾽ ἕσπετο (1.125); εἰσῆγον (4.43); ἕπεο προτέρω ([5.91]; *Il.* 18.387); ἕποντο (10.231); εἰσαγαγοῦσα (10.233, 314); ἑπόμην (10.313); ἕπεο (14.45); ἡγήσατο (14.48); εἰσαγαγών (14.49); προτέρω ἄγε (*Il.* 9.199); ἐς δ᾽ ἄγε (*Il.* 11.778); πρόσω ἄγε (*Il.* 18.388). This gesture of escorting a stranger from the outside, over the threshold, and into the house, symbolizes a reciprocal contract between the two: the visitor agrees to submit to the host's authority; the host agrees to protect the visitor while in his house. It is notable, then, that whereas Eumaeus "leads" (ἡγήσατο, εἰσαγαγών 14.48–49) the disguised Odysseus into his hut, when Telemachus, his recognized master, arrives soon thereafter, he does not lead him in; Telemachus simply enters the swineherd's hut of his own accord (εἴσελθε 16.25; ἵεν 16.41).

VIII. Seat

Once inside the house, a host's first provision for a visitor is a seat. A proper host offers a seat at the place of honor: Telemachus apparently offers to Athena-Mentes his own seat (1.130–32), as does Achilles to Priam (*Il.* 24.515, 522, 553, 597) and Metaneira to Demeter (*H.Dem.* 191); in Pylos, Pisistratus seats Telemachus beside his father, Nestor, and his brother Thrasymedes (3.36–39); in Sparta, Telemachus and Pisistratus are seated beside Menelaus (4.51); in Scheria, Alcinous makes room for Odysseus at the place of his own son Laodamas (7.169–71; cf. 7.468).

Several different formulae are used to describe the seating of visitors. Sometimes a simple invitation to sit suffices: ἑδριάασθαι ἄνωγον (3.35; *Il.* 11.778; *H.Dem.* 191). The actual seating is signified by a form of the verbs ἕζομαι, ἵζω, ἱδρύω, εἷσα, and καθεῖσα (1.130, 145; 3.37, 389; 4.51; 5.86; 7.169, 469; 10.233, 314, 366; 14.49; 15.134; *Il.* 9.200; 18.389; 24.522, 553). A rather longer formulaic expression occurs with some variety: ἐξείης ἕζοντο κατὰ κλισμούς τε θρόνους τε (1.145; 3.389; cf. 24.385), alternatively modified to ἐξέσθην δ᾽ ἄρ᾽ ἔπειτα κατὰ κλισμούς τε θρόνους τε (15.134) and εἷσεν δ᾽ εἰσαγαγοῦσα κατὰ κλισμούς τε θρόνους τε (10.233). The most elaborate expression for seating is a two-verse formula, with some variation in the first verse, which adds a description of a footstool (1.130–31; 10.314–[15] = 366–67; *Il.* 18.389–90):

αὐτὴν δ᾽ ἐς θρόνον εἷσεν ἄγων, ὑπὸ λῖτα πετάσσας,
καλὸν δαιδάλεον· ὑπὸ δὲ θρῆνυς ποσὶν ἦεν.

εἷσε δέ μ᾽ εἰσαγαγοῦσα ἐπὶ θρόνου ἀργυροήλου,
καλοῦ δαιδαλέου· ὑπὸ δὲ θρῆνυς ποσὶν ἦεν.

τὴν μὲν ἔπειτα καθεῖσεν ἐπὶ θρόνου ἀργυροήλου,
καλοῦ δαιδαλέου· ὑπὸ δὲ θρῆνυς ποσὶν ἦεν.

Niceties of etiquette may be observed in the types of seats offered to visitors: θρόνος, κλισμός, and δίφρος. The θρόνος, a chair with upright back and armrests, is usually reserved for gods and nobles (gods 5.86, 195; *Il.* 8.199, 442; 14.238; 15.124, 142; 18.389, 422; 20.62; *H.Ap.* 9; nobles 6.308; 7.95; 8.422; 16.408; 17.32; 18.157; 20.150; 21.139, 166; 22.23; 23.164; *Il.* 11.645; 24.515) and for guests who are invited to take the seat of honor (1.130; 4.51; 5.86, 195; 7.162, 169; 8.65, 469; 10.314, 352, 354, 366; *Il.* 18.389; 24.522, 533), but it is never used by women. The κλισμός, a chair with a reclined back, is used by men when feasting or relaxing (17.90; *Il.* 9.200; 11.623; 24.597) and by women (4.136; 17.97; *H.Dem.* 191, 193). The δίφρος, a stool, is used especially by subordinates and servants (17.330; 19.97, 101, 506; 20.259; 21.243; *Il.* 24.578; *H.Dem.* 198).[14]

It is indicative of Telemachus' generous hospitality that he offers Athena-Mentes a θρόνος with a footstool (θρῆνυς) for her feet, while he takes a κλισμός for himself (1.130–32). Achilles likewise shows proper etiquette by offering his θρόνος to Priam (*Il.* 24.515, 522, 553) and taking for himself a κλισμός (*Il.* 24.597); meanwhile, Priam's herald is made to sit on a δίφρος (*Il.* 24.578). Metaneira offers her own κλισμός to Demeter, but the goddess prefers a seat more in line with her disguise as a humble servant woman, so she accepts only a δίφρος (*H.Dem.* 191, 198). Upon his homecoming, Odysseus' own elevation in stature from beggar to master is visualized concretely by his change in seats from a δίφρος (19.97, 101, 506; 20.259; 21.243, 420) to a θρόνος (23.164).

IXa–c. Feast

The sharing of a feast is one of the most intimate means by which a stranger is welcomed into a home, for the banquet is the primary locus for participation in *xenia;* significantly, the term ξείνια, ξεινήϊα may specifically denote the food offered to a guest (4.33; [5.91]; *Il.* 11.779–80; 18.387, 408). Homer economically constructed his tale so that a visitor usually arrives at someone's house precisely at a time of feasting, either

---

14. On the distinction between these types of seats, see Athenaeus *Deipnosophists* 192e–f; Laser 1968, 34–56.

during the feast's preparation or during its actual consumption; thus the visitor may be immediately and effortlessly accommodated.

a. Preparation

Great attention is given to the details of the preparation of feasts. The epic diction is very rich in formulae for describing feast preparation, from the simple τετύκοντό τε δαῖτα (8.61; 16.478; 24.384; *Il.* 1.467; 2.430; 7.319) to the elaborate and variously described preparation of a banquet in conjunction with a sacrifice (e.g., 3.418-63, 470-72; 14.418-52; 20.250-55; *Il.* 1.457-66; 2.419-29; 9.206-20; 24.621-26). The most distinctive description of feast preparation for the entertainment of guests is a formulaic five-verse block that details the duties of the handmaid, who provides water for handwashing and a table, and the housekeeper, who serves bread and other food (1.136-40 = 4.52-56; 7.172-76; [10.368-72]; 15.135-[39]; 17.91-95):

χέρνιβα δ' ἀμφίπολος προχόῳ ἐπέχευε φέρουσα
καλῇ χρυσείῃ, ὑπὲρ ἀργυρέοιο λέβητος,
νίψασθαι· παρὰ δὲ ξεστὴν ἐτάνυσσε τράπεζαν.
σῖτον δ' αἰδοίη ταμίη παρέθηκε φέρουσα,
εἴδατα πόλλ' ἐπιθεῖσα, χαριζομένη παρεόντων.

An addendum of two or three verses, which adds the duties of a carver, who serves platters of meat, and a herald, who pours the wine, is sometimes attached to this five-verse block (1.141-43 (cf. [4.57-58]); 15.140-41):

δαιτρὸς δὲ κρειῶν πίνακας παρέθηκεν ἀείρας
παντοίων, παρὰ δέ σφι τίθει χρύσεια κύπελλα,
κῆρυξ δ' αὐτοῖσιν θάμ' ἐπῴχετο οἰνοχοεύων.

πὰρ δὲ Βοηθοΐδης κρέα δαίετο καὶ νέμε μοίρας·
οἰνοχόει δ' υἱὸς Μενελάου κυδαλίμοιο.

A truly generous host may "bestow great honor" (γεραίρω 14.437, 441; *Il.* 7.321) on his guest by relinquishing his own "designated portion" (γέρας 4.66), the fatty "chine" (νῶτον) of the cow, pig, sheep, or goat (4.65-66; 8.474-83; 14.437-41; *Il.* 7.321-22; 9.206-8).

b. Consumption

The preparation of the feast is generally described in great detail, but the actual consumption of the food merits only a simple, one-verse formula. In the *Odyssey*, the most common by far is οἱ δ' ἐπ' ὀνείαθ' ἑτοῖμα προκείμενα χεῖρας ἴαλλον (1.149; 4.67, 218; 5.200; 8.71, 484; 14.453; 15.142; 16.54; 17.98; 20.256; *Il*. 9.91, 221; 24.627). In the *Iliad*, the most common is δαίνυντ', οὐδέ τι θυμὸς ἐδεύετο δαιτὸς ἐΐσης (16.479; 19.425; *Il*. 1.468, 602; 2.431; 7.320; 23.56). The first-person dialogue of Odysseus' *Apologoi* requires the modification ἥμεθα, δαινύμενοι κρέα τ' ἄσπετα καὶ μέθυ ἡδύ (9.162, 557; 10.184, 468, [477]; 12.30). A few shorter formulaic phrases sometimes suffice to describe consumption: δαίνυντ' ἐρικυδέα δαῖτα (3.66; 13.26; 20.280; *Il*. 24.802), δαίνυνθ' ἑζόμενοι (3.471), πῖνε καὶ ἦσθε (5.94; 6.249; 7.177), κρέα τ' ἤσθιε πῖνέ τε οἶνον (14.109).

c. Conclusion

The feasting is concluded with a one-verse formula that also functions as a transition to the post-feast activities: αὐτὰρ ἐπεὶ πόσιος καὶ ἐδητύος ἐξ ἔρον ἕντο (1.150; 3.67, 473; 4.68; 8.72, 485; 12.308; 14.454; 15.143, 303, 501; 16.55, 480; 17.99; *Il*. 1.469; 2.432; 7.323; 9.92, 222; 23.57; 24.628); alternatively, αὐτὰρ ἐπεὶ δείπνησε καὶ ἤραρε θυμὸν ἐδωδῇ (5.95; 14.111), αὐτὰρ ἐπεὶ τάρπησαν ἐδητύος ἡδὲ ποτῆτος (5.201), πλησάμενος δ' ἄρα θυμὸν ἐδητύος ἡδὲ ποτῆτος (17.603), or σίτου καὶ οἴνοιο κορεσσάμενος κατὰ θυμὸν (14.46). The first-person dialogues of Odysseus' Apologoi and of Nestor's story require the modifications αὐτὰρ ἐπεὶ σίτοιό τ' ἐπασσάμεθ' ἡδὲ ποτῆτος (9.87; 10.58) and αὐτὰρ ἐπεὶ τάρπημεν ἐδητύος ἡδὲ ποτῆτος (*Il*. 11.780).

Homer freely modifies the conventional formulae of feasting to accommodate the particular circumstances of each scene. Most conspicuous, perhaps, are his modifications of the formulae for sacrificing cows in order to accommodate Eumaeus' sacrifice of a pig (cf. 14.75 and, e.g., 3.462; 14.418–56 and, e.g., *Il*. 1.447–74) and his modifications of the formulae for the serving of the feast in order to take into account the absence of meat-carvers, heralds, and servant girls in Eumaeus' hut (cf. 16.49–52 and, e.g., 1.141–43, 147). Sometimes Homer manipulates these conventional formulae with great poetic effect. The elaborate description of the feast preparation for Athena-Mentes in Ithaca, using the conventional five-verse block and addendum (1.136–43), is a striking contrast to the three-verse potpourri that describes the serving of the suitors (1.146–[48]); the juxtaposition of these two remarkably different descriptions of feast preparation serves to contrast Telemachus' generous reception of Athena-Mentes with his reluctant tolerance of the suitors. In describing Polyphemus' and the Laestrygonian Antiphates' treatment of their guests, Homer perverts the typical banquet scene, creating a black parody on a formal level, by applying the conventional diction of the banquet to their cannibalistic feast: ἑτάροις ἐπὶ χεῖρας ἴαλλε (9.288; cf. 1.149), ὁπλίσσατο δόρπον or ὁπλίσσατο δεῖπνον (2.20; 9.291, 311, 344; 10.116; cf. 16.453; 24.360).

X. After-dinner Drink

Immediately after the feast, either the host or the guest may fill a cup with wine and propose a toast. This wine drinking is distinct from the general eating and drinking of the feast (IXb), and it is separate from the libation that is occasionally shared between host and guest (XV). This formal element of an after-dinner drink takes many shapes: after the feast in Achilles' tent, Odysseus fills a cup of wine and salutes his host (*Il.* 9.224); after the feast in Odysseus' palace, Telemachus fills a cup with wine for the disguised Odysseus and seats him among the suitors for a time of drinking (20.260–62); after the feast in Eumaeus' hut, Eumaeus demonstrates the personal nature of his hospitality by refilling his own cup with wine and offering it to his disguised guest Odysseus (14.112–13); after Polyphemus' cannibalistic feast in the Cyclopeia, a parody of proper hospitality, Odysseus offers to the Cyclops the wine of Maron, which inebriates him and facilitates his blinding (9.345–61).

XIa–b. Identification

The revelation of a guest's identity is perhaps the most critical element in the development of a relationship of *xenia*, for it is the vital link that guarantees the host reciprocal hospitality as a guest in the future (cf. 9.16–18). It is understandable, then, that the manner in which a guest's name is requested and revealed takes on an almost ritualistic formality.

a. Host Questions the Visitor

A proper host requests his guest's name and inquires into his business only after providing him a meal; the stranger is to remain anonymous throughout the meal.[15] This point of etiquette may be observed in the hospitality of Telemachus (1.123-24; 16.54-59), Nestor (3.69-70), Menelaus (4.60-62), Arete (7.230-39), Eumaeus (14.45-47), the ruler of Lycia (*Il.* 6.171-77), Achilles (*Il.* 9.221-24), Charis and Hephaestus (*Il.* 18.385-87), and Metaneira (*H.Dem.* 206-12). The most paradigmatic hosts—Telemachus (1.123-24), Menelaus (4.60-62), and Eumaeus (14.45-47)—set their guests at ease on arrival by explicitly assuring them that they will not inquire into their identity or business until after the meal. Blame is attached to those who breach this convention: Hermes disregards Calypso's premature questions until after they have eaten (5.85-96); Odysseus gently reprimands Alcinous for probing into his identity before his belly is thoroughly satisfied (7.199-206, 215-21); and Polyphemus' role as a paradigm of perverted hospitality is reinforced by his demand for his guests' identity upon first setting eye on them (9.251-55).

The most routine formula of inquiry entails a request for information about a stranger's homeland and parentage: τίς πόθεν εἰς ἀνδρῶν; πόθι τοι πόλις ἠδὲ τοκῆες; (1.170; 10.325; 14.187; 15.264; 19.105; 24.298; cf. 7.238; *H.Dem.* 113). This question may be elaborated to include an inquiry into the stranger's means of transportation and business in the land (1.171-77; 14.188-90; 24.299-301; *H.Dem.* 114-17). When more than one stranger is present, and their means of transportation is assumed to be by ship, a different formula is used: ὦ ξεῖνοι, τίνες ἐστέ; πόθεν πλεῖθ᾽ ὑγρὰ κέλευθα; (3.71; 9.252; *H.Ap.* 452). This question too may be expanded to include an inquiry into the strangers' business (3.72-74; 9.253-55; *H.Ap.* 453-55). The host often expresses great concern that the stranger answer truthfully and accurately: ἀλλ᾽ ἄγε μοι τόδε εἰπὲ καὶ ἀτρεκέως κατάλεξον (1.169; 8.572; 24.287); καί μοι τοῦτ᾽ ἀγόρευσον ἐτήτυμον, ὄφρ᾽ ἐ ὗ εἰδῶ (1.174; 14.186; 24.297).

b. Visitor Reveals his Identity

In turn, the stranger's revelation of his identity and business is often preceded by assurances that this information will be true and accurate:

---

15. For comparative material evidencing this rule, see J.T. Kakridis 1975, 13-21.

τοιγὰρ ἐγώ τοι ταῦτα μάλ᾽ ἀτρεκέως ἀγορεύσω (1.179; 14.192; cf. 15.266; 16.61); τοιγὰρ ἐγώ τοι πάντα μάλ᾽ ἀτρεκέως καταλέξω (24.303); sometimes simply by καταλέξω (3.80; 9.14; 16.226), μυθήσομαι (9.16; *H.Dem.* 120), or ἐρέω (7.243; 15.402; 19.171). The information provided may include the stranger's name, parentage, homeland, means of transportation, and business (1.180–93; 3.81–101; 9.19–38, 259–71, 366–67, 504–5; 14.199–359; 15.403–84; 19.172–202; 24.304–14; *H.Dem.* 122–44; *H.Aphr.* 109–42). A prudent stranger will impose a sense of obligation on his host by strategically mentioning his relationship of *xenia* with a relative: Athena-Mentes claims to Telemachus that she is a *xenos* of his father (1.187–88), and the disguised Odysseus claims to Laertes that he is a *xenos* of his son, having once entertained him and given him gifts (24.265–79).

Homer demonstrates great flexibility and innovation by manipulating the formal elements of identification to accommodate each individual scene. In Arete's interrogation of Odysseus, the formulaic τίς πόθεν εἶς ἀνδρῶν; πόθι τοι πόλις ἠδὲ τοκῆες; is replaced by τίς πόθεν εἰς ἀνδρῶν; τίς τοι τάδε εἵματ᾽ ἔδωκεν; (7.238), reinforcing the theme of clothing central to this scene. Odysseus' revelation of his name, normally a form of countergift for a host's hospitality, proves to be a curse in the Cyclopeia: his false name Οὖτις tricks the Cyclops (9.364–414); his revelation of his real name at departure is framed as a taunt (9.502–5). The longest interrogation of a visitor in Homer is Alcinous' questioning of Odysseus (8.548–86); Odysseus' response is correspondingly lengthy, comprising the four-book Apologoi (9.1–11.330; 11.385–12.453).

Because gods can always recognize each other (5.79–80), there is no place for the formal element of identification in scenes of divine hospitality. Homer replaces the usual request for a stranger's identity with a request that the visiting deity state his business (5.87–90 ≈ *Il.* 18.424–27). The usual revelation of the stranger's identity is correspondingly replaced by the god's explanation for his visit (5.97–115; *Il.* 18.429–61).

Since one of the key themes of the *Odyssey* is that of recognition, and particularly the self-recognition of Telemachus and Odysseus, both of whom have difficulties coming to terms with their own identities (cf. 1.215–16), it is appropriate that their self-revelation as guests be occasionally replaced by an identification of them by their hosts. Sometimes this is a conscious act by the host, as in Helen's and Menelaus' identification of Telemachus (4.138–54) or Circe's identification of Odysseus (10.325–35). Sometimes the identification is inadvertent: Demodocus sings of Odysseus' exploits to the unknown stranger (8.73–82, 499–520); Eumaeus tells stories of Odysseus to his disguised guest (14.115–47); Penelope speaks of Odysseus to the disguised beggar (19.124–63); Penelope, Eurycleia, and Philoetius all remark on the similarities between the disguised beggar and Odysseus (19.357–81; 20.191–207).

XII. Exchange of Information

Information is as valuable a commodity as treasured guest-gifts. Sometimes the host provides specific information to an inquisitive visitor; other times the visitor provides news from abroad to a curious host, as though in exchange for material hospitality. This reciprocal exchange of information normally follows the feast and may include news, messages, instructions and advice, prophecies, and, very often, stories.

In the *Odyssey*, the exchange of information is often laden with irony because the hosts frequently fail to recognize the disguised Odysseus. Eumaeus informs the disguised Odysseus of the identity of his master (14.115–47) and fills him in on his supposed status (14.42–44, 133–36), and Odysseus in turn prophecies his own return (14.149–64, 321–33). Penelope tells the disguised Odysseus about her longing for her husband, whom she presumes dead (19.124–61), and Odysseus in turn tells a story about entertaining Odysseus in Crete (19.172–248) and prophecies his return and the death of the suitors (19.269–307, 555–58, 583–87). And the disguised Odysseus claims to Laertes, who craves information about his son, that he once entertained him in Alybas (24.266–314).

XIII. Entertainment

The after-dinner entertainment takes many forms. Song and dance are common accoutrements of the feast—μολπή τ' ὀρχηστύς τε˙ τὰ γάρ τ' ἀναθήματα δαιτός (1.152; cf. 8.246–65; 17.605–6)—but in the grandest palaces, the entertainment may also include exhibitions of athletic contests (boxing, wrestling, leaping, running, discus) or a special type of dancing while simultaneously throwing balls and performing gymnastic feats, as in Scheria and Sparta (8.100–131, 370–80; cf. 4.18–19). But by far the most prevalent form of entertainment after the feast is the telling of stories, sometimes by a professional bard to the accompaniment of a lyre (κίθαρις, φόρμιγξ 1.151–55, 325–27; 8.43–47, 62–70, 73–82, 241–369, 486–520; 13.27–28; 17.358–59, 605–6), sometimes by the host (3.102–98, 247–312; 4.76–112, 212–89, 347–586; 15.383–494), and sometimes by the guest (9.1–12.453; 10.14–16; 14.191–359, 462–506; 18.428–30). The favorite topics of storytelling are the events of the Trojan war and the adventures of the returns (νόστοι) in the war's aftermath (1.325–27; 3.102–98, 247–312; 4.76–112, 212–89, 347–586; 8.73–82, 486–520; 9.1–12.453; 10.14–16; 14.462–506), perhaps Homer's advertisement of his own repertoire.

Homer's handling of after-dinner entertainment often emphasizes the primary theme of vengeance underlying the *Odyssey*. In Ithaca, the bard Phemius is made to sing "under compulsion" (ἀνάγκη 1.154) by the suitors. Ironically, Phemius sings about the wrath of Athena, even as the goddess, in disguise as Mentes, is sitting in the corner conversing with Telemachus; and Phemius' song is about the return (νόστος) of the Achaeans, a subject of pressing concern to the suitors, who hope that the return of Odysseus will not be accomplished (1.325–27). The suitors' perverse hospitality toward the disguised Odysseus is demonstrated by their deriving amusement from a boxing match between him and the local beggar Irus for the right to beg in the palace (18.1–111), the "guest" in effect providing the after-dinner entertainment; athletic contests had functioned properly as part of the after-dinner entertainment in Scheria (8.100–131), but not here in Ithaca. The suitors' perversity is appropriately avenged, for in their final feast, Odysseus himself provides the entertainment: "the singing and the lyre" (μολπῇ καὶ φόρμιγγι 21.430), a vivid allusion to the bow with which he exacts retribution.

XIV. Visitor Pronounces a Blessing on the Host

A visitor abroad usually lacks the resources with which to compensate a host for his material provisions. He may reciprocate for the moment by providing news from abroad or entertainment by way of storytelling, and he may provide the means for his host to gain reciprocal hospitality in the future by revealing his name and country. He may also reciprocate for material provisions by pronouncing a blessing on his host; often the graciousness of the host's hospitality inspires such a blessing (7.148-50; 14.51-54, 439-41; 15.340-42; 17.353-55; *H.Dem*. 135-37, 224-25). The guest typically prays that his host be blessed with "glory" (κῦδος 3.55-59), with "the affection of Zeus" (φίλος Διὶ πατρὶ γένοιο 14.439-41; 15.340-42), with "material wealth" (ὄλβια 7.148-50; ὄλβιον 17.353-55; ἐσθλά *H.Dem*. 224-25), with a "prosperous and blessed posterity" (παισὶν ἐπιτρέψειεν ἕκαστος κτήματ'; τέκνα τεκέσθαι 7.148-50; *H.Dem*. 135-37), or rather generally, with "whatever he might desire" (ὅττι μάλιστ' ἐθέλεις 14.51-54; οἱ πάντα γένοιτο ὅσα φρεσὶν ᾗσι μενοινᾷ 17.353-55). Sometimes the guest invokes the gods generally (7.148-50; 14.51-54; *H.Dem*. 135-37, 224-25), sometimes Zeus specifically (14.51-54, 439-41; 15.340-42; 17.353-55)—and appropriately so, since he is the patron of suppliants and guests (6.206-8; 9.270-71, 477-79; 14.56-59, 283-84, 388-89).

Just as a guest may pronounce a blessing on a gracious host, so he may pronounce a curse on an ungracious one. When Antinous demonstrates his perverted hospitality by casting a footstool, an instrument of kind reception in normal circumstances, at the newly arrived Odysseus, he responds with a curse that is essentially a negation of the guest's usual prayer for a prosperous and blessed posterity: "If there are gods and Furies [ἐρινύες] for beggars, may death come upon Antinous before marriage." (17.475-76).

XV. Visitor Shares in a Libation or Sacrifice

Perhaps the most symbolically powerful gesture of a host's willingness to incorporate a stranger into the community, to transform an outsider into an insider, is an invitation to participate in the community's religious rituals. Shared participation in libations and sacrifices is a mark of the most generous hospitality. Nestor is particularly accommodating to Athena-Mentor and Telemachus on their arrival, encouraging them to participate in the sacrifices, libations, and prayers of the Pylian community (3.40-67, 338-42, 390-94, 418-63). Alcinous invites the newly arrived Odysseus to share in a libation to Zeus, "who protects revered suppliants" (ὅς θ' ἱκέτῃσιν ἅμ' αἰδοίοισιν ὀπηδεῖ 7.179-84). Eumaeus includes Odysseus in all his sacrifices and libations, humble though they be (14.407-48; 16.452-54). Amphinomus, who alone of the suitors shows proper respect toward guests, allows Odysseus to share in a libation (18.151-52). And

Achilles honors those who have come to him as mere messengers by inviting them to share in a sacrifice and meal (*Il*. 9.219-20).

XVI. Visitor Asks to Be Allowed to Sleep

The most hospitable hosts are so generous in their provisions of food, drink, and entertainment, especially in the form of stories—perhaps even to the point of being overbearing—that a guest often has to alert them that it is time for bed. The loquacious Nestor, having spent the entire day until the setting of the sun telling stories, is finally interrupted by Athena-Mentor, who encourages him to put an end to the sacrifice, "so that we may think of sleep, for it is the hour for such" (ὄφρα ... κοίτοιο μεδώμεθα· τοῖο γὰρ ὥρη 3.333-34). After Helen and Menelaus have entertained their guests throughout the evening with food, wine, and stories about Troy, Telemachus, in his first words to his hosts in Sparta, says, "Come, lead us to bed, so that we may even now lie down and delight in sweet sleep" (ἀλλ᾽ ἄγετ᾽ εἰς εὐνὴν τράπεθ᾽ ἡμέας, ὄφρα καὶ ἤδη ὕπνῳ ὕπο γλυκερῷ ταρπώμεθα κοιμηθέντες. 4.294-95). When Odysseus wishes to rest from the narration of his adventures to his Phaeacian hosts, he alerts them that "it is the hour for sleep" (ἀλλὰ καὶ ὥρη εὕδειν 11.330-31), but Alcinous, who is anxious for more stories, denies him: "This night is unspeakably long; not yet is it the hour for sleep in the hall" (νὺξ δ᾽ ἥδε μάλα μακρὴ ἀθέσφατος· οὐδέ πω ὥρη εὕδειν ἐν μεγάρῳ 11.373-74). Eumaeus, who is enjoying immensely his exchange of tales with Odysseus, encourages his guest to remain awake into the night: "These nights are immense" (αἵδε δὲ νύκτες ἀθέσφατοι 15.392), he says; "You should not lie down before it is time; much sleep is a vexatious thing" (οὐδέ τί σε χρή, πρὶν ὥρη, καταλέχθαι· ἀνίη καὶ πολὺς ὕπνος. 15.393-94). When at last Odysseus is reunited with his wife, he requests, "Let us go to bed, wife, so that even now we may lie down and take delight in sweet sleep" (λέκτρονδ᾽ ἴομεν, γύναι, ὄφρα καὶ ἤδη ὕπνῳ ὕπο γλυκερῷ ταρπώμεθα κοιμηθέντε. 23.254-55). Penelope assures him that he may go to bed whenever he wishes but then delays him, wanting to hear more about the prophecy of Teiresias. Priam uses similar language when, having tasted food and wine for the first time since his son's death and having spent the evening conversing with Achilles, he at last asks his host to let him sleep: "Lay me down quickly, god-born one, so that even now we may lie down and take delight in sweet sleep" (λέξον νῦν με τάχιστα, διοτρεφές, ὄφρα καὶ ἤδη ὕπνῳ ὕπο γλυκερῷ ταρπώμεθα κοιμηθέντες˙. *Il.* 24.635-36).

XVII. Bed

A bed for the guest is normally placed in the portico immediately outside the front door of the house (ὑπ᾽ αἰθούσῃ 3.399; 4.297; 7.336, 345; *Il.* 24.644; ἐν προδόμῳ 4.302; 20.1, 143; *Il.* 24.673); meanwhile, the host retreats to the innermost room of the house (μυχῷ 3.402; 4.304; 7.346; *Il.* 9.663; 24.675), where he sleeps beside his wife or concubine (3.403; 4.305; 7.347; *Il.* 9.664-68; 24.676).

The description of the bedding itself receives various degrees of elaboration. Although the general picture of Nestor's hospitality in Pylos as relatively humble is reinforced by the simple description of Telemachus' bed (τρητοῖς ἐν λεχέεσσιν 4.399), the personal nature of his hospitality is demonstrated by the provision of his own youngest son as Telemachus' bedmate in the portico (3.400-401). The material hospitality in Sparta is more lavish but less personal: Helen orders the servants to place a bed in the portico, to throw on it beautiful, purple rugs, to spread blankets above, and to put woolen mantles on top (4.296-99). The bed provided for Odysseus by the Phaeacians is equally elaborate (7.336-39 = 4.297-300), but the bedding scene is further augmented by an official announcement that the bed is ready (7.342). Achilles' wealth and generous hospitality, even in the harsh environment of the battlefield, are accentuated by Homer's use of the structure and formulae of the typical bedding scene of the palace to describe his provision of a bed for Phoenix and Priam in his shelter (*Il.* 9.617-22, 658-68; 24.643-55, 671-76; note that *Il.* 24.644-47 = *Od.* 4.297-300, 7.336-39; *Il.* 24.673 = *Od.* 4.302).

Manipulations of the bedding scene for poetic effect may be observed in the scenes of Odysseus' homecoming. Although the humbleness of Eumaeus' hospitality is accentuated by the substitution of sheepskins and goatskins for the usual rugs and blankets (14.519), his graciousness and loyalty is revealed by a reversal of the geography of the normal bedding scene: Eumaeus provides for Odysseus, the guest, a bed inside next to the fire, while he himself, the host, sleeps outside in the shelter of a hollow rock (14.518-33). Upon Odysseus' arrival at his own home, the geographical location of his bed acquires great symbolic value: at first Melantho suggests that he go away and sleep in a public lounging place for beggars (18.327-29); then Penelope acknowledges him as a guest and offers a bed in the portico (19.317-19, 598-99; 20.1); and once Odysseus has gained the upper hand against the suitors and has reestablished himself as master, he reclaims the bedroom in the innermost part of the house (23.295). His spatial progression from outside the house, to its periphery in the portico, to its innermost room, is symbolic of his elevation from beggar to guest to master.

XVIII. Bath

The provision of a bath for a guest is a normal part of proper hospitality, usually in conjunction with the preparation for a feast (1.310; 3.464-68; 4.48-50; 6.210-35; 8.426-27, 433-37, 449-57; 10.358-65, 449-51; 17.87-89; 19.317, 320, 343-60, 386-88, 503-7; 23.153-63). Usually the bath is provided well after the initial reception of the guest, sometimes even on the second day of the visit; rarely it is offered to the guest immediately on arrival (4.48-50; cf. 6.210-35; 17.87-90). It is usually the servant women who administer the bath (δμωαί; ἀμφίπολοι; ταμίη; 4.49; 6.209; 8.454; 10.348; 17.88; 19.317; 23.154; cf. 24.366), occasionally the mistress of the house (Helen 4.252; Calypso 5.264; Circe 10.449), and once the unmarried princess (Nestor's daughter Polycaste 3.464-65).

A typical Homeric bath entails heating water in a tripod (τρίπους); the attendant pours water from this tripod upon the guest, who is seated in a bathtub (ἀσάμινθος; cf. 8.426, 433-37; 10.358-63). The attendant then washes the guest and anoints him with olive oil (λοῦσέν τε καὶ ἔχρισεν λίπ᾽ ἐλαίῳ 3.466; cf. 4.49, 252; 8.454; 10.364, 450; 17.88; 23.154; 24.366). Finally, the attendant provides a fresh change of clothing (ἀμφὶ δέ μιν φᾶρος καλὸν βάλεν ἠδὲ χιτῶνα 3.467; cf. 4.50; 6.214; 8.455; 10.365, 451; 17.89; 23.155; 24.367).[16] Hence the Homeric bath is not a provision to be offered casually; it requires the active and intimate participation of a member of the host's household.

The quality of the bath is often indicative of the quality of the host's hospitality. In Sparta, the guests are offered a bath immediately on

---

16. Many of the elements of the Homeric bath are attested in the Linear B tablets: the tripod (ti-ri-po = τρίπους on the Pylos Ta series), the bath itself (a-sa-mi-to = ἀσάμινθος on Knossos Ws 8497), the employment of bath attendants of both sexes (re-wo-to-ro-ko-wo = λοετροχόοι on Pylos Ab 27 [553], Ad 676, Aa 783), and oil and cloaks reserved for guests (ke-se-ni-wi-jo, describing oil, on Pylos Fr 1231; pa-we-a ke-se-nu-wi-ja = φάρεα ξείνια on Knossos Ld 573). The clay bathtub (a-sa-mi-to = ἀσάμινθος) uncovered in the so-called palace of Nestor at Ano Englianos also evokes the Homeric bath.

arrival, perhaps an indication of the resources available to Menelaus, who can afford to keep a bath continuously heated in anticipation of the arrival of guests (4.48–50). In Pylos, the guest waits until the next day before a bath is offered, but the personal nature of Nestor's hospitality is demonstrated by the provision of his own unmarried daughter as bath attendant (3.464–68).

The transformative function of the bath is a key to the theme of disguise and recognition in the *Odyssey*. Often the guest rises from the bath with an enhanced appearance, sometimes "looking like a god" (δέμας ἀθανάτοισιν ὁμοῖος 3.468; 23.163; θεοῖσιν ἔοικε 6.243; cf. ἀθανάτοισι θεοῖς ἐναλίγκιον ἄντην 24.371), causing those who see him to "marvel" (θηεῖτο 6.237; θαύμαζε 8.459; cf. 24.370). Odysseus rightly fears that a bath will destroy his disguise and reveal his true identity; hence, he opts for a footbath (19.317, 320, 343–60, 386–88, 503–7). His eventual restoration as master of the house is symbolically realized later through the transformative function of a proper bath (23.153–63).

XIX. Host Detains the Visitor

Menelaus, an apparent model of hospitable behavior, advises his guest Telemachus (15.69–74):

νεμεσσῶμαι δὲ καὶ ἄλλῳ
ἀνδρὶ ξεινοδόκῳ, ὅς κ᾽ ἔξοχα μὲν φιλέῃσιν,
ἔξοχα δ᾽ ἐχθαίρῃσιν· ἀμείνω δ᾽ αἴσιμα πάντα.
ἶσόν τοι κακόν ἐσθ᾽, ὅς τ᾽ οὐκ ἐθέλοντα νέεσθαι
ξεῖνον ἐποτρύνει καὶ ὃς ἐσσύμενον κατερύκει.
χρὴ ξεῖνον παρεόντα φιλεῖν, ἐθέλοντα δὲ πέμπειν.

[I would be indignant at another man
who, receiving guests, acted excessively hospitable
or excessively hostile; all things are better in due measure.
It is as blameworthy to urge a guest to leave who does not
want to as it is to detain a guest who is eager to leave.
One must grant hospitality to a guest who is present and grant
conveyance to a guest who wants to leave.]

But generous hospitality often borders dangerously on forced detention, and the host's frequently reiterated invitation to stay ([ἐπι] μεῖναι) is often met by the guest's plea not to be detained (μὴ ... [κατ] ἔρυκε; cf. 1.309-13, 315; 3.343-55; 4.587-88, 593-608; 7.311-15; 9.303-5, 313-14, 340, 417-19, 517; 10.14-16, 467-74, 489; 11.338-41, 350-52; 13.28-35; 15.64-91, 199-201, 209-14, 335-36, 346; 16.82; 17.16-21; *Il.* 9.617-19; 24.682-88).

In the *Odyssey*, such hospitality threatens to obstruct the homecomings (νόστοι) of both Telemachus and Odysseus. To detain Telemachus in Sparta for as long as possible, Menelaus uses all the resources at his disposal: his stories, which delight Telemachus and tempt him to forget about home and stay in Sparta indefinitely (4.595-98); his offer of horses and a chariot as guest-gifts, gifts that would be useful only if Telemachus were to abandon his homecoming to rocky Ithaca and remain instead on the broad Lacedaemonian plain (4.600-608); the temptation of the wealth to be collected on his proposed leisurely tour through Hellas (15.75-85); and his scrupulous attention to the formalities of feasting, gift giving, libation, farewell speeches, and the interpretation of an omen, all of which delay his guest's inevitable departure (15.92-181). Telemachus expressly chooses to bypass Pylos altogether on his return home for fear that he will confront such obstructive hospitality in Nestor (15.195-219). This threat of detention is mirrored in the experiences of his father Odysseus, whose return home is constantly obstructed by elements associated with hospitality: the food of the Lotus-eaters and of Circe, the songs of the Sirens, the "guest-gift" of Polyphemus, and the beds of Circe and Calypso. These shared experiences of father and son create a sympathetic harmony between the two and reinforce the centrality of the theme of obstructed homecoming in the *Odyssey*.

XX. Guest-gifts

Gifts (ξεινήϊα, δῶρα, δωτίνη) are offered by a host to a guest, never vice versa, as a material symbol of their bond of friendship. In return, the host expects the guest to remember him (μεμνημένος 4.592; 8.431; μιμνήσκεται 15.54; μνῆμα 15.126), and as a purely practical consideration, to reciprocate with an equally valuable gift sometime in the future (ἀμοιβῆς 1.318; ἀμειψάμενος 24.285). It is the custom (θέμις 9.267-68; 24.285-86) that guest-gifts be exchanged back and forth, and gifts that fail to elicit countergifts are said to be given in vain (ἐτώσια 24.283).[17]

---

17. Homeric gift giving surely reflects a historical custom of gift exchange, perhaps of

The most prized type of guest-gift is treasure that can be stored up (κειμήλια). When Telemachus wishes to detain Athena-Mentes in Ithaca, he promises her the best kind of gift he can think of: "treasure . . . such as dear *xeinoi* give to *xeinoi*" (κειμήλιον . . . οἷα φίλοι ξεῖνοι ξείνοισι διδοῦσι 1.312–13). When Menelaus offers Telemachus a gift of horses and a chariot, Telemachus refuses them and insists, "let it be treasure" (κειμήλιον ἔστω 4.600). A gift of κειμήλια may include actual talents of gold (χρυσοῖο τάλαντον 8.393; cf. 8.440; 9.202; 13.11; 24.274), but it usually denotes items made of precious metals—bronze, silver, gold—such as weapons and armor (ἄορ 8.403–5; 19.241; ξίφος 8.406; 16.80; 21.34, 341; ἔγχος 21.34; ἄκων 21.340; τόξον 21.31; τεύχεα *Il.* 6.230; ζωστήρ *Il.* 6.219; θώρηξ *Il.* 11.19; κυνέη *Il.* 10.261) or various household utensils (κρητήρ 4.615; 9.203; 15.103; 24.275; ἄλεισον 8.430–31; τρίπους 13.13; λέβης 13.13; δέπας 15.102; *Il.* 6.220). It may also denote items of clothing (πέπλος 15.105–8; χλαῖνα 15.338; 16.79; 21.339; 24.276; χίτων 8.392, 425, 441; 15.338; 16.79; 19.241–42; 21.339; 24.277; φᾶρος 8.392, 425, 441; 24.277; ἐσθῆτα 8.440; εἵματα 13.10; τάπης 24.276; πέδιλα 16.80; 21.341).

Special value is attached to gifts that have a history behind them (i.e., gifts that have been passed down from someone else): Menelaus gives Telemachus a krater that he had received from Phaedimus, king of the Sidonians (4.613–19); Iphitus gives Odysseus a bow that he had received from Eurytus (21.31–33); Priam gives Achilles a cup that he had received from Thracian men (*Il.* 24.233–37); and the helmet that Meriones gives Odysseus is traced back through four previous exchanges (*Il.* 10.260–71).

Homer manipulates this typical element of gift giving to produce poignant parody on two occasions in the *Odyssey*. Polyphemus' cynical guest-gift (ξεινήϊον 9.370) to Odysseus is the privilege of being eaten last of the men. The suitor Ctesippus offers as an equally cynical guest-gift (ξείνιον 20.296) a pelting with an ox-hoof from the meat basket. This blatant disregard for the civilizing institution of *xenia* places Ctesippus and the suitors on the same level of savagery as the Cyclops.

---

the tenth and ninth centuries—so Finley 1955; Finley [1965] 1978, 58–164. Or perhaps it better reflects the institutions of the society contemporaneous with the poet—so Coldstream 1983, 201–7. For a salutary deemphasis of an underlying historical institution of gift exchange, see Hooker 1989. Gift giving is probably a genetically Indo-European institution—so Benveniste 1969, 65–101—although it is an equally prevalent custom in unrelated primitive and archaic societies—so Mauss 1924.

On the role of gift giving in ancient Greek myth and literature, see Gould 1973, 90–101; Nagy 1981; Donlan 1982a; Donlan 1982b.

XXI. Departure Meal

The didactic Menelaus advises Telemachus shortly before his departure that "it is an honor and a glory and a benefit, having dined, to go on a boundless trek" (ἀμφότερον κῦδός τε καὶ ἀγλαΐη καὶ ὄνειαρ δειπνήσαντας ἴμεν πολλὴν ἐπ᾽ ἀπείρονα γαῖαν. 15.78–79); and in practice, the provision of a meal for a departing guest appears to be a typical element. Yet this element plays a part in only the two most extensive hospitality scenes of the *Odyssey*: Telemachus' departure from Sparta (15.92–98, 133–43) and Odysseus' departure from Scheria (13.23–27). Elsewhere the departure of the guest is not elaborated, or as in Ithaca and Pylos, the hospitality scene is curtailed long before a proper departure scene can occur.

XXII. Departure Libation

The pouring of a libation is a regular element in departure scenes (cf. *Il.* 6.258–62; 9.171–77; 24.283–86). A libation specifically before a guest's departure plays a part in the two most extensive hospitality scenes of the *Odyssey*: Telemachus' departure from Sparta (15.147–50) and Odysseus' departure from Scheria (13.50–56). A libation is also performed upon Odysseus' and Aias' departure from Achilles' tent (*Il.* 9.656–57).

Homer's handling of the typical element of libation in these three scenes of guest departure is indicative of his practice of adapting conventional elements to their context. Upon Odysseus' and Aias' departure from Achilles' tent, the libation is mentioned cursorily, almost mechanically, reflecting the impatience of both guests and host to put an end to the visit. In an effective character sketch of the overly hospitable, even obstructive, Menelaus, Homer pictures him running after Telemachus and Pisistratus in order to perform a final libation, even as they are driving away on their chariot. Befitting the Phaeacians' extravagant hospitality, their libation upon Odysseus' departure from Scheria is the most elaborately described.

XXIII. Farewell Blessing

In the two most extensive hospitality scenes in the *Odyssey*, Telemachus in Sparta and Odysseus in Scheria, the hosts and guests exchange reciprocal blessings on departure. The host introduces his blessing by wishing his guest a farewell (χαῖρε 8.408, 461; 15.128, 151), then he prays specifically that his guest will enjoy a safe return to his family and homeland: "May Zeus accomplish your return home" (νόστον... Ζεὺς τελέσειεν 15.111-12); "May you fare well and return to to your well built home and to your fatherland" (σὺ δέ μοι χαίρων ἀφίκοιο οἶκον ἐϋκτίμενον καὶ σὴν ἐς πατρίδα γαῖαν. 15.128-29); "May the gods grant that you see your wife and come to your homeland, since you have suffered woes away from your loved ones for a long time" (σοὶ δὲ θεοὶ ἄλοχον ἰδέειν καὶ πατρίδ᾽ ἱκέσθαι δοῖεν, ἐπεὶ δὴ δηθὰ φίλων ἄπο πήματα πάσχεις. 8.410-11). The guest in turn echoes the host's farewell (χαῖρε 8.413; 13.39, 59), concurs with the prayer for his safe return (8.465-66; 13.38-43), then pronounces a reciprocal blessing upon his host: "May the gods grant you wealth" (θεοὶ δέ τοι ὄλβια δοῖεν 8.413); "May you, remaining here, take pleasure in your wedded wives and children, and may the gods grant you every excellence, and may there not be any evil for the city" (ὑμεῖς δ᾽ αὖθι μένοντες ἐϋφραίνοιτε γυναῖκας κουριδίας καὶ τέκνα· θεοὶ δ᾽ ἀρετὴν ὀπάσειαν παντοίην, καὶ μή τι κακὸν μεταδήμιον εἴη. 13.44-46); "Take delight in your house and in your children and people and in your king Alcinous" (σὺ δὲ τέρπεο τῷδ᾽ ἐνὶ οἴκῳ παισί τε καὶ λαοῖσι καὶ Ἀλκινόῳ βασιλῆϊ. 13.61-62).

Homer parodies the structure and diction of the typical departure blessing in the Cyclopeia, where Polyphemus curses rather than blesses his "guest," praying that he *not* arrive home (δὸς μὴ Ὀδυσσῆα πτολίπορθον οἴκαδ᾽ ἱκέσθαι 9.530), and that if he is fated "to see his loved ones and come to his well built home and to his fatherland" (φίλους ἰδέειν καὶ ἱκέσθαι οἶκον ἐϋκτίμενον καὶ ἑὴν ἐς πατρίδα γαῖαν 9.532-33), that "he arrive late and badly off" (ὀψὲ κακῶς ἔλθοι 9.534), and that "he find troubles at home" (εὕροι δ᾽ ἐν πήματα οἴκῳ 9.535). This negation of the diction of the conventional blessing reflects the Cyclops' negation of the civilizing institution of *xenia* generally.

XXIV. Departure Omen and Interpretation

It was traditional, both historically and in Homer's poetic cosmos, to seek a favorable omen before setting out on a journey (cf. *Il.* 24.290-321). In scenes of guest departure, a proper omen and interpretation occurs only once in the surviving epic corpus—in Telemachus' departure from Sparta. Just as Telemachus and Pisistratus prepare to depart, an eagle flies by on their right side, carrying a goose in its talons. Helen interprets this omen favorably, as a sign of Odysseus' return and vengeance on the suitors (15.160–81).

In a rather parodic inversion, Odysseus suffers an unfavorable omen as he departs from the land of the Cyclopes. Having divided up the spoils from the Cyclops' cave, Odysseus sacrifices his portion, Polyphemus' favorite ram, to Zeus (9.550–53). Although the sacrifice is intended to honor Zeus as protector of guests, since he has helped Odysseus avenge Polyphemus' violations of hospitality, Zeus refuses to accept the sacrifice (ὁ δ' οὐκ ἐμπάζετο ἱρῶν 9.553), apparently because the stolen ram is symbolic of Odysseus' violations of hospitality as a guest. It is with this unfavorable omen, then, that Odysseus proceeds on a journey that will prove disastrous.

XXV. Escort to Visitor's Next Destination

Escort (πομπή) to a visitor's next destination is the last obligation of a host to his guest. This obligation is fulfilled in various ways. Sometimes the host simply provides directions to the destination (10.508–40; 12.25–27). Sometimes supplies of food for the journey are provided: bread, wine, and cooked meats (3.479–80; 12.301–2; 13.69). Divinities may raise a favorable wind for the traveler (10.17–26; 10.507; 11.6–8; 12.148–50). But the most generous hosts escort their guests personally: Eumaeus himself acts as Odysseus' guide to the city (17.194, 201–3); Nestor offers Telemachus horses and a chariot and his own sons as guides (πομπῆες) for his journey to Sparta (3.324–26, 368–70, 474–86); the Phaeacians, who are famous for delivering their guests safely and speedily by ship even to distant destinations (πομποὶ ἀπήμονές εἰμεν ἁπάντων 8.566 = 13.174; cf. 7.191–98, 317–28; 8.30–38, 555–71), gather a select crew to accompany Odysseus to Ithaca (13.4–6, 47–52, 63–125).

The suitors, who are notorious for their inversions of various elements of hospitality, are eager to offer escort (πομπή) to Odysseus, but it is not the proper πομπή to the guest's desired destination, that for which the Phaeacians are deservedly praised; to the suitors, πομπή means "to expel by force" from the house (ἐκπέμψασθε θύραζε 20.361; δώματος ἐκπέμψῃσι 18.336) or "to send as a slave" to Egypt, Cyprus, Sicily (17.448; πέμψωμεν 20.382–83), or, worse yet, king Echetus (πέμψομεν 21.307–9), who is notorious for cutting off the noses, ears, and genitals of his victims (18.84–87).

The Problem of Concordance Interpolations

Anyone who wishes to treat the Homeric epics as orally generated and orally performed poems must face squarely the fact that they have been transmitted for more than two and a half millennia in written form, largely by scribes and scholars who appreciated even less than we do today the mechanisms of oral poetry. The poems have thereby suffered excisions, accretions, and various other changes, sometimes through the accidents that are a normal part of the process of transmission, other times through conscious and purposeful manipulation by human hands.

In my view, the tightly knit and balanced structures of both epics and the remarkable homogeneity in the massive body of our inherited texts, lacking as they do any substantial variations in the overall plots of the tales, argue against any large scale post-Homeric omissions or additions; yet changes on a smaller scale, the inevitable result of a long textual, and at times perhaps oral, transmission, are to be expected. There is little we can do to detect changes in the text, whether from rhapsodic embellishment and curtailment or from scribal expansion and omission, before the standardization of the text by Aristarchus in the second century B.C.; and we should take note, as a reminder of our ignorance and as a caution to any generalizations we might wish to make, of the considerable textual variants attested in early quotations of Homer and in the Ptolemaic papyri.[18]

We can take some comfort in Aristarchus' exceptional caution as an editor; while he did omit verses from the already heavily interpolated texts that he inherited, he almost always did so on the basis of external, documentary evidence, omitting only those verses that were absent from a majority of manuscripts.[19] Like his Alexandrian predecessors, he did frequently *athetize* verses on internal grounds (i.e., he left the verse in the text, but with an obelus marked in the left column to indicate some doubt as to authenticity). He did not understand the oral nature of the poetry and therefore objected to the repetition of identical verses, freely athetizing on these grounds; he also athetized on stylistic grounds, because of incongruities, because he was offended by certain religious

---

18. On the early quotations of Homer, see van der Valk 1964, 264–369; van der Valk 1949, 278–85; Allen [1924] 1969, 249–70. On the pre-Aristarchean papyri, see S. West 1967; Allen [1924] 1969, 271–301.

19. Apthorp 1980a, 47–125.

points, or because he considered a verse inappropriate. But such *atheteses,* far from being evidence of a verse's inauthenticity, are ironically a testimony of authenticity; at least one can be certain that such verses are ancient, since the Alexandrians read them in their manuscripts.[20]

Our basis for suspecting pre-Aristarchean interpolation, therefore, is not the *atheteses* but the record of the scholia regarding the readings of various pre-Aristarchean authorities. To this record we may apply the same criterion that is productively applied to post-Aristarchean interpolations—namely, that weakness of attestation in pre-Aristarchean editions constitutes grounds for suspicion. There are two added difficulties, however: (1) rather than having the manuscripts themselves, we are relying on the report of the scholia; (2) pre-Aristarchean critics, unlike post-Aristarchean copyists, did in fact omit verses on internal grounds; hence, we must take into account possible motives for their omission of weakly attested verses.

We can do much more about the considerable post-Aristarchean interpolations that have made their way into our inherited texts. We have inherited more manuscripts of Homer than of any other ancient text except the New Testament; and although this plethora of manuscripts multiplies the variants, resulting in many complexities, this very multiplicity furnishes a sound basis on which to evaluate the authenticity of variant readings. In the last century, we have been particularly fortunate to add to our manuscripts the evidence of many early papyri, the discovery of which has substantially increased our knowledge of the state of the Homeric text at various periods. The accumulated evidence suggests that interpolations are a real and prevalent problem in the post-Aristarchean period. But these are not generally difficult to identify. I have based my evaluation of weakly attested verses on the criteria established by G.M. Bolling and refined by M.J. Apthorp,[21] which acknowledge the clearly demonstrated tendency that in the transmission of Homer's epics, as in the transmission of other sacred or highly regarded texts, accretion, not deletion, is the normal habit of copyists. The manuscript tradition of Homer, therefore, not only retained all of Aristarchus' vulgate text but acquired a fair amount of new material. The proof of this is in the consistent correlation between weakly attested verses in later manuscripts and the absence of these verses in earlier papyri. These observations led Bolling to the conclusion that the *numerus versuum* of

20. On this point, see Janko 1992, 20–29.
21. Bolling [1925] 1968, 3–30; Apthorp 1980a, 35–125.

the Aristarchean text could be reconstructed by omitting from the vulgate all weakly attested verses that show no sign of surface corruption. This conclusion appears fundamentally sound; consequently I have generally regarded weakly attested verses, particularly those absent in early manuscripts and those to which there are no Aristarchean scholia attached, as interpolations, unless there is a possibility of a copyist's error evidenced by *homoeoarchon, homoeomeson,* or *homoeoteleuton.* Occasionally, though, I have considered reasons other than mechanical ones for the omission of a verse, attempting to guess at possible contextual motives for omission; hence, while sometimes retaining suspected verses for consideration, I have tried not to make such verses a mainstay of my arguments.

Whenever we make general statements or construct elaborate theories about the intentions of Homer as a historical poet, about the nature of an original oral performance, or about the resonance of repeated formulae or the thematic echoes between reiterated type-scenes, we should keep an eye on the apparatus of our modern editions, lest we base our theories about Homer on late scribal additions. We should not regard our inherited texts, and the modern editions in which they are most readily accessible, as identical to a Homeric performance. The Wolfian vulgate, from which perhaps the most popular edition today, Allen's Oxford edition, differs but little—the Oxford edition adds *Od.* 18.111a and omits *Il.* 8.548, 550-52; 9.458-61; 11.543—has achieved such sacred status that many scholars naively accept this (or other modern eclectic editions) as canonical, without any acknowledgment of manuscript problems. In fact, some seventy-six weakly attested verses still reside in the Oxford *Iliad,* some ninety-four in the Oxford *Odyssey,*[22] and these late scribal interpolations are frequently marshaled as evidence in identifying verbal echoes, tracing thematic patterns, or supporting a particular theory of oral poetics.[23]

---

22. Apthorp 1980a, xvii.

23. A few representative examples will suffice:

Brown (1966), arguing that in order to be successful a formal curse must repeat the name and address of the object of the curse, relies heavily on *Od.* 9.531, Polyphemus' repetition of Odysseus' father's name and his address in Ithaca. But this verse is surely a concordance interpolation (from *Od.* 9.505); it is attested in only two very late manuscripts (P³ and P⁷).

Block (1985), tracing the theme of clothing requested by, and offered to, Odysseus, marshals as evidence two interpolated verses (*Od.* 14.154, 516; see Block, 5-6). By thus choosing to follow the Oxford text, even against overwhelming manuscript evidence of

At first glance, the interpolation of some 170 verses out of 27,803 total verses in the epics might not appear to present a serious problem. But to the detriment of treatments of type-scenes and themes, such as my analysis of conventional elements in hospitality scenes, these interpolations are concentrated in the most conventional passages of the poems, for it is here that a scribe, incorrectly construing an absence of a verse in a shorter than normal version of a type-scene as an omission, is most likely to interpolate the verse from a parallel passage (i.e., to make a *concordance interpolation*). Consequently almost every hospitality scene in the *Odyssey*, because of its largely conventional nature, contains serious manuscript problems.

This problem of concordance interpolations is critical, for example, in the feasting scenes of the *Odyssey*. The typical five-verse block that describes the preparation of a feast occurs six times in our inherited text (1.136–40; 4.52–56; 7.172–76; 10.368–72; 15.135–39; 17.91–95):

χέρνιβα δ' ἀμφίπολος προχόῳ ἐπέχευε φέρουσα
καλῇ χρυσείῃ, ὑπὲρ ἀργυρέοιο λέβητος,
νίψασθαι· παρὰ δὲ ξεστὴν ἐτάνυσσε τράπεζαν.
σῖτον δ' αἰδοίη ταμίη παρέθηκε φέρουσα,
εἴδατα πόλλ' ἐπιθεῖσα, χαριζομένη παρεόντων.

[A handmaid brought water and poured it from an ewer,
a beautiful, golden one, into a silver basin,
to wash with; and set out beside them a polished table.
A respected housekeeper brought bread and set it beside them,
adding many dishes, gracious with her provisions.]

Four of the scenes in which this five-verse block occurs have suffered various degrees of interpolation. The entire scene of Circe's feast preparation is a concordance interpolation (10.368–72), and the addendum to the feast preparation scene in Sparta appears to be interpolated (4.57–58). In two other scenes, the textual problems are complicated owing to

---

interpolation, Block causes the theme to appear more pervasive in this scene than it should.

W.C. Scott (1971), analyzing the scenes of feasting in Ithaca, with frequent recourse to parallel scenes of feasting in the *Odyssey*, fails to recognize that *Od.* 1.148, 4.57–58, 10.368–72, 15.139, and 21.270 are all very likely concordance interpolations. This failure casts some doubt on his resulting theory of the nature of oral composition and performance.

For further examples of failures to recognize interpolated verses, see Apthorp 1980a, 195–227.

a confusion in antiquity over the meaning of εἴδατα (misconstrued as "leftover meat") and whether it can appropriately be served in conjunction with freshly cut meat (1.139–40; 15.139).[24]

The disagreement over the meaning of εἴδατα goes at least as far back as Aristarchus. The HMQ scholia to 4.55–56 relate Aristarchus' suspicion of 1.139–40: εἰκότως δὲ νῦν τὰ περὶ τῆς ταμίας παράκειται· οὐ γὰρ ἐν τῷ ξενίζεσθαι παρὰ Τηλεμάχῳ τὴν Ἀθηνᾶν. ἐπεισεληλύθασι γὰρ οὗτοι τοῖς περὶ τὸν Μενέλαον, ἐξ ἀρχῆς δὲ παρὰ τῷ Τηλεμάχῳ πάρεστιν ὁ Μέντης. Apparently the problem entailed a misunderstanding of εἴδατα to mean "leftover meat," which would be appropriate in Sparta, where Telemachus and Pisistratus arrive after the initial feast has been served, but inappropriate in Ithaca, where Athena-Mentes arrives at the beginning of the preparation of the feast. This misunderstanding of εἴδατα led Athenaeus too (*Deipnosophists* 193b) to suspect 4.55–57 (and perhaps 1.139–41): διαμαρτάνουσι δὲ πολλοὶ παρὰ τῷ ποιητῇ ἐφεξῆς τιθέντες τούτους τοὺς στίχους· [quotes 4.55–57 = 1.139–41] εἰ γὰρ εἴδατα παρέθηκεν ἡ ταμίη, δῆλον ὡς κρεάτων λείψανα τυγχάνοντα, τὸν δαιτρὸν οὐκ ἔδει παρεισφέρειν. διόπερ τὸ δίστιχον ἀπαρκεῖ. More important here than Athenaeus' bungled textual criticism is that, whereas Aristarchus gives no indication that he suspected 1.139–40 on external grounds, we may infer from Athenaeus' words (διαμαρτάνουσι δὲ πολλοὶ) that he (or his source) knew of some manuscripts that did not have 4.57 (and perhaps 1.141). The absence of 4.57–58 in many medieval manuscripts suggests their spuriousness, raising suspicion that Athenaeus' source probably noted that 4.57–58 were missing in some manuscripts and present in others (a result of simple concordance interpolation) and attributed this weakness of attestation to falsely deduced internal evidence. The authenticity of 1.141–42, on the other hand, remains unquestionable. S. West surprisingly perpetuates Athenaeus' definition of εἴδατα as "leftover meat" and purports to solve the perceived inconcinnity in 1.139–42 by doing away with the ταμιή (1.139–40)—like Aristarchus, entirely on internal grounds.[25] But surely the omission of 1.139 by L⁴ is a mistake, for the omission of the single verse leaves 1.140 stranded.

My own, fairly simple view is that εἴδατα is a generic word for food and does not necessarily mean leftover food. After all, do the Lotus-

---

24. In 4.57–58 and 15.139, there is some difficulty in determining whether the textual problems result from simple concordance interpolation or from a lexical misconception.

25. S. West, in Heubeck, West, and Hainsworth 1988, 1.139–40n.

eaters enjoy "flowery leftovers" (ἄνθινον εἶδαρ *Od.* 9.84)? Do the horses of the gods eat "ambrosial leftovers" (ἀμβρόσιον εἶδαρ *Il.* 5.369; 13.35)? The serving of εἴδατα with fresh meat, as at 1.140–41 and 15.139–40, would not strike a Homeric audience as incongruous, and the fact that both εἴδατα and the cutting of the meat by a δαιτρός occur in the first feasting scene of the *Odyssey* only serves to show that the poet was elaborating this scene a little more than some of the others.

My conclusions about the authenticity of the six occurrences in the *Odyssey* of this five-verse block (and of some of the verses immediately after this block) follow.

(1.136–43). All verses are authentic. The omission of 1.139 by L⁴ is a mistake. Both ancient and modern objections to 1.139–41 on internal grounds are the result of a misunderstanding of εἴδατα.

(4.52–58). Athenaeus' objection to 4.57 (and presumably 4.58) on internal grounds is ill-founded, but in his report, he incidentally betrays that manuscripts at his (or his source's) disposal did not contain 4.57–58. Many medieval manuscripts, including L⁸, omit the verses, and there are no scholia attached to them. They are probably post-Aristarchean concordance interpolations (from 1.141–42); yet, it is with some tentativeness that I regard these verses as spurious, since an influential pre-Aristarchean edition may have omitted them on the same internal grounds that aroused Athenaeus' suspicion of 4.57–58 and Aristarchus' suspicion of 1.139–40.

(7.172–76). All verses are authentic.

(10.368–72). The entire passage is absent in the oldest manuscripts—Π⁸ (1–2 A.D.) and L⁴ in Allen's families e, f, i, j, k, and in Pal., T, and Z. It is in the margins of Allen's families e and j. It is bracketed in P³, V⁴, and Br. Further, there are no scholia attached to any of these verses, and Eustathius does not mention them in his commentary. The entire scene is clearly a post-Aristarchean concordance interpolation.

(15.135–41). All medieval manuscripts except Allen's families d, f, g, and h omit 15.139, and there are no scholia attached to the verse, strongly suggesting that it is a post-Aristarchean interpolation. Yet I am reluctant to strike off the last verse of a five-verse block that has maintained its integrity in every other case, especially since 15.139 is a clause dependent both grammatically and contextually on 15.138. Moreover, the same falsely deduced argument against 1.139–41 could account for the suspicion attached to 15.139; namely, that since Boethoides (= Eteoneus) is carving fresh meat at 15.140, the "leftovers" (εἴδατα) at 15.139 do not make sense. 15.135–41 are structurally similar to 1.136–43: after the five-verse block, someone carves and distributes meat, then someone else passes around the wine. I think the addendum to the five-verse block was a conventional element with which the poet could elaborate the scene. Thus, despite manuscript evidence to the contrary, I tentatively regard 15.139 as authentic.

(17.91–95). All verses are authentic.

In sum, when we consider the transmission of the Homeric epics, we face a problem that everyone who works on Homer must confront—namely, that we can never be absolutely certain of the authenticity of our inherited texts; everything we say must be affixed by an imaginary asterisk denoting that our conclusions are conditional. But these difficulties should not cause us to abandon hope of saying anything meaningful about Homer, nor should they necessarily compel us to take cover behind the protective shield of literary theories that claim to consider only the text "as we have it." In the following analyses of Homeric hospitality scenes, I base my conclusions on as early and as reliable a text as the resources available permit; beyond this I can do little more than be admittedly tentative about conclusions based on problematic verses, while studiously avoiding all the forms of dogmatism for which Homeric scholarship has become so notorious.

Chapter 2

Ithaca (*Od.* 1.103–324)

καί τε θεοὶ ξείνοισιν ἐοικότες ἀλλοδαποῖσι,
παντοῖοι τελέθοντες, ἐπιστρωφῶσι πόληας,
ἀνθρώπων ὕβριν τε καὶ εὐνομίην ἐφορῶντες.

[Even the gods, likening themselves to guests from abroad,
taking on all forms, frequent the cities,
observing both the violence and the orderliness of men.]
—(*Od.* 17.485–87)

In the first scene of hospitality in the *Odyssey*, Athena, disguised as Mentes, a guest-friend of Odysseus, visits the palace in Ithaca. Though the simple purpose of her visit, as expressed in the council of the gods (1.80–95), is to encourage the disheartened Telemachus and to set into motion his journey to Sparta and Pylos, this scene is complicated and enriched, and its tension heightened, by its drawing on the common folktale motif in which a god in disguise visits the house of mortals in order to test their hospitality. This type of theoxeny appears in folktales universally,[1] is well attested in Greek and Roman myth generally,[2] and is an often reiterated motif in the *Odyssey* itself: the Phaeacians suspect Odysseus of being a god in disguise (7.199–206); Telemachus, in awe at his father's sudden change in appearance, fears that he is a god (16.178–79); and the suitors raise the possibility that the newly arrived beggar

---

1. Thompson 1955–58, K1811, Q1.1, Q45.

2. The motif occurs in its most standard form in Jupiter's and Mercury's visit to Baucis and Philemon (Ovid *Met.* 8.611–724), Jupiter's visit to Lycaon (Ovid *Met.* 1.211–41), Zeus' and Apollo's visit to Macello (Nonnus *Dionysiaca* 18.35; scholia to Ovid *Ibis* 475; Servius on *Aeneid* 6.618), and Jupiter's, Neptune's, and Mercury's visit to Hyrieus (Ovid *Fasti* 5.495–536). On the possibility of Greek antecedents to the tale of Baucis and Philemon, see Malten 1939; Fontenrose 1945; Hollis [1970] 1985, 106–12. For Greek antecedents to the tale of Jupiter and Lycaon, see Apollodorus 3.8.1–2 and Eratosthenes *Catasterismi* 8. For a complete list of the various types of theoxenies in Greek and Roman myth, see Burnett 1970, 24–25n.8. On Odysseus' return home as a theoxeny, see chapter 8.

may be a god in disguise, come to observe the conduct of men (17.485–87). Molding the scene of Athena-Mentes' visit to Ithaca—in its simplest form merely a messenger scene—into the framework of a theoxeny increases the suspense surrounding her reception, and it accentuates the contrast between Telemachus' proper, indeed generous, hospitality and the suitors' blatant disregard for the stranger, a contrast further sharpened on the occasion of Odysseus' homecoming. Telemachus passes the divine test; the suitors do not. This contrast is articulated at every level of the Homeric diction, from the short formulaic phrases to the larger elements of the conventional type-scene. Thus the poet draws the contrast between Telemachus and the suitors on the level of form as well as content.

Athena-Mentes arrives in Ithaca and stands for a long time at the threshold of the courtyard (V; 1.103–4; cf. 119–20). A description of the residence, which commonly occurs in guest-arrival scenes (IIIa), is entirely omitted here. A description of the palace in Ithaca is reserved for the return of Odysseus himself, who describes in touching detail the home from which he has been too long absent (17.263–68). Here the poet has chosen instead to focus attention on the suitors, giving a full description of their activities (IIIc). Completely oblivious to the arrival of the stranger, they remain seated on the skins of oxen that they have slaughtered, playing games while they await the beginning of a feast (1.106–12).[3] Here, in his first portrayal of the suitors, the poet draws attention to the most improper aspect of their behavior—their consumption of Odysseus' and Telemachus' livelihood. The simple relative clause "which they themselves slaughtered" (οὓς ἔκτανον αὐτοί 1.108) poignantly encapsulates their outrageous behavior.

Though deep in contemplation, Telemachus is the first to notice Athena-Mentes (VIIa), and he hastens to greet her (VIId), indignant that a stranger should be suffered to stand so long at the door (1.113–20). It is a Homeric convention that the youngest son of the master of a house be the first to notice and greet a guest: Nestor's youngest son Pisistratus is the first to greet Telemachus in Pylos (3.36); the young Achilles is the first to notice and greet Nestor and Odysseus when they visit Phthia (Il.

---

3. Athenaeus claims to have read in a work of Apion of Alexandria, who had in turn heard from Cteson of Ithaca, that the suitors were playing a game of lots in order to determine who would win Penelope's hand (*Deipnosophists* 1.16e–17b). This is an absurd conjecture, of course, but it draws a captivating picture of the boldness of the suitors—a boldness the *Odyssey* itself portrays.

11.777); and Telemachus is the first to notice Eumaeus upon his arrival at the palace (17.328). In this scene, Telemachus' attention to the newly arrived Athena-Mentes is a striking contrast to the suitors' obliviousness: he is "by far the first" (πολὺ πρῶτος 1.113) to notice the stranger.

Telemachus' greeting is a very proper and conventional one. He takes the stranger by the right hand (VIIf), relieves her of her spear (VIIh), and bids her welcome (VIIg), saying (1.123–24):

Χαῖρε, ξεῖνε, παρ' ἄμμι φιλήσεαι˙⁴ αὐτὰρ ἔπειτα
δείπνου πασσάμενος μυθήσεαι ὅττεό σε χρή.

[Greetings, stranger, you will be welcomed by us; but when you have partaken of the meal, you will tell us what you need.]

This greeting exemplifies an important precept of proper etiquette: a meal must precede any mention of business (χρή 1.124), and even any inquiry into the stranger's identity.⁵

But Telemachus' hospitality is not merely conventional and adequate. He lavishes special attention on his guest, placing her spear against a pillar, in a stand among Odysseus' own spears (1.127–29). This gesture of relieving a guest of a spear, though not a regular element in the surviving epic corpus, appears to be a conventional motif. It serves the practical function of disarming a potentially dangerous stranger and also symbolizes the host's position as master of that particular domain. Elsewhere, in response to Theoclymenus' supplication, Telemachus invites him on board his ship and shrewdly relieves him of his spear (15.282–83). In a scene devoid of any potential danger, Eumaeus welcomes Telemachus at his hut and, as though to assert his mastery in that place, relieves him of his spear (16.40). But upon Telemachus' arrival at his

---

4. The significance of the verb is that the stranger, a ξεῖνος (outsider), will be treated as a φίλος (insider). This also appears to be the significance of the following related phrases: ξεῖνε φίλ' (1.158; 19.350); φίλοι ξεῖνοι (1.313); ξείνων φιλίων (19.351; 24.268). Cf. Lydian bilis, "one's own," as a possible cognate of φίλος.

5. Cf. the observation of this point of etiquette by Nestor (3.69–70), Menelaus (4.60–62), Arete (7.230–39), Eumaeus (14.45–47), Telemachus (16.54–59), the ruler of Lycia (Il. 6.171–77), Achilles (Il. 9.221–24), Charis and Hephaestus (Il. 18.385–87), and Metaneira (H.Dem. 206–12); for breaches of this rule, cf. the Cyclops (9.251–55), Calypso (5.85–96—here Hermes disregards her questions until after they have eaten), and Alcinous (7.199–206, 215–21—here, although having been served a feast, Odysseus expresses reluctance to begin a conversation until his belly is full).

own home, in the absence of a proper master of the house, he puts away his spear himself (17.29). In this scene, then, Telemachus' gesture of taking Athena-Mentes' spear serves the practical function of disarming an unknown stranger and also asserts his authority in the house. But the gesture is elaborated here to emphasize Telemachus' role as a proper, indeed an exceptional, host, special attention being given to the touching detail of Telemachus' placement of the spear into his father's own spear stand. One may compare this to Leto's affectionate welcome of her son Apollo: upon his arrival home, she alone of the gods welcomes him, relieving him of his bow and hanging it from a golden peg on her father's pillar; only then does she lead him to his seat (*H.Ap.* 5-9).

Telemachus' provision of a seat for his guest is also exceptionally generous (VIII). He seats her on a θρόνος, the most formal and honorable type of the various Homeric chairs. He spreads a beautifully crafted cover on the chair and provides a footstool (θρῆνυς) for his guest's feet, while he himself sits down on the humbler κλισμός (1.125-32). One may compare this to Achilles' display of proper etiquette in offering his own θρόνος to the suppliant Priam, taking for himself the more lowly κλισμός (*Il.* 24.515, 522, 553, 597).[6]

The contrast between the behavior of Telemachus and that of the suitors is sharpened in the feasting scene that follows. Lest his guest become annoyed at the uproar of the suitors and lose her appetite, Telemachus seats her "apart from the other suitors" (ἔκτοθεν ἄλλων μνηστήρων 1.132-33). This phrase conveys both the spatial and the moral distance that separates the two groups, for while Telemachus and Athena-Mentes diligently observe the rituals that define the reciprocal nature of the relationship of *xenia*, the suitors demonstrate by their behavior—and the poet demonstrates by his formal description of their behavior—that they enjoy this reciprocal relationship neither with Telemachus nor with the newly arrived stranger. The quiet conversation between Telemachus and his guest in the corner of the hall represents the only glimmer of civilization in the topsy-turvy realm of Ithaca.

Whereas Telemachus displays proper etiquette toward his guest by leading her into the house, relieving her of her spear, and seating her on an elaborately decorated θρόνος, the suitors display no such etiquette

---

6. Priam's herald is made to sit on the δίφρος (*Il.* 24.578), the most humble of the three seats. On this scene, see R.M. Frazer 1971. Telemachus' exceptional manners here have been noted since antiquity. The scholia to 1.130 praise his speech, his manners, his taking of the guest's spear, and his offer to the stranger of his own seat.

and remain oblivious to the guest's arrival. And Telemachus does not extend such courtesy to them; they simply enter the palace and seat themselves of their own accord (1.144-45):

Ἐς δ᾽ ἦλθον μνηστῆρες ἀγήνορες. οἱ μὲν ἔπειτα
ἑξείης ἕζοντο κατὰ κλισμούς τε θρόνους τε.

[The arrogant suitors came in. Then they
sat down in order on seats and on armchairs.]

The preparation of the feast (IXa), while understood to be simultaneously enjoyed by all participants, is narrated as two consecutive events. By this formal presentation of the feast preparation in two separate narratives, the poet suggests that while Telemachus and Athena-Mentes are participating in the ritual of proper *xenia* the suitors are merely consuming yet another meal at the expense of their unwilling host.[7] The preparation of Telemachus' and Athena-Mentes' feast is narrated first, and it is described at great length: a handmaid brings water for washing their hands and sets a table beside them, a housekeeper serves bread and other food, a carver serves platters of meat, and a herald pours their wine (1.136-43). More importantly, the poet uses here a conventional block of formulaic verses that in the *Odyssey* almost always appear as a unit (1.136-40 = 4.52-56; 7.172-76; [10.368-72]; 15.135-[39]; 17.91-95):[8]

χέρνιβα δ᾽ ἀμφίπολος προχόῳ ἐπέχευε φέρουσα
καλῇ χρυσείῃ, ὑπὲρ ἀργυρέοιο λέβητος,
νίψασθαι· παρὰ δὲ ξεστὴν ἐτάνυσσε τράπεζαν.
σῖτον δ᾽ αἰδοίη ταμίη παρέθηκε φέρουσα,
εἴδατα πόλλ᾽ ἐπιθεῖσα, χαριζομένη παρεόντων.

[A handmaid brought water and poured it from an ewer,

---

7. Consecutive narration of simultaneous events is a common technique in Homeric epic, but something more sophisticated seems to be occurring in this scene. W.C. Scott (1971) notes the differences between the two scenes with regard to their length and elaboration, and their variation in the use of repeated verses. He suggests that these are deliberate devices on the part of the oral poet to show the different treatment that Athena-Mentes and the suitors receive.

8. For the manuscript problems of 10.368-72 and 15.139, see chapter 1. No theories about the nature of oral composition and performance should be based on these apparently late additions to the Homeric text.

a beautiful, golden one, into a silver basin,
to wash with; and set out beside them a polished table.
A respected housekeeper brought bread and set it beside them,
adding many dishes, gracious with her provisions.]

The consecutively narrated description of the suitors' feast preparation
is much less fully elaborated, and it does not draw on the formulae of
the conventional feast preparation type-scene (1.146–[48]):

τοῖσι δὲ κήρυκες μὲν ὕδωρ ἐπὶ χεῖρας ἔχευαν,
σῖτον δὲ δμῳαὶ παρενήνεον ἐν κανέοισι,
[κοῦροι δὲ κρητῆρας ἐπεστέψαντο ποτοῖο.]⁹

[Heralds poured water upon their hands,
and servant girls heaped up bread in baskets,
[and young boys filled up mixing bowls to the brim with wine.]]

Verses 1.146 and [1.148] are the normal introduction not to a feasting
scene but to a libation scene (cf. 3.338–39; 21.270–71; *Il.* 9.174–75), and
verse 1.147, which interrupts the progress of the libation sequence, is
unattested elsewhere in Homer (although it is clearly conventional: a
modification of this verse appears in the description of Eumaeus' meal
preparation at 16.51).¹⁰

An audience steeped in the conventions of Homeric oral poetry would

---

9. A strong case, based on external grounds, can be made against the authenticity of
1.148 (as well as 1.148a νώμησαν δ' ἄρα πᾶσιν ἐπαρξάμενοι δεπάεσσιν). 1.148 is absent
in the two oldest manuscripts to contain this passage (P¹⁰⁶ = Pack 1024 and L⁴), as well
as three others (L⁶, R⁵, R⁶). Further, in other manuscripts this verse is found in different
places (after 146, 147, 148a, and 149), suggesting that it was originally found in the margin
and was later inserted at different points in the text. The internal evidence is strong too.
There is nothing in the passage to provoke a copyist's error. The verse is a likely candidate
for concordance interpolation (1.148 = 3.339; 21.271; *Il.* 1.470; 9.175). Elsewhere the verse
is used only of libation scenes in a religious context, and so appears somewhat inappropriate
here. A motivation for its interpolation may be surmised in a perceived need for a mention
of drinks, given verse 1.150, though in fact the mixing of the suitors' wine has already
occurred at 1.110. Elsewhere 1.148 is always followed by 1.148a (3.339–40; 21.271–72),
indicating that the two verses should be taken as a pair and should stand or fall together—
hence, the case against 1.148a, which is very strong, strengthens the case against 1.148. I
regard both verses as interpolations.

10. Arend (1933, 71–72) notes the similarity of these verses to a conventional libation
scene. The scholia to 15.138 contrast the action of the ταμίη and that of the δμῳαί: "The
δμῳαί heap up bread because of the suitors' profligacy and greediness."

not fail to perceive the connotation. The potpourri of verses that describes the preparation of the suitors' feast would seem abrupt, perhaps a bit jarring, in the face of the elaborately wrought description of the serving of Telemachus and Athena-Mentes. An experienced audience had no doubt heard the conventional feast preparation type-scene numerous times and, immediately realizing the conventional nature of the serving of Telemachus and Athena-Mentes, would have anticipated the subsequent verses as soon as the first verse was uttered, comfortably assured that Telemachus was conducting himself properly as host. In each case in the *Odyssey* where this conventional block of verses is used, exceptional hospitality is being offered: Menelaus' extravagant hospitality (4.52–56; 15.135–[39]); Alcinous' belated, but generous, hospitality (7.172–76); Circe's propitiatory banquet ([10.368–72]); and Penelope's welcome of Telemachus at his homecoming (17.91–95). The recollection of scenes like these would have colored the audience's perception of this scene, reassuring them that Telemachus was conducting himself properly.

Verse 1.149, which describes the actual consumption of the feast (IXb), raises a pertinent question (1.149):

οἱ δ' ἐπ' ὀνείαθ' ἑτοῖμα προκείμενα χεῖρας ἴαλλον.

[They stretched forth their hands to the food that was spread out ready.]

Does this verse refer only to the suitors or to both groups? The ambiguity here appears deliberate, for it complements the effect created by the consecutive narration of the two feast preparations. In effect, the poet has portrayed, on the level of form as well as on the level of content, a situation in which Telemachus, Athena-Mentes, and the suitors partake physically of the same food but do not partake in the intimacy of a shared feast.

After the feast, the suitors turn their attention to another conventional element of hospitality, "song and dance, the delights of the banquet" (XIII; 1.152). Just as Demodocus provides entertainment among the Phaeacians, so does Phemius among the Ithacans; the conventional diction used here to describe the herald bringing the lyre to the bard and the bard striking up a song is very close to the diction in the scene of Demodocus (cf. 1.153–55; 8.261–62, 266). But the situation in Ithaca is anything but usual; this element of the banquet is perverted by the suitors, who force the bard Phemius to play and sing "under compulsion" (ἀνάγκῃ 1.154). The abnormality of this situation is further accentuated by the fact that the guest, Athena-Mentes, takes no part in the song and dance but continues to sit apart with Telemachus. Phemius, unlike Demodocus, performs not for the guest but for the suitors. It is perhaps with some irony that the poet has portrayed a scene in which the disguised Athena is relating to Telemachus the imminent return (νόστος) of Odysseus (1.195–205), while in the background Phemius is entertaining the enraptured suitors with songs about the bitter return (νόστος) that Athena had inflicted on the other Achaeans (1.325–27).

In accordance with proper etiquette, Telemachus requests his guest's identity only after the conclusion of the feast (XIa). His formal request is expressed in conventional diction (1.170–73: 170 = 10.325; 14.187; 15.264; 19.105; 24.298; cf. 7.238; H.Dem. 113; 1.171–73 = 14.188–90; cf. 16.57–59; each of these three passages describes the questioning of strangers on the island of Ithaca):[11]

τίς πόθεν εἰς ἀνδρῶν; πόθι τοι πόλις ἠδὲ τοκῆες;
ὁπποίης τ᾽ ἐπὶ νηὸς ἀφίκεο᾽ πῶς δέ σε ναῦται
ἤγαγον εἰς Ἰθάκην; τίνες ἔμμεναι εὐχετόωντο;
οὐ μὲν γάρ τί σε πεζὸν ὀίομαι ἐνθάδ᾽ ἱκέσθαι.

[What men are you from? Where are your city and parents?

---

11. Verses 1.171–73, Telemachus' questions to Athena-Mentes, and 1.185–86, her corresponding answers, were suspected in antiquity. Aristarchus probably placed an obelus and asterisk by 1.171–73, since the scholia note that he placed an asterisk by 14.188–90, which he evidently believed to be the source of this passage. According to the scholia to 1.171–73, Aristarchus thought the passage more appropriate in the episode with Eumaeus and Odysseus, and the scholia to 14.188–90 tell why: ὅτι νῦν ὡς πρὸς ῥάκεσιν ἠμφιεσμένον ὀρθῶς λέγονται᾽ ὡς δὲ πρὸς τὴν Ἀθηνᾶν ὁμοιωθεῖσαν Μέντῃ καὶ Βασιλικὴν ἔχουσαν στολὴν οὐ πάνυ (i.e., these are the types of questions one asks of a beggar, not of a prince; the scholia to 16.57–59 reassert this). Objection to the verses' appropriateness, as well as the common objection to repeated verses, may very well account for the omission of 1.171–73 in some pre-Aristarchean manuscripts, as the scholia to 1.171–73 report. 1.185–86 were understandably athetized by Aristophanes and Aristarchus, since they respond to 1.171–73. The scholia to 1.185–86 report that some editions did not contain these verses.

The evidence of the scholia, then, raises the possibility of pre-Aristarchean interpolation. Yet the scholia suggest that these verses were omitted on internal grounds that strike one familiar with the nature of oral poetry as unreliable. Further, while 1.185 could have been interpolated from elsewhere in the Odyssey (24.308), 1.186 is unique.

I favor the authenticity of all these verses, though with sufficient tentativeness to avoid making them an important part of my argument.

Upon what sort of ship did you come, and how did the sailors
bring you to Ithaca? Who did they claim to be?
For I do not think that you came here on foot.]

But the addendum to his questions (1.175-77), in which he asks specif-
ically whether Athena-Mentes is a *xenos* of his father Odysseus, is unique,
and therefore worthy of closer attention. Telemachus is clearly concerned
about his obligation to this stranger; if Athena-Mentes is a *xenos* of his
father, he too shares the relationship, with all its benefits and
obligations.[12]

Accordingly, in her answer (XIb) Athena-Mentes perspicaciously
stresses her relationship of *xenia* with Odysseus. She claims to be a *xenos*
of Odysseus through their fathers (1.187-88):

ξεῖνοι δ᾽ ἀλλήλων πατρώϊοι εὐχόμεθ᾽ εἶναι
ἐξ ἀρχῆς.

[We claim to be hereditary guest-friends of each other
from long ago.]

She supports this claim by demonstrating her awareness of Laertes' and
Odysseus' circumstances (1.189-205) and by remarking on Odysseus'
and Telemachus' similarity in physical appearance (1.208-9). She makes
a point of the frequent contact she and Odysseus had enjoyed (θαμὰ
τοῖον ἐμισγόμεθ᾽ ἀλλήλοισι 1.209), directing Telemachus' attention to
a specific occasion on which Odysseus had been offered hospitality,
including a gift, by her father (1.257-64).

While Athena-Mentes is recapitulating her relationship of *xenia* with
Odysseus, she is cultivating a similar relationship with Telemachus him-
self. By providing news of Odysseus' whereabouts (1.195-99), a prophecy
of his imminent return (1.200-205), and advice regarding the resolution
of the situation in Ithaca (1.269-302), she is already reciprocating for

---

12. One of the most striking aspects of the institution of *xenia* is its inheritability. A
vivid illustration occurs in *Il.* 6.119-236, where the opposing warriors, Glaucus and Dio-
medes, discover that their grandfathers, Bellerophon and Oeneus, had been *xenoi* and had
exchanged gifts—gifts that Diomedes, for his part, still possesses. In a dramatic scene,
Glaucus and Diomedes decide not to fight but to renew their inherited relationship by
exchanging gifts themselves, demonstrating that the institution of *xenia* transcends even
political loyalties. Cf. *Od.* 4.104-12, 169-80; 15.195-98.

Telemachus' hospitality. News, messages, instructions and advice, prophecies, and stories are integral elements in the exchange of information between guest and host, and they often function, as here, as a form of reciprocity for the host's material hospitality (XII).

Athena-Mentes' zealous disclosure of her relationship with Odysseus gives rise to an ironic, and rather pathetic, scene. She apparently knows Odysseus better than does his own son. Telemachus has never seen his father, and he is even uncertain about his true parentage (1.215–16). Athena-Mentes' request for Telemachus' identity (1.206–7), then, is not merely a frivolous departure from convention (in which the host normally demands the identity of his guest, not vice versa) but a poignant commentary on an unusual and pathetic situation. Telemachus is unsure of his own identity, and his guest, who can at least observe the physical similarities between father and son (1.207–9), is better qualified than he to make a judgment as to his identity.

At this point in the narrative, Athena-Mentes' sudden announcement that she will return to her ship (1.303–4) threatens to bring this hospitality scene to an abrupt and unexpected end. In a fully narrated hospitality scene, a bed (XVII), a bath (XVIII), a presentation of guest-gifts (XX), and an offer of conveyance to the next destination (XXV) would still await the guest (see Appendix). But Athena-Mentes' unexpected announcement precludes the fulfillment of these rituals, and the conscientious Telemachus is justifiably concerned, lest he be unable to fulfill all the obligations of a proper host. He protests that she should remain until he can offer a bath and a guest-gift—a "precious" and "very beautiful" one (τιμῆεν, μάλα καλόν 1.312), which will be a "treasure" (κειμήλιον 1.312).

The poet must extricate himself from a delicate situation here. On the one hand, Athena-Mentes' purpose in coming to Ithaca has been achieved, and there is nothing to be gained by extending the scene further; as a simple messenger scene, it is complete. Moreover, as a divinity, Athena-Mentes cannot continue to participate in the exclusively human institution of *xenia*: acceptance of a bath would be awkward; acceptance of a guest-gift would result in an unacceptable obligation to her human host. The gods do not normally participate in the banquets of men or in the human ritual of gift exchange; their relationship to man is a vertical rather than a horizontal one; they get their share of the banquet through sacrifice and their share of gifts through offerings, which they reciprocate with blessings.[13] On the other hand, a blatant refusal of Telemachus' gift would be a serious breach of proper etiquette. In the Homeric world, refusal to accept a gift would signal refusal to participate in any relationship that entailed reciprocal obligation. Such refusal would halt the flow of the economy; it would be comparable, on a social level, to refusal to marry or to give one's daughters in marriage.[14] The poet delicately skirts these difficulties by having Athena-Mentes postpone the gift rather than refuse it. She tells Telemachus that she will fetch it on her homeward journey, and she advises him to make it a gift "worthy of a reciprocal exchange" (σοὶ δ' ἄξιον ἔσται ἀμοιβῆς 1.318).

---

13. This vertical relationship is clearly defined in the myth of Prometheus (Hesiod *Theog.* 535-57). After the intervention of Prometheus, the gods no longer endured the feasts of men, taking their share of the banquet in the form of sacrifice (cf. *Il.* 4.48-49 = 24.69-70). The only Homeric incident of a mortal and an undisguised god feasting together is the meal shared by Odysseus and the nymph Calypso, in which case an explicit contrast is drawn between the human food of Odysseus and the nectar and ambrosia of the goddess (*Od.* 5.196-99). The Ethiopians and Phaeacians, with whom the gods share in the banquet undisguised, have superhuman status (*Il.* 1.425; 23.205-7; *Od.* 1.22-26; 7.201-3). See Vernant 1977, 910-12; Saïd 1979, 17-18.

14. Finley 1955; Finley [1965] 1978, 58-164; Gould 1973, 90-101.

Chapter 3
Pylos (*Od.* 3.4–485; 15.193–214)

οὔ θην δὴ τοῦδ' ἀνδρὸς 'Οδυσσῆος φίλος υἱὸς
νηὸς ἐπ' ἰκριόφιν καταλέξεται, ὄφρ' ἂν ἐγώ γε
ζώω, ἔπειτα δὲ παῖδες ἐνὶ μεγάροισι λίπωνται,
ξείνους ξεινίζειν, ὅς τίς κ' ἐμὰ δώμαθ' ἵκηται.

[By no means will the dear son of this man Odysseus
spend the night on the deck of his ship, so long as I
live, and so long as children are left in my halls
to grant hospitality to guests who come to my house.]
—(*Od.* 3.352–55)

In sharp contrast to the anarchy in Ithaca, where the suitors entirely disregard the rituals of hospitality, Telemachus finds in Pylos a stable and well-ordered society, whose ruler takes great pride in his scrupulous observation of every detail of these rituals. Nestor is exceptionally pious: sacrifices, libations, and prayers abound in this scene, and they are essential ingredients of Nestor's expression of hospitality toward his guests, often complementing, or even substituting for, the conventional elements of feast preparation and consumption in more secular hospitality scenes. Nestor's hospitality is also warm and intensely personal, although his provisions for his guests are somewhat simple; this is a contrast to the extravagant, but less personal, hospitality soon to be offered by Menelaus in Sparta. In many respects, the hospitality scenes in Pylos and Sparta function as paradigms of proper hospitality with which all other scenes of hospitality in the *Odyssey* can be compared or contrasted; they are the standard by which the perversions and inversions of hospitality in subsequent scenes, particularly in Odysseus' wanderings, can be recognized. As part of his overall design of the monumental *Odyssey*—a chronological hysteron-proteron, in which the travels of Telemachus are narrated before the chronologically earlier wanderings of Odysseus—Homer has artistically, and informatively, placed these models of proper hospitality early in the epic.

This, at least, is the apparent situation; in fact, under closer scrutiny, the behavior of both Nestor and Menelaus proves to be less than exemplary because of the very zealousness of their hospitality. Both hosts become so possessive of their guest that they try to detain him, becoming potential obstacles to his return home. This overzealousness serves thematically to create a sympathetic harmony between Telemachus and Odysseus: both son and father are abroad at the same time, experiencing adventures in exotic surroundings, both ultimately desiring a return home (νόστος) but confronting obstacles to it. While Odysseus confronts Lotus-eaters and Sirens, who would detain him with food and song, and goddesses and witches, who detain him with their charms, Telemachus confronts a more innocent, but no less effective, obstacle—his hosts' excessive hospitality, which obstructs his expeditious return home. This aspect of their hospitality is not immediately apparent in books 3 and 4, but it becomes clear when the narrative returns to Telemachus in book 15, after the theme of the detention of guests has become familiar from the adventures of Odysseus in books 9–12. I believe this is the deliberate design of a poet who had good control over the architectonics of his entire epic.

It is remarkable that both the description of Telemachus' and Athena-Mentor's arrival at Pylos and the description of the activities of the Pylians—both conventional elements of a typical scene of hospitality (II, IIIc)—are narrated not once but twice. First they "arrive" (ἷξον 3.5) on their ship at the shores of Pylos, where the Pylians are performing a sacrifice (3.5–9); then they "arrive" (ἷξον 3.31) on foot at a gathering of Pylians, where Nestor is sitting with his sons and companions, preparing a feast (3.32–33). On the level of content, these two arrivals are to be understood as one and the same; on the level of form, this double narration first draws attention to the general populace of Pylians, then focuses attention on Nestor and his family, who, being the objects of Telemachus' quest, are of primary importance.

The description that follows of the reception of the strangers is analogous. When the gathered Pylians catch sight of the strangers (VIIa), the entire company approaches en masse (VIId; ἀθρόοι ἦλθον ἅπαντες 3.34), greets them with their hands (VIIg; 3.35), and bids them to sit (VIII; 3.35).[1] Then Pisistratus, Nestor's youngest son, approaches "first"

---

1. This communal reception is a stark contrast to the reception in Ithaca, where Telem-

(VIId; πρῶτος 3.36), takes them by the hand (VIIf; 3.37), and seats them in the place of honor beside his brother and father (VIII; 3.36–39).[2] The two descriptions refer to the same reception, of course, but the narratives are formally distinct. The double narration further focuses attention on Pisistratus, who will prove to be Telemachus' most intimate companion. By using double narration to tell of the strangers' arrival and reception, the poet has created an aesthetically pleasing visual effect, slowly focusing attention, as though through a zoom lens, first on the general populace of Pylians, then on a smaller group comprised of Nestor and his family, and finally on Pisistratus himself. This device of narrative focusing signifies, on the level of form, the incorporation of these strangers into the social group; in the final picture, they are intimately surrounded by their accommodating hosts, seated in the place of honor, next to the ruler of the land.

The incorporation of these strangers into the social group is powerfully expressed by Pisistratus' invitation to participate in the performance of religious rituals: sacrifice, libation, and prayer (XV; 3.40–64). Such an incorporation of outsiders (ξεῖνοι) into the household (οἶκος) is the raison d'être of the institution of *xenia,* and here it is achieved through shared participation in the Pylians' favorite pastime.

The prevalence of religious rituals in this scene is even more striking when one observes that scenes of sacrifice and libation are functional replacements for the more usual scenes of feast preparation and consumption. In more secular hospitality scenes, a description of feast preparation (IXa) normally ensues after the reception (VII) and seating (VIII) of a guest. But here in Pylos, a long description of sacrifice, libation, and prayer intervenes (3.40–64), overshadowing the subsequent description of feasting (3.65–67). The guests are given "portions of entrails" (σπλάγχνων μοίρας 3.40) to taste instead of bread and meat, and the wine that is offered is designated for libations rather than for drinking. The description of the feast that follows is very short, its preparation, consumption, and conclusion comprising only three verses (IXa-b-c; 3.65–67):

οἱ δ' ἐπεὶ ὤπτησαν κρέ' ὑπέρτερα καὶ ἐρύσαντο,
μοίρας δασσάμενοι δαίνυντ' ἐρικυδέα δαῖτα.

---

achus alone greets Athena-Mentes, the suitors remaining oblivious to the stranger's arrival; here in Pylos, the entire community shares in the hospitality.

2. For the convention of the youngest son of the master of the house being the first to notice and greet a guest, cf. Telemachus (1.113; 17.328) and the young Achilles (*Il.* 11.777).

αὐτὰρ ἐπεὶ πόσιος καὶ ἐδητύος ἐξ ἔρον ἔντο,

[When they had roasted the outer flesh and unskewered it,
dividing up the portions, they partook of the glorious feast.
But when they had cast aside their desire for food and drink,]

Moreover, verses 3.65–66 are not the ones normally used to describe the preparation and consumption of feasts; elsewhere in Homer these verses always occur in the context of sacrifice (3.65 = 3.470; 20.279; 3.66 = 20.280). Verse 3.67, the normal conclusion for a feast of any kind (Homer 22x), is the only formal element used elsewhere in Homer to describe secular feasting scenes.

This theme of Nestor's piety is further reinforced in the following scene, which describes the arrival of the Pylians and their guest at Nestor's palace. They all enter the palace and take their seats (3.389):

ἑξείης ἕζοντο κατὰ κλισμούς τε θρόνους τε,

[They sat down in order on seats and armchairs,]

In every other occurrence of this formula in Homer, a scene of feasting ensues (1.145; 10.233; 15.134; 24.385), but not here; instead Nestor administers a libation and prayer to Athena (3.390–94).

The final feasting scene in Pylos on the following day follows a similar pattern. The description of the preparation and performance of the sacrifice is greatly elaborated (3.418–63) at the expense of the feast itself, which is very simply described (3.470–73).

In sum, religious rituals are the most conspicuous of the typical elements in this scene. Nowhere else in the *Odyssey* are so many or such elaborate sacrifices, libations, and prayers described (3.5–9, 40–64, 332–42, 380–84, 390–95, 418–63). Moreover, on a formal level, they complement, and in some instances actually replace, the typical descriptions of the feast. Feasting in Pylos is always done in conjunction with sacrifice, drinking with libation. This is a stark contrast to Sparta, where no sacrifices are performed,[3] and to Ithaca, where the suitors' feasting and drinking conspicuously lack a religious dimension.[4]

---

3. Bethe (1922, 31) makes a poignant contrast: "Nestor der Patriarch, Menelaos der Weltmann."

4. In the suitors' orgy of feasting and drinking, sacrifice and libation are absent. See Vidal-Naquet 1970, 1291; Saïd 1979, 32–41.

Only after the sacrifice, libations, and prayers have been completed and after all have had their fill of the subsequent feast, does Nestor, proper host that he is, inquire into his guests' identity (XIa; 3.69–74):

Νῦν δὴ κάλλιόν ἐστι μεταλλῆσαι καὶ ἐρέσθαι
ξείνους, οἵ τινές εἰσιν, ἐπεὶ τάρπησαν ἐδωδῆς.
ὦ ξεῖνοι, τίνες ἐστέ; πόθεν πλεῖθ᾽ ὑγρὰ κέλευθα;
ἤ τι κατὰ πρῆξιν ἢ μαψιδίως ἀλάλησθε
οἷά τε ληϊστῆρες ὑπεὶρ ἅλα, τοί τ᾽ ἀλόωνται
ψυχὰς παρθέμενοι, κακὸν ἀλλοδαποῖσι φέροντες;[5]

[Now it is better to inquire and ask
guests who they are, when they have taken delight in food.
O strangers, who are you? From where do you sail the watery ways?
Are you on some business or do you wander aimlessly,
like pirates, who wander over the sea,
risking their lives, bringing evil to foreigners?]

Nestor's questions may strike a modern reader as a blatant discourtesy, but this formula should be regarded as a routine epic inquiry into the business of unexpected guests (3.71–74 = 9.252–55; *H.Ap.* 452–55). Apparently the rituals of hospitality were so hallowed that a proper host like Nestor was obligated to offer hospitality to his guests regardless of who they were, even to pirates.[6]

---

5. Verses 3.72–74 and the parallel verses at 9.253–55 (=*H.Ap.* 453–55) fell under suspicion in antiquity. According to the scholia on 3.71–74, Aristophanes thought the questions inappropriate in the mouth of the Cyclops (9.253–55) because the Cyclops "would not be such a chatterbox"; hence, he thought verses 9.253–55 were interpolated from 3.72–74. Aristarchus took the opposite view: that the questions were less appropriate in the mouth of Nestor because "Telemachus would not appear to be a pirate." Both scholars' judgments are based on internal, and therefore highly subjective, grounds; there is no external manuscript evidence against either passage. A further argument for the authenticity of 3.72, at least, is Telemachus' direct response to the question at 3.82, a verse whose authenticity was not questioned by Aristarchus.

6. The critical difference between Nestor's and Polyphemus' interrogation of their guests is not the content of their questions, which are identical (3.71–74 = 9.252–55), but the position of the interrogation in the sequence of events: Nestor, as is proper, questions his guests only after the completion of the feast (cf. 1.123–24; 4.60–62; 7.230–39; 14.45–47; 16.54–59; *Il.* 6.171–77; 9.221–24; 18.385–87; *H.Dem.* 206–12); Polyphemus rudely interrogates his guests immediately upon arrival (cf. 5.85–96; 7.199–206, 215–21). See further chapter 6.

But Telemachus is not a pirate. He is the son of Odysseus, a faithful companion and guest-friend of Nestor (3.126–29; cf. 3.352–55). Like Athena-Mentes in Ithaca (1.178–212), Telemachus perspicaciously refers to this relationship, identifying himself as the son of Odysseus and mentioning Odysseus' friendship with, and past favors to, Nestor (3.83–85, 98–101). Since *xenia* is an inheritable relationship, Nestor and Telemachus are now *xenoi,* and Nestor begins to regard his guest no longer as an outsider, a potentially hostile stranger, but as an insider. Henceforth Nestor addresses Telemachus as φίλος (3.103, 184, 199, 211, 313, 352, 375).

Nestor's attitude toward his guests is well expressed by his outburst when Telemachus and Athena-Mentes make as if to depart for their ship for the night (3.346–55):

Ζεὺς τό γ' ἀλεξήσειε καὶ ἀθάνατοι θεοὶ ἄλλοι,
ὡς ὑμεῖς παρ' ἐμεῖο θοὴν ἐπὶ νῆα κίοιτε
ὥς τέ τευ ἢ παρὰ πάμπαν ἀνείμονος ἠὲ πενιχροῦ,
ᾧ οὔ τι χλαῖναι καὶ ῥήγεα πόλλ' ἐνὶ οἴκῳ,
οὔτ' αὐτῷ μαλακῶς οὔτε ξείνοισιν ἐνεύδειν.
αὐτὰρ ἐμοὶ πάρα μὲν χλαῖναι καὶ ῥήγεα καλά.
οὔ θην δὴ τοῦδ' ἀνδρὸς Ὀδυσσῆος φίλος υἱὸς
νηὸς ἐπ' ἰκριόφιν καταλέξεται, ὄφρ' ἂν ἐγώ γε
ζώω, ἔπειτα δὲ παῖδες ἐνὶ μεγάροισι λίπωνται,
ξείνους ξεινίζειν, ὅς τίς κ' ἐμὰ δώμαθ' ἵκηται.

[May Zeus and the other immortal gods prevent this:
that you go away from me to your swift ship,
as though from someone altogether without clothing or poor,
in whose house there are neither mantles nor many blankets,
neither for himself nor for his guests to sleep in softly.
But I do have mantles and lovely blankets.
By no means will the dear son of this man Odysseus
spend the night on the deck of his ship, so long as I
live, and so long as children are left in my halls
to grant hospitality to guests who come to my house.]

A number of characteristics, both of Nestor's behavior and of the rituals of hospitality in general, are illuminated in this speech. For the first time in the *Odyssey,* Zeus' special interest in hospitality is expressed, for it is Zeus in particular whom Nestor invokes (3.346). The most powerful god oversees this most vital institution of human civilization— Zeus Xeinios, protector of suppliants and strangers (9.270–71; cf. 6.206–8; 9.477–79; 14.56–59, 283–84, 388–89):

Ζεὺς δ᾽ ἐπιτιμήτωρ ἱκετάων τε ξείνων τε,
ξείνιος, ὃς ξείνοισιν ἅμ᾽ αἰδοίοισιν ὀπηδεῖ.

[Zeus is the protector of suppliants and guests,
Zeus Xeinios, who attends to revered guests.]

In this speech, Nestor also emphasizes an aspect of *xenia* that was previously touched on by Athena-Mentes during her visit to Ithaca—the inheritability of the relationship of *xenia*. Nestor declares that not only as long as he lives but as long as his sons inhabit his house *xenoi* will be offered *xenia* (3.352–55). His declaration proves to be prophetic, since Telemachus and Pisistratus later claim a relationship of *xenia* with each other based on their own shared experiences as well as on their fathers' relationship (15.196–98).

Somewhat unexpected is Nestor's emphasis on his financial resources. Perhaps he assumes that his moral rectitude has already been established by his proper reception of his guests and by his pious observance of religious rites, and he can conceive of no reason for his guests' desire to leave other than that they think him poor. To counter this, he vehemently claims that he possesses sufficient clothing and bedding to make them comfortable.[7] But the general impression of Nestor in Pylos is not of a rich king in a luxurious dwelling, as is the case of Menelaus in Sparta. Although Nestor has demonstrated, and will continue to demonstrate, a scrupulous adherence to the rituals of hospitality, his provisions for his guests are not extravagant, particularly in contrast to Menelaus' lavish hospitality. Yet his reception continues to be characterized by a warmth and personal affection largely lacking in Sparta.

Scrupulous adherence to the rituals of hospitality by Nestor, and by the Pylians generally, distinguishes this scene as a paradigm of proper hospitality (see Appendix). The Pylians' initial reception of their guests

---

7. The historical custom of providing mantles for guests is attested in the Linear B tablets. Knossos Ld 573 runs: e-ru-ta-ra-pi pa-we-a | ke-se-nu-wi-ja re-u-ko-nu-ka, ideogram for mantle, 35 (ἐρυθρᾶφι φάρεα ξείνια λευκ[όνυχα?]), "thirty-five mantles for guests with white [borders?] and with red [somethings]").

is exemplary: they catch sight of them immediately (VIIa), rush to them (VIId), take them by the hand (VIIf), greet them (VIIg), and offer them seats in the place of honor next to Nestor himself (VIII; 3.34–39). They incorporate these guests into their community through shared participation in sacrifice, libation, prayer, and feast (IX, XV; 3.40–66). As is proper, Nestor does not inquire into his guests' identity until after they have satisfied their appetites (XIa; 3.67–74). In the exchange of information that follows the feast (XII), Nestor offers both good entertainment and sound advice, relating stories about the returns (νόστοι) of various Iliadic heroes (XIII; 3.102–98, 253–312), and exhorting Telemachus to be brave like Orestes (3.199–200) and to hasten to Sparta in search of additional news (3.313–23). When the Pylians and Telemachus return to the palace, Nestor provides his guest the usual sleeping accommodations, a bed in the portico (XVII; ὑπ' αἰθούσῃ 3.399; cf. 4.297; 7.345; *Il.* 24.644). On the next day, Telemachus is given a bath, anointed with oil, and provided a fresh change of clothing (XVIII). Then he is seated at the place of honor beside Nestor (VIII), where he partakes of another feast (IX; 3.464–72). Finally, Nestor provides his guest conveyance (πομπή) to his next destination: horses, chariot, and supplies for the journey (XXV; 3.475–85). The only conventional element of hospitality conspicuously absent from this scene is a presentation of guest-gifts upon departure (XX); presumably Nestor expects to meet this obligation upon Telemachus' return.

But as scrupulous as is Nestor's attention to the details of *xenia,* his provisions for his guests are relatively simple, particularly in comparison with the luxurious accommodations provided by Menelaus in Sparta. In Sparta, heralds, servants, and handmaids attend to the guests; in Pylos, these duties fall on members of Nestor's family. In Sparta, the description of the palace upon the guests' arrival is greatly elaborated (4.43–46); in Pylos, a description of the palace is almost entirely lacking (3.388). In Sparta, the preparation and consumption of two lavish feasts are described at length (4.52–68; 15.135–44); in Pylos, the description of the serving of food is secondary to the description of sacrifice (3.65–67, 470–73). In Sparta, the description of a luxurious bed for Telemachus is greatly elaborated (4.296–301); in Pylos, a very simple bed is described (3.399). In Sparta, Telemachus receives precious guest-gifts of gold and silver (4.613–19; 15.102–29); in Pylos, as events turn out, he receives nothing.[8]

---

8. Some of the simplicity in this scene is due to the Pylians' circumstances: they are

Yet what Nestor lacks in wealth and luxury he makes up for in warmth and personal affection. In Sparta, the guests are received rather coldly by a herald (4.22–36); in Pylos, they are warmly greeted by Nestor's relatives and sons (3.31–42). In Sparta, the housemaids bathe the guests (4.48–50); in Pylos, Nestor's own youngest daughter Polycaste performs this duty (3.464–68).[9] In Sparta, servants perform most of the tasks of the feast (4.52–58; 15.92–98, 135–41); in Pylos, Nestor and his sons prepare food and serve wine (3.32–33, 390–94). There is no one in Sparta to correspond to Nestor's youngest son Pisistratus, who becomes Telemachus' closest companion and personal guide (3.36–39, 400–401, 415–16, 481–85).

Yet, for all its paradigmatic qualities, Nestor's hospitality is marked by his overzealousness, his wish to detain his guest in Pylos, ultimately even against his will. This theme of detention (XIX) is first observed, though in a completely positive light, in Athena-Mentor's advice to Nestor that he should put an end to the day's activities and allow his guests to go to bed (3.331–36). While this is a compliment to Nestor's abilities as a story-teller—his stories of various νόστοι have occupied an entire day—it also characterizes him as an overly garrulous and confining person.[10]

The theme of detention is next observed, again in a positive light, in Nestor's response to his guests' imminent departure. When Athena-Mentor and Telemachus make as if to go back to their ship for the night, Nestor "detains" (κατέρυκε 3.345) them in order to offer them more comfortable accommodations in his own home. This gesture can be understood simply as a sign of generous hospitality; yet the verb κατέρυκε is pregnant with meaning in the *Odyssey,* being most immediately

---

sacrificing on a beach rather than feasting in a palace. Hence a simple seat on fleeces in the sand replaces the more elaborate thrones of palaces (3.38). This may also account for the omission of the usual description of the palace, the later arrival at Nestor's palace being secondary in this scene.

9. Usually the slave women administer the bath (4.49; 6.209; 8.454; 10.348; 17.88; 19.317; 23.154; cf. 24.366), occasionally the mistress of the house (4.252; 5.264; 10.449). It is very special treatment to have an unmarried daughter of the king bathe a stranger; the only remotely comparable scene in Homer is when Hebe, daughter of Zeus and Hera, bathes her brother Ares on Olympus (*Il.* 5.905).

10. Often a tired guest interrupts the activities of the evening by asking to be allowed to sleep (XVI): so Athena-Mentes asks Nestor (3.333–34), Telemachus asks Menelaus (4.294–95), Odysseus asks the Phaeacians (11.330–31, 373–74) and Penelope (23.254–55), and Priam asks Achilles (*Il.* 24.635–36). Always the host, not the guest, wishes to stay up (cf., in addition to the above, Eumaeus at 15.390–402, Penelope at 19.509–11). Only once in Homer does a host unasked urge a guest to go to bed (Arete at 7.334–43).

associated with Calypso's treatment of Odysseus, whom she "detains" against his will (κατερύκει 1.55; 23.334; cf. 1.197; 4.498, 552). The verb is also used in a very revealing speech by Menelaus upon Telemachus' imminent departure from Sparta (15.68–74):

Τηλέμαχ', οὔ τί σ' ἐγώ γε πολὺν χρόνον ἐνθάδ' ἐρύξω
ἱέμενον νόστοιο· νεμεσσῶμαι δὲ καὶ ἄλλῳ
ἀνδρὶ ξεινοδόκῳ, ὅς κ' ἔξοχα μὲν φιλέῃσιν,
ἔξοχα δ' ἐχθαίρῃσιν· ἀμείνω δ' αἴσιμα πάντα.
ἶσόν τοι κακόν ἐσθ', ὅς τ' οὐκ ἐθέλοντα νέεσθαι
ξεῖνον ἐποτρύνει καὶ ὃς ἐσσύμενον *κατερύκει*.
χρὴ ξεῖνον παρεόντα φιλεῖν, ἐθέλοντα δὲ πέμπειν.

[Telemachus, I will not detain you here for long,
since you are desirous for your return home; I would be indignant
    at another man
who, receiving guests, acted excessively hospitable
or excessively hostile; all things are better in due measure.
It is as blameworthy to urge a guest to leave who does not want
to as it is to *detain* a guest who is eager to leave.
One must grant hospitality to a guest who is present and grant
    conveyance to a guest who wants to leave.]

This theme of detention is not fully developed until Telemachus returns to Pylos on his journey home in book 15. After his too lengthy stay in Sparta, Telemachus is in a hurry to return home and asks Pisistratus to assist him in avoiding a meeting with his father (15.199–201):.

μή με παρὲξ ἄγε νῆα, διοτρεφές, ἀλλὰ λίπ' αὐτοῦ,
μή μ' ὁ γέρων ἀέκοντα κατάσχῃ ᾧ ἐνὶ οἴκῳ
ἱέμενος φιλέειν· ἐμὲ δὲ χρεὼ θᾶσσον ἱκέσθαι.

[Do not lead me past the ship, Zeus-nourished, but leave me there,
lest the old man detain me unwilling in his house
in his desire to grant hospitality. But I must go quickly.]

Pisistratus complies with Telemachus' request, realizing the threat his father poses to his friend's expeditious return (15.209–14):

σπουδῇ νῦν ἀνάβαινε κέλευέ τε πάντας ἑταίρους,
πρὶν ἐμὲ οἴκαδ᾽ ἱκέσθαι ἀπαγγεῖλαί τε γέροντι.
εὖ γὰρ ἐγὼ τόδε οἶδα κατὰ φρένα καὶ κατὰ θυμόν·
οἷος κείνου θυμὸς ὑπέρβιος, οὔ σε μεθήσει,
ἀλλ᾽ αὐτὸς καλέων δεῦρ᾽ εἴσεται, οὐδέ ἕ φημι
ἂψ ἰέναι κενεόν· μάλα γὰρ κεχολώσεται ἔμπης.

[Embark now in haste and urge on all your companions
before I go home and report to the old man.
For well do I know this in my mind and heart,
how overweening his heart is; he will not let you go,
but he will come here himself to summon you, and I do not think
he will go back empty-handed, for he will be extremely angry.]

The final and lasting impression of Nestor is as an overbearing host.
What was in book 3 a somewhat humorous trait of a garrulous old man
has in book 15 developed into a serious obstacle to Telemachus' return.
Telemachus is so fearful of detention that he even forgoes the expected
guest-gifts in order to accomplish his νότος surreptitiously. Nestor's own
son calls his father "overweening" (ὑπέρβιος 15.212), a word elsewhere
applied in the *Odyssey* only to the suitors' activities (7x) and to Odysseus'
men when they eat the cattle of Helius (12.379). Nestor's overly zealous,
and consequently obstructive, hospitality is a fault, and at least by the
standards of Menelaus' didactic speech to Telemachus, it is deserving of
"blame" (κακόν 15.72).

This blameworthiness in Nestor's hospitality serves a function in the
interplay of themes in the larger structure of the *Odyssey*. By placing
this scene, as well as the scene of Telemachus' difficult departure from
Sparta, after the narration of the wanderings of Odysseus, Homer has
created a sympathetic harmony between father and son. By book 15, the
ubiquitous obstacles to Odysseus' return have become a familiar theme;
now there arise similar obstacles to Telemachus' return. Nestor and
Menelaus are as potentially effective as obstacles to Telemachus' νόστος
as Calypso and Circe are to Odysseus'. Telemachus plans to sneak away
from Sparta (15.44–55) and in fact does so from Pylos. Both father and
son, who are abroad at the same time, the one in a world of monsters
and witches, the other in a world of ancient Iliadic heroes, overcome
obstacles to achieve their νόστοι, arriving in Ithaca at about the same
time, to be reunited in the lowly hut of the swineherd Eumaeus after
twenty years.

Chapter 4

Sparta (*Od.* 4.1–624; 15.1–184)

ἀμείνω δ' αἴσιμα πάντα.
ἰσόν τοι κακόν ἐσθ', ὅς τ' οὐκ ἐθέλοντα νέεσθαι
ξεῖνον ἐποτρύνει καὶ ὃς ἐσσύμενον κατερύκει.

[All things are better in due measure.
It is as blameworthy to urge a guest to leave who does not
want to as it is to detain a guest who is eager to leave.]
—(*Od.* 15.71–73)

Accompanied by Pisistratus, Telemachus next seeks the hospitality of Menelaus in Sparta. This hospitality scene, one of the longest and most elaborate in the *Odyssey,* and one that in many ways functions as a paradigm of proper hospitality, occupies most of book 4 and a large portion of book 15. Like the scene in Pylos, it is interrupted by the long ten-book narrative of Odysseus' homecoming. This involved narrative structure was no doubt an innovation of Homer, and it is one that has elicited much admiration. But as ingenious and sophisticated as was Homer's innovation in enveloping the narrative of Odysseus' "Return" (books 5–14) within the narrative of Telemachus' adventures (i.e., the "Telemachy"; books 1–4, 15.1–184), the joining of these two narratives has resulted in some chronological difficulties, for the amount of time that elapses in the two narratives is different. According to the account of sunsets, dawns, and the passing of days, the narrative leaves Telemachus as a guest of Menelaus in Sparta on the sixth day of the action of the epic (4.624) and returns to him on the dawn of the thirty-sixth day (15.1).[1] Is the audience to understand that Telemachus has spent a

---

1. See Delebecque 1958, 31–41, chart opposite 12; Hellwig 1964, 42–44. They agree in their chronologies, except Delebecque puts an end to the *Odyssey* at 23.296, and so he calculates a total of forty days instead of Hellwig's forty-one. Stanford (1958–59, x–xii, 15.1ff.n) calculates that Athena reaches Sparta on the dawn of the thirty-fifth day, in order

71

month in Sparta? Or is it to understand that time has been at a standstill for Telemachus during Odysseus' homecoming, and that when Homer turns his narrative back to Sparta in book 15 it is the day after the events narrated in book 4?

The scholarly debate on this problem of chronology has centered on the question of whether time is understood to stop in one place (e.g., Telemachus in Sparta) when the narrative shifts to another (e.g., Odysseus on his travels from Ogygia to Ithaca) or whether time is understood to continue at a relatively similar rate in both places. In view of the variety of ways in which Homer indicates the chronological relationship of different scenes, the apparent confidence with which many have taken one side or the other in this debate seems unjustified.[2] For a long time, it has been recognized that Homer often narrates simultaneous events as if they had occurred successively; hence, while the events of scene A are being narrated, the audience is to understand that nothing is happening, that time is at a standstill, in scene B, and vice versa.[3] This appears to be the case in *Iliad* 15.143-261, where the simultaneous dispatches of Iris to Poseidon and Apollo to Hector are narrated as if the events had occurred successively, and in *Odyssey* 1.80-95 and 5.28-42, where the simultaneous dispatches of Athena to Telemachus and Hermes to Odysseus are narrated successively, as if Athena's duties had been accomplished (in books 1-4) before Hermes set out (in book 5). In each case, time appears to be suspended for one party (Apollo and Hermes) while it continues for the other (Iris and Athena) and vice versa.

---

to avoid the inconsistency of Telemachus' spending two nights on his voyage home while Odysseus spends one night with Eumaeus. But this calculation creates a problem more serious than the one it solves, since it would entail Athena arriving in Sparta (15.1) before she has departed from Ithaca (13.439-40). This would also unravel Homer's intricate interweaving of the Return and the Telemachy, whereby he leaves Odysseus sleeping at night in Ithaca at the end of book 14, and returns to Telemachus sleeping at night in Sparta at the beginning of book 15. Homer's clever synchronization of the two narratives would be destroyed by Stanford's calculation, since it assumes that it is one night earlier for Telemachus than for Odysseus.

2. Favoring a long stay by Telemachus in Sparta are Rothe (1914, 119), Shewan (1926, 31-37), Woodhouse (1930, 15-16, 163-64), Focke (1943, 1-24), Heubeck (1954, 58-63), Delebeque (1958, 18-30), Eisenberger (1973, 84-87, 92), and Apthorp (1980b, 1-22).

Those who argue that the Homeric concept of time is such that Telemachus' stay in Sparta may be regarded as a short one include Fränkel ([1931] 1960), Hölscher (1939, 1-3), Page (1955, 64-67, 77-79), Austin (1969, 48-52), Erbse (1972, 39-41), and Hoekstra, in Heubeck and Hoekstra (1989, 15.1-3n).

3. The seminal work is by Zielinski (1899-1901), who attributes this type of narration to a primitive conception of time that could not embrace two actions at once.

These two examples of narrating simultaneous events as if they had occurred successively have often been marshaled as evidence against a long stay by Telemachus in Sparta, since by using them as criteria time should be understood to be suspended in Sparta while the events of Odysseus' homecoming are narrated.[4] But the chronological relationship between the Telemachy and the Return is essentially different from these two examples. Homer does not indicate at 15.1 that the events to follow are to be understood as simultaneous with the events preceeding (i.e., the Return), as he does in *Iliad* 15.220-35 by narrating a second dispatch and in *Odyssey* 5.1-42 by narrating a second council of the gods and a second dispatch. On the contrary, Homer indicates that the events to follow are to be understood as occurring simultaneously with the events involving Odysseus at home in Ithaca, leaving a temporal vacuum of about a month during which Telemachus has been lingering in Sparta.

This method of narrating simultaneous events (in which time is understood to be suspended in one place while continuing in another) is not the only, or even the most common, method found in the epics. Very often, Homer narrates simultaneous events as if they occupy the same time, simply by using the common adverb *meanwhile* (τόφρα; e.g., *Il.* 4.220-21; 13.81-84; 15.343-45, 390-94; *Od.* 3.301-3, 464-65; 8.438-40; 23.288-90; 24.365-67).[5] In these cases, time appears to continue at a relatively equal rate in both scenes.

Very often, too, Homer narrates a change of scene paratactically, sometimes abruptly (even in midverse), without a connecting adverb (e.g., *Il.* 3.448-50; 16.1-2, 101-2; *Od.* 4.624-25; 6.1-3; 13.185-89; 17.166-69; 20.240-42). It is left to the audience to determine the chronological relationship of the two scenes. Usually this poses no difficulties, and though the chronological relationship is usually of little or no concern, it is generally understood that time goes forward in both scenes at a similar rate. This is manifestly clear on the many occasions when a switch is made from scene A to scene B and back to scene A again; time continues in scene A even when the narrative shifts to scene B (e.g., *Il.* 3.116-245; 6.116-237; 9.656-69; 11.611-44; 15.405-16.2; 17.700-18.2; 18.148-369; *Od.* 2.337-4.625; 15.296-497; 15.547-16.323).

The joining in book 15 of the two major narratives of the *Odyssey,* the Telemachy and the Return, appears to be of this last type. The narrative simply leaves Odysseus in Ithaca at the end of book 14 and

---

4. See, for example, Page 1955, 65-67.
5. See Bassett's salutary corrective of Zielinski (1938, 34-39).

describes Athena's arrival in Sparta at the beginning of book 15. In the rather minor actions in the examples listed above, the question of how much time has elapsed in the transition is rarely a matter for concern. The only example that aproaches the magnitude of the change in book 15 is the change of narrative from Ithaca to Pylos-Sparta and back to Ithaca again (*Od.* 2.337–4.625). Using it as a criterion, it would seem to support the impression of a long stay by Telemachus in Sparta, for time clearly elapses in Ithaca while Telemachus is abroad.[6]

The narration of Odysseus' homecoming has taken an extraordinarily long time—the events of thirty days narrated in ten books—placing some stress on Homer's usual methods and creating a potential for a certain amount of bewilderment on the part of the audience. Additional stress is created by Homer's desire to synchronize the chronologies of the narratives of Odysseus and Telemachus precisely at the point at which they join. He does this by leaving Odysseus asleep at night in Ithaca (14.523) and returning to Telemachus asleep at night in Sparta (15.5), as though it were the same night. This effectively precludes the audience from regarding the narrative of book 15 as recording the events of the day after the events narrated in book 4. There is left the impression that Telemachus' stay in Sparta has been a lengthy one.

What do these questions of chronology have to do with the theme of hospitality? It seems that Homer has anticipated the potential for bewilderment on the part of his audience about the chronological relationship of the Telemachy and the Return and has prepared the way since the beginning of book 4 by making a long stay in Sparta thematically plausible. Homer has made a point of describing the attractiveness of Sparta: the splendor of the palace (4.43–47, 71–75) and the escape from the harsh realities of Ithaca (4.164–67, 317–21) provided by Helen's drug (4.220–26) and Menelaus' stories (4.595–98). When the narrative leaves Telemachus in Sparta and returns to the suitors in Ithaca (4.625), Telemachus' intentions are left unclear; although he ostensibly refuses Menelaus' invitation to remain in Sparta for awhile (4.587–88, 594, 598–99), he expresses a desire to stay "even for a year" (εἰς ἐνιαυτόν 4.595), listening to Menelaus' stories (4.595–98). When the narrative returns to Sparta ten books, and thirty days, later, it is not surprising to find Telemachus still lingering there.

Homer most effectively makes a long stay in Sparta plausible by his

---

6. So Delebecque 1958, 42–55; Apthorp 1980b, 3–4.

development of the theme of guest detention. This theme is seen in embryonic form early in book 4, but it is more elaborately developed in book 15. Just as Telemachus is attracted to Sparta, so Menelaus, who has just lost his only legitimate child to marriage, is overjoyed at the prospect of granting hospitality to the son of a former comrade (4.60–64, 169–70). The potential for guest detention is first observed in Menelaus' wish that he had settled Odysseus and Telemachus near him in Argos, where they would have delighted in each other's company until they died (4.171–80). His expressed jealousy of Nestor, with his abundance of sons (4.209–11), is a further indication of his potential for guest detention: he is now childless, and Telemachus is thought fatherless. The attractions of Helen's drug and Menelaus' stories, and therefore their potential as obstacles to Telemachus' return home, are parallel to the attractions/obstacles to Odysseus of the drugs of the Lotus-eaters and Circe and the songs of the Sirens.

The similarities between the experiences of father and son, and the echoes in the formulaic language that describes these experiences, suggest that Telemachus' return, like his father's, will be fraught with obstacles. At the end of book 4, just before the narrative leaves Telemachus in Sparta, Menelaus invites him to stay for "eleven or twelve days" (4.588), and he offers him guest-gifts designed to prevent rather than facilitate his return home (4.589–92, 600–608). When the narrative returns to Telemachus in book 15, this theme of guest detention becomes even more pronounced. Menelaus seems entirely unable to appreciate Telemachus' anxiety to leave, ignoring his repeated pleas for a speedy return (15.65–66, 88–91) and instead performing in minute detail all the rituals involved in a formal leave-taking: gift giving, feasting, libation, and farewell speeches. He even tries one last time to persuade Telemachus to stay and take a trip through Hellas and Argos with him (15.80–85). It is no wonder that upon hearing Athena's message Telemachus intends to sneak away from Sparta without a formal farewell (15.44–55), an intention realized in the case of his departure from Nestor in Pylos (15.195–214).

From a practical point of view, then, this theme of guest detention is Homer's answer to the chronological problems posed by the joining of the two major narratives in the *Odyssey*. But this is only a partial explanation for the development of the theme. A more important, and more artistic, reason for its development is its place among the many parallels between the experiences of Telemachus in Sparta and the experiences of Odysseus during his return. These shared experiences create a sympathetic harmony between father and son, and they connect the two major threads of the *Odyssey* thematically.[7] Both father and son are wandering far from home, encountering strangers to whom they cautiously reveal their identities. They meet various attractions and dangers, both of which pose obstacles to their expeditious homecomings. In the scenes of hospitality, these attractions and dangers take on the form of a temptation of the guest to stay and, ultimately, of a forceful detention of the guest. Both father and son experience temptation and detention as they are entertained, predominately by powerful women hosts; both are tempted by the delights of food, drink, drugs, stories, and song to forget their homecoming and enjoy an easy life far from the troubles of Ithaca; both must be reminded of their homecoming; and both must sagaciously extricate themselves from the lavish entertainment of their hosts, overcoming the temptation to remain secure in a blissful but unreal utopia. When their hosts become overbearing or forceful, this theme of temptation progresses, for both father and son, into a theme of guest detention. Homer has created a sympathetic harmony between father and son by means of these thematic analogues; moreover, he has made this sympathetic harmony very acute by artistically arranging his narrative so that Odysseus is telling the stories of former obstacles to his return (books 9–12) and is experiencing present obstacles to his return (in Scheria) at the same time that Telemachus is experiencing similar obstacles in Sparta. Telemachus is stranded in Sparta for ten books with good reason.

This theme of guest detention, and its contribution to the development of a sympathetic harmony between father and son in the two major threads of the *Odyssey*, is certainly not the only, nor perhaps even the most important, theme in this scene of hospitality in Sparta. I emphasize it only because it seems relatively neglected, and because it shines a curiously illuminating light on the controversial question of Homeric chronology. The commentary that follows will address in detail many other interesting themes and problems in this scene of hospitality: the various manipulations and transformations of the conventions of hospitality; the paradigmatic quality of Menelaus' hospitality; the comparison of the hospitality in Sparta with that in Pylos, which immediately

---

7. On the common experiences of father and son, see Seitz 1950, 131–37; Rose 1967, 391–98; Rüter 1969, 141–42, 238–40; Fenik 1974, 5–60; Austin 1975, 181–200; Powell 1977, 50–56. Apthorp (1980b, 12–22) treats more specifically the common obstacles to both of their returns.

precedes, and with that of Odysseus in Scheria, which immediately follows; the motif of the slow *anagnorisis* of the guest; and the place of this scene in the overall structure of the epic.

(4.1–19). Homer creates a very revealing first impression of Sparta that anticipates themes to be worked out later in the scene. It is an impression of immense wealth and splendor, yet at the same time one of melancholy and sterility—all is not well in the land of the Lacedaemonians. They are celebrating the double wedding of Menelaus' daughter Hermione and son Megapenthes, replete with neighbors and kin as guests and with a bard and tumblers for entertainment. But it is a sad occasion too, for Menelaus' only legitimate child is being sent far away to Neoptolemus' kingdom, and Helen is unable to bear him any more children (4.12–14).[8] For this reason, the wedding is marked by a sense of sadness and loss, resembling in a curious way its polar opposite, a funeral.[9] In spite of its splendor, Sparta appears at first glance a bittersweet place.

(4.20–36). Sparta lacks the warm affection of Nestor and his brood in Pylos. In Sparta, it is not, as in Pylos, or even as in Ithaca, a family member who first sees the guests and rises to greet them (VIIa, c, d; 3.36–39; 1.113–24; cf. Achilles in *Il.* 11.777–79); it is the official herald of the palace, Eteoneus. And, quite unexpectedly, rather than "go to" his guests (VIId), "stand near them, and address them with winged words" (VIIg), as Telemachus does in Ithaca (βῆ δ᾽ ἰθὺς ... ἐγγύθι δὲ στάς ... ἔπεα πτερόεντα προσηύδα 1.119–22), Eteoneus, while his actions are described in the same formulaic language, does precisely the reverse. He "goes" (βῆ δ᾽ ἴμεν 4.24), "stands near" (ἀγχοῦ δ᾽ ἱστάμενος 4.25), and "addresses with winged words" (ἔπεα πτερόεντα προσηύδα 4.25), but these actions are directed not to the guests but to his master Menelaus; he leaves Telemachus and Pisistratus standing in the doorway while he consults with his master as to whether they should be granted hospitality or sent elsewhere (VIIb). This is remarkably rude behavior, especially in view of Telemachus' earlier expression of indignation that his own guest should be left standing for a long time in the doorway

---

8. Homer makes a point of the fact that Menelaus' bastard son Megapenthes ("Much Grief") was born of a slave.

9. This is perhaps related to the historical reality of archaic Greece, where the marriage of a daughter was, from a parent's perspective, tantamount to her funeral, since it involved her "loss," that is, her removal to another's household (οἶκος).

(1.119–20). It is a very strange behavior too, the motivation for which is difficult to decipher. Does the herald hesitate to greet the guests because of the special circumstances of the wedding celebration?[10] Is his hesitation due to the notorious results of a previous experience with a guest in Sparta (i.e., Paris; cf. *Il*. 3.351–54)?[11] Or is the herald's hesitation a poetic device designed to provide an opportunity for displaying Menelaus' indignation at his servant's lack of hospitality—Eteoneus' impropriety acting as a foil for Menelaus' magnanimous hospitality? This seems to be the effect intended here, for to Eteoneus' question as to whether they should accept the guests or send them elsewhere, Menelaus answers "very indignantly" (μέγ᾽ ὀχθήσας 4.30), calling Eteoneus a "fool" (νήπιος 4.31) who speaks like a "child" (πάϊς 4.32), that just as they had received "much hospitality" (ξεινήϊα πολλά 4.33) during their travels, so should they offer it to these guests.

Menelaus' instructions to Eteoneus initiate one of the longest and most elaborate scenes of hospitality in the *Odyssey,* and one that is paradigmatic of proper hospitality in many respects. This scene contains all the conventional elements of the two previous hospitality scenes, but it extends the ritual to its proper conclusion of gift-giving and formal leave-taking, adding some unique elements as well. Moreover, it elaborates these conventional elements far more than did the previous two scenes.

(4.37–43). Before Telemachus and Pisistratus are ushered into the palace, Eteoneus and a retinue of attendants look after the needs of the horses. This is one of only two incidents of horse hospitality in Homer (VIIe; cf. *Il*. 8.432–35).[12] It is analogous to scenes of human hospitality, corresponding closely to the hospitality offered subsequently to Telemachus and Pisistratus: the unyoking of the horses corresponds to the change of clothing offered to the human guests (4.39, 50); the leading of the horses to the manger, to the seating of the human guests (4.40, 51); the description of the horses' meal of emmer and white barley, to the description of the human feast (4.41, 52–66). Even the leaning of the chariots against the wall is vaguely analogous to the leaning of a human guest's

---

10. So S. West, in Heubeck, West, and Hainsworth 1988, 4.20ff.n.

11. So scholia to 4.26.

12. The simple stopping, unyoking, and feeding of horses is a typical scene (*Il*. 5.368–69, 775–77; 8.49–50, 440–41), but only *Il*. 13.34–38, the description of Poseidon's tending to his own horses, approaches the elaborated form of these two scenes.

spear against a pillar or wall (4.42; 1.127-29; cf. 17.29; *Il.* 13.260-61).
Only on Olympus are horses provided for so generously (*Il.* 8.432-35).

(4.43-47). A description of the residence (IIIa) is a recurrent element in
arrival scenes (5.57-76; 7.81-102, 133-34; 9.218-23; 10.210-11; 14.5-22;
17.264-68; *Il.* 6.242-50, 313-17; 18.369-71; 24.448-56). Upon their arri-
val in Sparta, Telemachus and Pisistratus marvel at how Menelaus' palace
"gleams like the sun or the moon" (4.45), and they "take great delight
in looking at it" (4.47). After a brief interruption for a bath and meal,
this description continues at 4.71-75, where Telemachus remarks on the
splendor of the bronze, gold, amber, silver, and ivory, comparing Mene-
laus' palace to the home of Zeus on Olympus. Elsewhere in the *Odyssey*,
only the splendor of Alcinous' palace in Scheria matches this description
(7.81-135: 7.84 = 4.45; 7.85 ≈ 4.46; 7.134 ≈ 4.47).

(4.48-50). A bath, anointing, and provision of fresh clothing, which
follow the arrival scene, are also conventional elements of hospitality
(XVIII), but this is one of very few occasions in Homer on which the
guests are offered a bath immediately on arrival.[13] Elsewhere the bath
occurs later, sometimes even on the following day (1.310; 3.464-67; 8.454-
56; 10.364-65, 449-51; 19.317). The availability of a bath on arrival
points to the exceptional quality of Menelaus' hospitality; his ability to
maintain a heated bath continuously is also a reflection of his high
standard of living.[14]

(4.51-68). After the bath, the guests are led to the seat of honor beside
the master of the house (VIII; 4.51; cf. 1.130-32; 3.37-39, 469; 7.169-
71).[15] There ensues the familiar block of verses describing the preparation

---

13. Upon Odysseus' arrival in Scheria, Nausicaa's handmaids provide him with oil and
bid him to bathe himself in the river (6.214-16); upon Telemachus' and Theoclymenus'
arrival at the palace in Ithaca, they are bathed by the servants (17.87-90).

14. So S. West, in Heubeck, West, and Hainsworth 1988, 1.310n.

15. The wedding celebrations have been entirely forgotten; they are never again men-
tioned. This has disturbed some readers. Diodorus the Aristophanean regarded the wedding
scene as spurious (Athenaeus, *Deipnosophists* 180e). Modern scholars have recognized the
infelicity of such wholesale expurgation based solely on internal evidence, and by regarding
the inherited text here as genuine, they have come to appreciate the artistic shift, brought
about by the arrival of the two guests, from a wedding scene to a funeral scene (i.e., that
of Odysseus), from an epithalamium to a dirge, from a ritual involving insiders (φίλοι)
to one involving outsiders (ξεῖνοι); see Bergren 1981, 203-5.

and serving of the feast (IXa; 4.52-56 = 1.136-40; 7.172-76; [10.368-72]; 15.135-[39]; 17.91-95):[16]

χέρνιβα δ᾽ ἀμφίπολος προχόῳ ἐπέχευε φέρουσα
καλῇ χρυσείῃ, ὑπὲρ ἀργυρέοιο λέβητος,
νίψασθαι· παρὰ δὲ ξεστὴν ἐτάνυσσε τράπεζαν.
σῖτον δ᾽ αἰδοίη ταμίη παρέθηκε φέρουσα,
εἴδατα πόλλ᾽ ἐπιθεῖσα, χαριζομένη παρεόντων.

[A handmaid brought water and poured it from an ewer,
a beautiful, golden one, into a silver basin,
to wash with; and set out beside them a polished table.
A respected housekeeper brought bread and set it beside them,
adding many dishes, gracious with her provisions.]

As is proper, Menelaus assures his guests that he will inquire into their identity only after they have eaten (XIa; 4.60-62; cf. 1.123-24; 3.69-70; 7.230-39; 14.45-47; 16.54-59; *Il.* 6.171-77; 9.221-24; 18.385-87; *H.Dem.* 206-12), and he shows special graciousness by offering them the fatty chine of the cow, which was his own "portion" (γέρας 4.66; cf. 8.474-83; 14.437-41; *Il.* 7.321-22; 9.206-8). The consumption and conclusion of the feast are described by the same formulaic verses used in the preceding two hospitality scenes (IXb-c; 4.67-68 = 1.149-50; 4.68 = 3.67):

οἱ δ᾽ ἐπ᾽ ὀνείαθ᾽ ἑτοῖμα προκείμενα χεῖρας ἴαλλον.
αὐτὰρ ἐπεὶ πόσιος καὶ ἐδητύος ἐξ ἔρον ἕντο

[They put forth their hands to the food lying ready before them.
But when they had cast off desire of drink and food,]

(4.69-167). In the two previous scenes, the feast was followed by an inquiry into the guests' identity (XIa; 1.169-77; 3.69-74), but in this scene, the identification of the guest is considerably delayed, its details slowly worked out while Telemachus expresses further amazement at the splendor of Menelaus' palace (4.71-75), Menelaus tells the tale of his own return home (νόστος) and of the fates of other Iliadic heroes (4.78-

---

16. The addendum to this block of verses, 4.57-58, is probably a concordance interpolation. On the general manuscript problems of this type-scene, see chapter 1.

112), Telemachus weeps for his father (4.113–16), and Helen makes her grand entrance (4.120–37). Only then is the question of Telemachus' identity addressed, first by Helen's suspicions (4.138–46), then by Menelaus' (4.147–54), and finally by Pisistratus' confirmation of these suspicions (4.155–67); Telemachus plays the role of the silent stranger throughout the scene. The complexity and length of Telemachus' *anagnorisis* here (4.60–157) is remarkable in contrast to the relative simplicity of the two previous identification scenes (1.169–212; 3.69–101).[17]

The delayed *anagnorisis* here facilitates the continuation of the theme of Telemachus' physical resemblance to his father (cf. 1.206–12; 3.120–25). Rather than Telemachus identifying himself, as is the norm in the simple type-scene of guest identification (XIb), he is identified by Helen and Menelaus, who remark on his physical likeness to Odysseus. This is of great psychological importance to Telemachus, whose journey abroad is in many ways educative, particularly with regard to his own identity. He had earlier expressed doubt about being the son of Odysseus, whom, after all, he has never even seen (1.213–20).[18] Helen and Menelaus can, and do, provide confirmation of his identity. Thus, as do many other themes in the *Odyssey*, this theme of self-recognition provides a link between the experiences of father and son.

Odysseus too is often recognized or referred to by his hosts even before he tells them his name: Demodocus sings of Odysseus' exploits to the unknown stranger (8.73–82, 499–520); Circe recognizes Odysseus because of his cleverness (10.330); Eumaeus, the swineherd, tells stories about Odysseus to his disguised guest (14.115–47); Penelope speaks about Odysseus to the disguised beggar (19.124–63), and she even remarks on the beggar's physical likeness to Odysseus (19.357–60), as does Eurycleia (19.361–81); and Philoeteus, the goatherd, is also reminded of Odysseus when he sees the beggar (20.191–207). Thus Odysseus' hosts, like Telemachus' in this scene, provide confirmation of his identity, a confirmation

---

17. The ancients were impressed by the novelty of this scene: the scholia to 4.69 contrast the "common" (κοινός) pattern of identification, as in the episode at Pylos, with the "novel" (καινός) pattern here; Eustathius (1487, 15ff.) attributes the difference between the two scenes to "Homer's being fond of variety" (πολυσχήμων).

18. Of the various reasons for Telemachus' journey to Pylos and Sparta, its educative function and its contribution to the boy's maturation are the most frequently cited: scholia to 1.93, 284; J.A. Scott 1917, 420–28; Schwartz 1924, 253; Woodhouse 1930, 210–12; Jaeger 1945, 29–34; Reinhardt 1948, 47; Millar and Carmichael 1954, 58–64; Delebecque 1958, 137; Kirk 1962, 359; Clarke 1963, 129–45; Klingner [1944] 1964, 39–79; Austin 1975, 181–200.

for which Odysseus is yearning as intently as is his son, for his return home (νόστος) is a metaphor for his psychological return to self-recognition.[19] Recognition by his hosts confirms to him that he is no longer "No-man" (Οὖτις 9.366) but is in fact Odysseus.

Another result of Telemachus' delayed *anagnorisis* is the delightful irony it produces, particularly in Menelaus' speeches. First, Menelaus compliments the lineage of his guests (4.62–64), not realizing how noble and well-known to him their lineage actually is. Next, after telling briefly of his own return from Troy, and of his own troubles, he remarks that his guests "will have heard these things from your fathers" (4.94–95)— not true in Telemachus' case. Conversely, Menelaus himself will tell Telemachus shortly about the troubles of his father. Finally, in the most ironic speech of all, Menelaus declares his close relationship with, and his indebtedness to, Odysseus, as well as his extreme grief over Odysseus' fate, even mentioning in passing the grief of Laertes, Penelope, and Telemachus himself (4.104–12). Thus Menelaus unknowingly, and therefore without any possibility of guile, builds a bond of friendship with Telemachus, based on the inheritability of *xenia*. By means of his delayed *anagnorisis,* Telemachus finds in Menelaus a trustworthy host, just as Odysseus, by means of his disguise, finds in Eumaeus a trusted servant (13.397–415). Most ironic, of course, is Menelaus' mention of Telemachus himself (4.112), a situation with many parallels in the experiences of his father (8.73–83, 492–520; 14.37–184; 19.124–381). In the pathetic culmination of this scene—pathos is often the outcome of irony—Menelaus' mental image of Telemachus grieving at home incites Telemachus to begin weeping in reality.

In a scene with many parallels to this one, that of Odysseus in Scheria, Homer constructs a similar situation of delayed *anagnorisis,* leading to a similar profusion of irony.[20] In both scenes, the usual spontaneous reception of guests is replaced by an initial hesitation to grant hospitality: in Sparta, by the herald Eteoneus; in Scheria, by Alcinous himself (VIIb; 4.22–29; 7.153–54). In both scenes, the agents of this impropriety are quickly reprimanded (4.30–36; 7.155–66), and the guests are hospitably received (4.37–68; 7.167–84). And in both scenes, the guests are amazed

---

19. Frame 1978.

20. The similarities between the two scenes have long been recognized. See the scholia to 4.113; 8.43, 489, 492; Eustathius 1489, 35ff.; Hölscher 1939, 66; Seitz 1950, 132; Rüter 1969, 238–40; Fenik 1974, 20–28; Austin 1975, 179–200; Powell 1977, 30–32, 52–53; Apthorp 1980b, 12–22; Richardson 1983, 223–25.

at the splendor of the palaces, which glitter with the brilliance of gold, silver, and bronze (4.43–47, 71–75; 7.81–135). Homer uses the same simile to describe their splendor (4.45–46 ≈ 7.84–85):

ὥς τε γὰρ ἠελίου αἴγλη πέλεν ἠὲ σελήνης
δῶμα καθ᾽ ὑψερεφὲς Μενελάου κυδαλίμοιο.
(μεγαλήτορος Ἀλκινόοιο.)

[For there was a gleam like that of the sun or moon
beneath the high-roofed house of glorious Menelaus.
(of great-hearted Alcinous.)]

Finally, in both scenes, the *anagnorisis* of the guest is delayed, resulting in dramatic irony. Just as Telemachus, at Menelaus' mention of his and his father's troubles, begins to weep and cover his eyes with his purple cloak (4.113–16), so Odysseus, at Demodocus' story about his troubles, weeps and covers his eyes with his purple cloak (8.83–92, 521–31). Just as Telemachus' weeping is observed by Menelaus, leading him to suspect his guest's identity (4.116–19, 147–54), so Odysseus' weeping is observed by Alcinous, leading him to inquire into his guest's identity (8.93–95, 532–86). Homer has artistically linked these two scenes, creating a sympathetic harmony between father and son, as they share common experiences at the hands of their respective hosts.

(4.168–82). With the confirmation of Telemachus' identity (4.157), his relationship of *xenia* with Menelaus, inherited through his father, is established. Menelaus makes this clear in his welcoming speech: "Surely the son of a φίλος has come to my house" (4.169–70). Menelaus also implies his indebtedness to Odysseus, hence to Telemachus, by recalling Odysseus' service to him: "[Odysseus], who endured many trials on my behalf" (4.170). He claims further that if Odysseus had returned, he would have "granted him hospitality" (φιλησέμεν 4.171) above the other Argives, even emptying one of his cities in the Peloponnese to accommodate the wholesale resettlement of Odysseus and all his people from Ithaca (4.174–77). Settled thus nearby each other, they would have frequently "come in contact" (ἐμισγόμεθα 4.178), living out their lives "befriending each other and delighting in each other's company" (φιλέοντέ τε τερπομένω τε 4.179). Such a wholesale resettlement of a population is unprecedented in Homer—Agamemnon's offer to Achilles of seven cities in the Peloponnese does not entail Achilles' move there (*Il.* 9.149–56)—and one may reasonably pause to wonder whether or not Odysseus would have been altogether happy about the prospect of moving all his possessions, family, and people, from Ithaca to the Peloponnese in order to fraternize with Menelaus. And though Menelaus' offer could be understood simply as a hyperbolic demonstration of his affection for Odysseus, it takes on added significance later in Telemachus' visit, when Menelaus persists in making every effort to dissuade Telemachus from leaving Sparta (4.587–88, 599; 15.75–85), and when Telemachus in turn expresses his willingness to stay even for a year (4.595–96). The now childless Menelaus, living only with his sterile wife and his memories of a glorious past to comfort him, begins, even in the early stages of this scene, to reveal his desire to detain Telemachus in Sparta; if he cannot resettle Odysseus there, he can perhaps resettle his son. Thus the theme of guest detention begins its development very early in this scene (XIX).

(4.183–215). This theme of detention is raised again in a subtle way in the conversation that follows. In response to Pisistratus' polite request to put a stop to the weeping, this time by the entire group, Menelaus praises him for his wise words and remarks, with a perceptible tone of jealousy, on Nestor's fortune in his birth, marriage, and fine sons, surrounded by whom he will grow old comfortably in his house (4.204–11). This is a poignant contrast to Menelaus himself, who has been particularly unfortunate both in his marriage and in his offspring.

(4.216–39). After the resumption of the meal, the theme of detention receives further attention in Helen's provision of a grief-soothing drug accompanied by delightful stories (XIII). Though apparently innocuous in itself, the provision of drugs and stories, especially by a woman, takes on a sinister quality when viewed in the light of Odyssean parallels. Just as powerful, even divine, women play the role of host to Odysseus (Circe, Calypso, Arete), so here the semi-divine Helen takes over from her husband the responsibility of entertaining the guest. Just as the fruit of the lotus causes Odysseus' men to "forget" (λαθέσθαι 9.97) their homecoming and Circe's "drugs" (φάρμακα 10.236) cause Odysseus' men to "forget" (λαθοίατο 10.236) their fatherland, so Helen's "drug" (φάρμακον 4.220) brings about "forgetfulness" (ἐπίληθον 4.221). Admittedly, Helen's drug, unlike Circe's, is a "good" one (ἐσθλά 4.228) rather than a "baneful" one (λυγρά 10.236), since it effects the "cessation of grief and anger" (νηπενθές τ᾽ ἄχολόν τε 4.221) and the "forgetfulness of all misfortune" (κακῶν ἐπίληθον ἁπάντων 4.221), and since its effect is "ephemeral" (ἐφημέριος 4.223). But there is still something sinister about a drug that will allow a man to endure tearlessly the death of his mother and father and the murder of his own brother or son (4.224–26). Helen's provision of stories for her guest brings to mind another Odyssean parallel, the songs of the Sirens. Helen invites her guests to "take delight" (τέρπεσθε 4.239) in her stories about the suffering of the Greeks at Troy, just as Odysseus "takes delight" (τερπόμενος 12.52; τερψάμενος 12.188) in the songs of the Sirens, which also recount the suffering of the Greeks at Troy (12.189–90). One begins to wonder if this enchantress Helen, with her exotic drugs and delightful stories, presents as serious an obstacle to the homecoming of Telemachus as do the Lotus-eaters, Circe, and the Sirens to the homecoming of his father.

(4.240–64). In her story, Helen recounts how she recognized and be-friended Odysseus—just as she is now recognizing and befriending Telem-achus—when he came, disguised as a beggar, to spy on the Trojans. Her self-portrait is designed to impress her guest and to endear herself to him. She depicts herself as more clever even than Odysseus—for the only person more clever than the master of disguise is the one who is able to see through that disguise. She also establishes a relationship of *xenia* with Telemachus by emphasizing how she befriended his father (cf. 1.187–89; 4.104–12, 169–80), bathing, anointing, and clothing him, as is proper for a host. She claims that Odysseus confided in her the plans of the Greeks, that she aided him in his escape back to the ships, and that she rejoiced in his killing the Trojans, since she had had a change of heart and wanted to return home to her husband and fatherland. Aphrodite, she claims, was the cause of her delusion.

(4.265–89). In Menelaus' story of the wooden horse, which immediately follows—a doublet of Helen's story, even beginning with the same for-mulaic verse (242 ≈ 272)—he debunks her portrayal of herself.[21] The only point of agreement is that she must have been under the spell of some divinity. In answer to her claim of sympathy for the Greeks, he tells about how she disguised her voice to sound like the wives of the Greeks

---

21. The juxtaposition of these two apparently contradictory stories has elicited much commentary: Nestle 1942, 73; Anderson 1958; Kakridis 1971; Barck 1971, 23–26; Schmiel 1972; Dupont-Roc and Le Boulluec 1976; Andersen 1977; Bergren 1981; Olson 1989.

hidden in the horse and called to them by name, and he pointedly mentions that Deiphobus, the Trojan whom she had married after Paris' death, accompanied her.[22] In answer to her claim that she was more clever than Odysseus, he points out that this time Odysseus saw through her disguise and prevented the men from betraying their positions. He makes no direct reply to her claim that she had offered *xenia* to Odysseus, but one begins to wonder if this too is not part of her fabrication, the "things suited to the occasion" (ἐοικότα 4.239), which she promised to tell. The inherent implausibility of a princess bathing and entertaining a vagrant beggar becomes more striking after Menelaus' counterstory. The overall result of this pair of stories is that one is left somewhat less comfortable about Helen's relationship with Telemachus, for if she were a threat to Odysseus, as Menelaus claims, rather than a proper host, as she claims, she might be a threat to Odysseus' son.

(4.290–95). Having taken upon themselves the duties of the bard, Menelaus and Helen have provided the evening's entertainment with stories about Troy (XIII). But Telemachus' response to their storytelling is curt. Having remained silent throughout the evening, his first words to his hosts in Sparta are a request to be allowed to go to bed (XVI). He is not cheered by stories about Odysseus' cleverness, since it has not saved him. "But come," he says, "send us off to bed so that we can delight ourselves with sweet sleep" (4.294–95). Wearied by stories that have brought him only tears and pain, Telemachus would rather "take delight in sweet sleep" (ὕπνῳ ὕπο γλυκερῷ ταρπώμεθα 4.295) than follow Helen's suggestion to "take delight in stories" (μύθοις τέρπεσθε 4.239).

(4.296–305). The provision of a bed (XVII) for Telemachus is described by a type-scene that recurs twice in the *Odyssey* (Telemachus at Pylos 3.397–403; Odysseus at Scheria 7.335–47) and twice in the *Iliad* (Phoenix at Achilles' hut 9.658–68; Priam at Achilles' hut 24.643–76).[23] While the basic structure of the type-scene is the same in all five occurrences—a

---

22. The scholia to 8.517 attribute the story of the marriage of Helen and Deiphobus to the Epic Cycle (οἱ μεταγενέστεροι). Proclus mentions the marriage in his summary of the *Ilias Parva* of Lesches. But the *Odyssey* itself seems already to assume the marriage, both here and at 8.517–20.

23. Eumaeus' provision of a bed for Odysseus in disguise (14.518–33) and Penelope's offer of a bed for Odysseus in disguise (19.317–19) are fundamentally different in diction and structure.

bed is provided in the portico for the guest, while the master sleeps inside with his wife/concubine—none is identical in every detail. Homer expands, curtails, and otherwise refashions the details of the type-scene to fit each situation. Here in Sparta the type-scene is expanded and elaborated more than it was in Pylos. Whereas in Pylos Nestor himself had provided a bed, as well as his own son as a bedmate (3.400–401), here Helen relegates the duty of making the bed to the women servants, and a herald leads the guests to bed. Whereas the bed in Pylos had been described with the barest of details (τρητοῖς ἐν λεχέεσσιν 3.399), here the description of the bedding occupies three verses (4.297–99). In both scenes, the masters of the house lie down in the innermost rooms with their wives, but Nestor's wife had remained anonymous, while Helen is adorned by a full verse of epithets (4.305). Homer has manipulated the elements of the type-scene so as to paint a picture of a scene of hospitality considerably more elaborate, though somewhat less personal, in Sparta than in Pylos.

(4.306–31). Not until the next morning does Menelaus ask Telemachus specifically about the purpose of his visit, for Telemachus had arrived in Sparta in the evening, a time for feasting and stories, not for business, which is normally conducted in the morning (cf. 2.1–7; 8.1–5). Telemachus responds by describing his troubles at home and by supplicating Menelaus, begging for news of his father, just as he had supplicated Nestor earlier in Pylos (4.322–31 = 3.92–101). The situation seems to call for Menelaus to come to Telemachus' aid: the suitors had suspected that Telemachus was going to Sparta for this purpose (2.325–27); Pisistratus had told Menelaus earlier that Telemachus had come to get his counsel "either for word or for deed" (ἔπος . . . ἔργον 4.163); and here (4.316–31), although asking explicitly only for news of his father, Telemachus presents a dismal picture of his troubles at home and appositely reminds Menelaus of Odysseus' favors to him in Troy "both in word and in deed" (ἔπος . . . ἔργον 4.329)—the very favors that resulted in Odysseus' present troubles—implying that Menelaus should reciprocate in kind.[24] From the perspective of the epic's structure as a whole, the vengeance

---

24. On Menelaus' failure to intervene in the affairs in Ithaca, see scholia to 4.163, 167. Telemachus had earlier raised the question of Menelaus' failure to intervene in the treacherous murder of his brother (3.248–52). Perhaps this characterization of Menelaus was the inspiration for Euripides' characterization of him in his *Orestes* (esp. 682–716), where he refuses to come to the aid of his nephew.

motif to be worked out later leaves no room for Menelaus' intervention; yet in the immediate context, Menelaus' failure to help Telemachus resolve the situation in Ithaca and his attempt to encourage Telemachus to stay in Sparta instead reflect badly on his behavior as a *xenos* of Odysseus, hence of Telemachus.

(4.332–586). Although Menelaus expresses much indignation at the suitors in Ithaca and predicts their death upon Odysseus' return, he not only fails to offer physical aid (ἔργον) but is unable to give an adequate answer (ἔπος) to Telemachus' request for news of his father. Instead of relating the tale of the νόστος of Odysseus, he tells at great length the tale of his own νόστος (4.351–586) and even those of Agamemnon and Aias. He has only the scantiest information about Odysseus—that, bereft of companions, he is unwillingly detained on Calypso's island (4.555–60). Again, from the perspective of the epic's overall structure, Menelaus' inability to provide adequate information about Odysseus and his substitution of his own, Agamemnon's, and Aias' νόστοι for Odysseus' are easily accounted for by noting Homer's intention of having Odysseus recount his own νόστος later (books 9–12). Moreover, the tales of the νόστοι of the various heroes were of great interest to Homer's audience, and this scene provided an excellent opportunity to complement Nestor's earlier tales. In the immediate context, however, one wonders if Homer is not trying to depict Menelaus' own audience, Telemachus, who professes to enjoy the stories (4.597–98), as somewhat put off by their length, since Menelaus is unable to provide adequate news of his father.

(4.587–619). Menelaus' stories could go on forever. At the end of his long account of his νόστος, Menelaus invites Telemachus to remain in Sparta "for eleven or twelve days" (4.588), and Telemachus responds that he could stay "for a year," without even thinking of home, so much does he delight in Menelaus' stories (4.595–98). He appears ambivalent, struggling between his sense of duty and his desire for his own return home, on the one hand, and the considerable attractions of Sparta, on the other. In a remarkable exchange of speeches between host and guest, the theme of guest detention becomes very pronounced.

Menelaus ends the story of his νόστος by relating how the gods granted him a swift journey back home (τοί μ᾽ ὦκα φίλην ἐς πατρίδ᾽ ἔπεμψαν 4.586). But he is not willing to grant his guest the same favor. Rather, he encourages Telemachus to "stay" (ἐπίμεινον 4.587)—a verb used elsewhere in the *Odyssey* of detaining a guest against his will (1.309; 11.351; cf. μεῖνε 4.733)—in his house for "eleven or twelve more days" (i.e., "for some time"),[25] promising to send him on his way thereafter with glorious guest-gifts (XX). But even the guest-gifts that he promises are designed to detain Telemachus in Sparta: three horses, a chariot, and a libation cup (4.590–91). The gifts of horses and chariot are not only inappropriate for Telemachus' situation but deceptive. As Telemachus shrewdly points out, these gifts are suitable on the broad Lacedaemonian plain, but they are entirely useless on rocky Ithaca (4.600–608). And these are precisely Menelaus' intentions: the gifts are symbolic of his attempt either to resettle Telemachus in Sparta—a desire that he has already expressed (4.174–77)—or at least to detain him on the plain of Lacedaemonia for a time—a suggestion that he later makes explicitly (15.80–85).

Telemachus understands Menelaus' intentions and immediately pleads with him not to "detain him there for a long time" (μὴ δή με πολὺν χρόνον ἐνθάδ᾽ ἔρυκε 4.594; cf. σὺ δέ με χρόνον ἐνθάδ᾽ ἐρύκεις 4.599). The verb ἐρύκω is pregnant with meaning in the *Odyssey*, evoking Calypso's detention of Odysseus in Ogygia (1.14; 9.29; cf. κατερύκω 1.55, 197; 4.498, 552; 23.334). Telemachus assures Menelaus of his own desire to stay (4.595–98), attributing his anxiety to leave to his concern for his men, who are awaiting him in Pylos (4.598–99). But Telemachus' response to Menelaus' offer of guest-gifts is startling: he refuses them, and he requests "treasure" (κειμήλιον 4.600) as a substitute; he will not take horses back to Ithaca, a land suitable only for goats (4.601–8).[26] According to the standards of Homeric society, and, consequently, according to the poetic conventions of the traditional type-scene of hospitality, this refusal of guest-gifts is an anomalous, indeed unique, behavior. Just as Telemachus will later attempt to leave Sparta surreptitiously, without collecting Menelaus' guest-gifts (15.44–55), and just as he will thereafter avoid Pylos entirely on his journey home, in his haste depriving Nestor of an opportunity to fulfill his obligation to provide guest-gifts (15.195–219), so here he refuses inappropriate guest-gifts so as to expedite his return home.

Telemachus' refusal is startling, but it is treated by Menelaus as an appropriate response to his offer of inappropriate gifts. To Telemachus'

---

25. On this expression, see Focke 1943, 3–4.

26. The scholia to 4.602 and Eustathius 1510, 50ff. compare Odysseus' yielding of the Thracian steeds to Diomedes at the end of *Iliad* 10.

request for a substitute gift of treasure (κειμήλιον), the type of gift generally preferred by guests (cf. 1.309-13), Menelaus good-naturedly assents and offers him the "most beautiful and honorable" (κάλλιστον καὶ τιμήεστατον 4.614) treasure in his possession—a krater of silver and gold, the work of Hephaestus, which had been given to him as a guest-gift by Phaedimus, king of the Sidonians (4.613-19). This is a gift worthy of his guest, one Telemachus can in turn pass on to someone else if he wishes. The nature of gift exchange in Homeric society is such that gifts with a history have extraordinary value (*Il.* 10.260-71; 24.233-37; *Od.* 9.196-215; 21.31-33; cf. Stesichorus fr. 234 *PMG*).

(4.620-24). At this juncture in the *Odyssey*, the narrative shifts abruptly back to Ithaca, where the suitors are entertaining themselves in the house of Odysseus. It does not return to Telemachus in Sparta until book 15, the interval being occupied by the ten-book account of Odysseus' return home. In book 4 (620-24), we leave Telemachus and Menelaus speaking to each other while they await the preparation of yet another feast, and in book 15 (4-6), we return to Telemachus in bed at night in the portico of Menelaus' palace. According to the narrative of books 5-14, Odysseus' journey from Ogygia to Ithaca has taken about a month. When we return to Telemachus in book 15, are we to understand that he has lingered in Sparta for an equal time? Or are we to understand the night in book 15 to be the night following the feast in book 4? It seems to me that Homer was sensitive to the chronological problem and tried to preclude any bewilderment on the part of his audience by leaving Telemachus' future unclear in book 4. This is achieved by the development of the theme of guest detention (XIX), largely through the progression of Menelaus' overbearing hospitality, even from the beginning of Telemachus' visit in Sparta. By the time the narrative shifts back to Ithaca, a long stay by Telemachus in Sparta seems quite plausible.

(15.1-42). The description of Athena's arrival in Sparta at the beginning of book 15 in order to urge Telemachus to depart does nothing to destroy this impression. She comes (15.3)

νόστου ὑπομνήσουσα καὶ ὀτρυνέουσα νέεσθαι.

[in order to remind (Telemachus) of his homecoming and to urge (him) to go.]

Telemachus, like his father, is to have a νόστος, and Athena must "remind" (ὑπομνήσουσα 15.3) him of it, just as Odysseus' men must "remind" (μιμνήσκεο 10.472) Odysseus of his fatherland after having dallied with Circe for a year (10.467–71). The verbal correspondence suggests that Telemachus has spent an unacceptable length of time in Sparta: longer than a day and a half, in any event, as those who regard book 15 as describing the night following the events of 4.624 must believe (see n. 2). Athena must "urge him on" (ὀτρυνέουσα 15.3; cf. ὄτρυνε 15.14); ὀτρύνω is another verb used numerous times in the context of Odysseus' delayed νόστος (1.85; 7.151; 8.30; 9.518; 11.357).

In her admonition to Telemachus, Athena echoes the warning that Nestor had given him in Pylos (15.10–13 ≈ 3.313–16):

Τηλέμαχ᾽, οὐκέτι καλὰ δόμων ἄπο τῆλ᾽ ἀλάλησαι,   15.10
(καὶ σύ, φίλος, μὴ δηθὰ δόμων ἄπο τῆλ᾽ ἀλάλησο)   3.313
κτήματά τε προλιπὼν ἄνδρας τ᾽ ἐν σοῖσι δόμοισιν   15.11 = 3.314
οὕτω ὑπερφιάλους· μή τοι κατὰ πάντα φάγωσι   15.12 = 3.315
κτήματα δασσάμενοι, σὺ δὲ τηϋσίην ὁδὸν ἔλθῃς.   15.13 = 3.316

[Telemachus, no longer is it good to wander far from home
(As for you, friend, do not for long wander far from home)
leaving behind your possessions, and in your house
such violent men, lest they divide and devour all
your possessions, and you go on a vain journey.]

Again, the implication is that Telemachus has stayed away too long, neglecting to follow Nestor's advice.

Athena's description of the situation back in Ithaca also suggests a rather long absence by Telemachus. She warns that the situation has changed considerably since he left, that Penelope is on the verge of changing her mind and complying with the wish of her father and brothers to marry Eurymachus (15.15–23). Even though Athena's warning appears to consist of a lie, in order for the lie to be believable, if only to Telemachus, a rather long stay must be understood. Telemachus' immediate concern for his mother upon returning to Ithaca shows that Athena's description of this scenario has thoroughly persuaded him. He asks Eumaeus whether his mother is still at home, or whether someone has already married her, leaving the bed of Odysseus empty and gathering spiders' webs (16.33–35).[27]

---

27. On Athena's message to Telemachus in Sparta, see further Rothe 1914, 119; Shewan

(15.43–55). Athena's message incites Telemachus to immediate action. As soon as she is gone, he wakens Pisistratus and urges him to harness the horses for departure. Telemachus' surreptitious departure is apparently intended to avoid any further obstruction by Menelaus, just as his later bypassing of Pylos is intended to avoid any obstruction by Nestor. Though Telemachus' intentions are understandable, this surreptitious departure not only is entirely improper by the standards of Homeric manners but does not even accord with Athena's advice, which was to ask Menelaus for a hasty return (15.14–15). Reminding him not only that it is impossible to drive by night but that proper conduct requires that he await the gift giving (XX), the formal farewell (XXIII), and the host's escort to his next destination (XXV), Pisistratus quotes a proverbial expression (15.54–55):

τοῦ γάρ τε ξεῖνος μιμνήσκεται ἤματα πάντα
ἀνδρὸς ξεινοδόκου, ὅς κεν φιλότητα παράσχῃ.

[For a guest remembers forever
the guest-receiving man, who provides hospitality.]

(15.56–66). Telemachus assents; but as soon as it is morning, he approaches Menelaus and asks him in the most urgent terms to send him home (15.65–66):

ἤδη νῦν μ' ἀπόπεμπε φίλην ἐς πατρίδα γαῖαν·
ἤδη γάρ μοι θυμὸς ἐέλδεται οἴκαδ' ἱκέσθαι.

[Now, at last, send me back to my dear fatherland,
for my heart already desires to return home.]

Telemachus' words, ἤδη νῦν ... ἤδη, imply that he has been in Sparta for some time and is now anxious to leave. We may well compare the exhortation of Odysseus' men, who, after a year on Circe's island, plead with Odysseus to remember his fatherland (10.472):

Δαιμόνι', ἤδη νῦν μιμνήσκεο πατρίδος αἴης

[Strange man, now, at last, remember your fatherland.[28]]

1926, 32–33; Focke 1943, 2, 10, 20, 58; Heubeck 1954, 62–63; Delebecque 1958, 26–27; Apthorp 1980b, 5–8.

28. Shewan (1926, 394) and Apthorp (1980b, 6) also compare ἤδη νῦν at *Il.* 1.456.

(15.67–74). In response to Telemachus' urgent request, Menelaus waxes eloquent with a lesson on the proper duties of a host (15.68–74):

Τηλέμαχ', οὔ τί σ' ἐγώ γε πολὺν χρόνον ἐνθάδ' ἐρύξω
ἱέμενον νόστοιο· νεμεσσῶμαι δὲ καὶ ἄλλῳ
ἀνδρὶ ξεινοδόκῳ, ὅς κ' ἔξοχα μὲν φιλέῃσιν,
ἔξοχα δ' ἐχθαίρῃσιν· ἀμείνω δ' αἴσιμα πάντα.
ἶσόν τοι κακόν ἐσθ', ὅς τ' οὐκ ἐθέλοντα νέεσθαι
ξεῖνον ἐποτρύνει καὶ ὃς ἐσσύμενον κατερύκει.
χρὴ ξεῖνον παρεόντα φιλεῖν, ἐθέλοντα δὲ πέμπειν.

[Telemachus, I will not detain you here for long,
since you are desirous for your return home; I would be indignant
    at another man
who, receiving guests, acted excessively hospitable
or excessively hostile; all things are better in due measure.
It is as blameworthy to urge a guest to leave who does not
want to as it is to detain a guest who is eager to leave.
One must grant hospitality to a guest who is present and grant
    conveyance to a guest who wants to leave.]

This is a proverbial expression of proper conduct for a host (cf. Hesiod *Erga* 327–60). But it is ironic in this context, for the hospitality that Telemachus receives in Sparta is not "in due measure" (αἴσιμα). He has experienced to some extent both "excessive hostility" (ἔξοχα δ' ἐχθαίρῃσιν), in his initial reception by Eteoneus, and "excessive hospitality" (ἔξοχα μὲν φιλέῃσιν), in Menelaus' constant obstructions to his expeditious return. Menelaus has "detained" (ἐρύξω, κατερύκει) him despite his expressed "eagerness to leave" (νέεσθαι...ἐσσύμενον; cf. 4.594, 599). Even Menelaus' garrulity here, which is accentuated by this excessively long and trite speech, is an ironic contrast to his professed intention to expedite Telemachus' return (15.68).

(15.75–85). Menelaus' subsequent words confirm his failure both to appreciate the urgency of his guest's request and to regard the very instructions that he himself has given:

Wait until I bring you beautiful gifts and place them on the chariot . . . until I tell the women to prepare a feast in the house . . .

and if you wish to take a trip through Hellas, I will harness the horses for you, so that I myself may accompany you, and I will guide you to the cities of men, and no one will send us away empty-handed, but everyone will give something to carry off: tripods, caldrons, mules, goblets. (paraphrase of 15.75–85)

Not only do Menelaus' proposals impose further delays on Telemachus' return, but Menelaus even offers an escort (πομπή; XXV) in the wrong direction, a tour through the "cities of men" in Hellas. This proposed tour is reminiscent of Menelaus' seven-year tour during his own νόστος (4.81–91), both being designed to accumulate treasure in the form of guest-gifts.

(15.86–91). Menelaus' previous tour in search of treasure prevented him from avenging his brother's murder at the hands of a lawless suitor, Aegisthus. Telemachus' response to Menelaus' proprosal is therefore well advised. He answers tersely, reiterating his desire to return home (15.88):

βούλομαι ἤδη νεῖσθαι ἐφ᾽ ἡμέτερ"...

[I wish to return home at once...]

He punctuates his speech with the emphatic ἤδη for the third time (cf. 15.65–66) and pointedly implies that the possessions he has left unattended at home are of greater concern to him than the acquisition of more (15.88–91). Verse 15.88 is not a conventional phrase; it is notable that in order to accommodate the repeated ἤδη Homer has resorted to a linguistically late and very rare contraction of νέεσθαι, the only example in the surviving epos of a metrically necessary contraction of this verb. This suggests that this is not merely a repetition of the common type found in formulaic verses; it suggests rather that Homer made a conscious decision to repeat ἤδη (15.65, 66, 88) in order to emphasize Telemachus' urgency to extricate himself from his overbearing host.

(15.92–132). Unaffected by Telemachus' urgency, Menelaus, as planned, bids his wife and the maidservants to prepare a feast in the house (XXI) and bids Eteoneus to start a fire and roast the meat. Menelaus, Helen, and Megapenthes go to the storeroom of the palace to fetch guest-gifts for Telemachus (XX), Menelaus fetching a double-handled goblet, Megapenthes a silver krater, and Helen a peplos for Telemachus' future wife. The goblet is presumably the one that Menelaus had promised in book 4 (4.591).[29] The krater too (15.103-4) appears to be the same one promised by Menelaus and described in detail in book 4 (4.613-19). The promise of these gifts in book 4 anticipates their presentation in book 15, providing a thematic bridge over the long, ten-book interval.

Some time during the transmission of the Homeric text, someone thought that a stronger connection between book 4 and book 15 could be made by repeating the long description of the krater in 4.613-19; or perhaps someone merely wanted to make it clear that the krater presented to Telemachus in book 15 was the same one promised in book 4. Consequently, verses 15.113-19 have made their way into the inherited text. The manuscript evidence provides conclusive proof, however, that 15.113-19 are interpolated.[30]

---

29. Whereas δέπας is used here (15.102) and ἄλεισον in 4.591, the two terms are semantically interchangeable, their use being determined by the meter (e.g., 3.50-51).

30. The verses are absent in Allen's families b and i and in manuscripts H³ and L⁵. More significantly, they are apparently absent in Π²⁸ (Pack² 1106, 3rd-4th c.), which, though fragmentary in this portion of the text, reveals by comparison with the average number of verses per page that in the codex several verses (surely 15.113-19) are lacking between 15.91 and 15.127; see further Hunt 1911, 114, 170. The verses are also apparently absent in *P. Amh.* 2.18 (Pack² 1211, 1st-2nd c.), which, while containing very thorough scholia on the epic diction of *Od.* 15, appears to neglect entirely to gloss any words between 15.109, perhaps even 15.111 (see Apthorp 1980a, 201-2) and 15.121, though many words in this hiatus are ripe for exegesis; see further Grenfell and Hunt 1901, 9-16. It is somewhat less significant, but notable nonetheless, that Dindorf's collection of scholia, though generally scanty in the later books of the *Odyssey,* fails to remark on any verses of this passage. In sum, while the earliest manuscript to include the passage dates from the 10th-11th c. (L⁴), two manuscripts from the 1st-4th c., as well as the scholia generally, testify to its absence at a very early stage of transmission. The manuscript evidence strongly suggests that Aristarchus did not include these verses in his edition. They show every sign of being a post-Aristarchean interpolation: a concordance passage is available at 4.613-19; the manuscript evidence against the passage is extensive enough in itself to reduce almost to nothing the possibility of post-Aristarchean excision or accidental omission; there are no homoeographic grounds for suspecting accidental omission; moreover, the probability of an accidental omission coinciding exactly with a concordance passage (i.e., 4.613-19) is extremely minute. We may be quite confident that the seven verses were interpolated, probably in order to make clear that the krater given to Telemachus in book 15 was the same one promised him in book 4.

The evidence of Stesichorus fr. 209 *PMG,* a lyric adaptation of Telemachus' departure scene, which, after describing the omen and its interpretation by Helen, continues in the second column to describe what appears to be a parting gift to Telemachus of a gold and silver object, casts little doubt on the view that *Od.* 15.113-19 is an interpolation. Stesichorus demonstrates so much freedom in his adaptation of other details of the Odyssean scene that we need not infer from his description of a silver and gold guest-gift that he is

If we omit verses 15.113–19, the gift-giving scene takes on a slightly different color and a quite different symmetry. In the fetching of the gifts from the storeroom, the descriptions of Menelaus' goblet and Megapenthes' krater are very simple, while the description of Helen's peplos is elaborated—she made it herself; it is the most beautiful and the largest; it shines like a star; it lies at the bottom of the chest (i.e., it is the most valuable).[31] Likewise, in the presentation of the gifts to Telemachus (15.111–30, omitting 15.113–19), Menelaus' and Megapenthes' gifts are presented simply, while Helen's is presented with an elaborate five-verse speech. The overall impression created by this symmetry is that, just as Helen had earlier taken over from her hesitant husband the responsibility of greeting and entertaining their guest (4.120–305), and just as she will soon thwart Menelaus' attempt to interpret the bird-omen by anticipating him with her own interpretation (15.167–78), so now the presentation of Helen's gift overshadows that of Menelaus. Like Arete in Scheria, she, not her husband, is the dominant figure in the scene.

The entire gift-giving scene is very formal and proper. The gifts are not only appropriate; they are the most valuable that Menelaus and Helen can provide: Menelaus' "most beautiful" (κάλλιστον 4.614) treasure, which was, in turn, a guest-gift to him; Helen's "most beautiful" (κάλλιστος 15.107) possession, which she had made with her own hands. The speeches that accompany the gift giving are also formal. Menelaus prays that Zeus (patron of guests) will accomplish a return for Telemachus (15.111–12), and Helen wishes him a bon voyage (XXIII; 15.128–29).

(15.133–43). The final feast in Sparta ensues (XXI), described in the same conventional diction as the first feast (4.51–68), with only slight elaboration: the seating (VIII; 15.134); the formulaic five-verse block describing the meal preparation (IXa; 15.135–[39]),[32] here followed by a unique addendum describing the distribution of meat by Eteoneus, Menelaus' attendant, and the pouring of wine by Megapenthes, Menelaus' son (15.140–41); the consumption of the food (IXb; 15.142); and the conclusion of the feast (IXc; 15.143).

---

modeling it on his knowledge of these verses. Stesichorus may be elaborating the simple description of the krater in 15.103–4 on the basis of his recollection of the longer description of it in 4.613–19 (though the gift is definitely not a krater in Stesichorus, since it is modified by a feminine adjective); or he may be freely inventing the details; see further Reece 1988.

31. Cf. the description of the peplos that Hecabe selects for Athena in *Il.* 6.288–95.

32. For the possibility that verse 15.139 is an interpolation, see chapter 1.

(15.144-84). Immediately following the meal, Telemachus and Pisistratus harness the horses, climb onto the chariot, and drive out the front doorway (15.145-46):

ἵππους τε ζεύγνυντ᾽ ἀνά θ᾽ ἅρματα ποικίλ᾽ ἔβαινον,
ἐκ δ᾽ ἔλασαν προθύροιο καὶ αἰθούσης ἐριδούπου.

[They harnessed the horses and mounted the well-wrought chariot, and drove out the doorway and the resounding portico.]

Telemachus has finally departed, at last overcoming the final obstacle to his return; or so it would seem, especially to an audience accustomed to these formulaic verses, which elsewhere always signal an actual departure (15.145-46 = 3.492-[93][33] = 15.190-91; cf. *Il.* 24.322-23). The audience would expect the subsequent verses to describe the speedy passage to their next destination (as in 3.494-4.2; 15.192-93). But instead, Menelaus runs after Telemachus and Pisistratus, holding a goblet of wine in his hand, in order to pour a libation before they leave (XXII). While the two guests remain in the chariot—somewhat awkwardly—a sequence of conventional elements occurs (15.150-81). Menelaus stands in front of their horses and exchanges farewell speeches with them (XXIII). Suddenly an omen appears (XXIV)—an eagle, clutching a goose in its claws. While Menelaus considers what to make of the omen, Helen interrupts, taking control of the situation, just as she did in the recognition scene and in the gift-giving scene, and she offers a favorable interpretation. Telemachus responds gratefully to her interpretation. Not until verse 15.182, thirty-six verses after Telemachus and Pisistratus have mounted the chariot and driven out the doorway, do they actually depart.

This awkward sequence of events results from a displacement of the conventional elements of a standard departure scene. Homer has narrated the mounting of the chariot and the driving away (15.145-46) too early in the scene. The two-verse formula should have followed the libation (XXII), farewell speeches (XXIII), omen, and interpretation (XXIV); it should have come immediately before verse 15.182, when the actual departure occurs. One may well compare Priam's departure scene (*Il.* 24.281-323), where the sequence is harnessing of the horses (24.281-82),

---

33. Verse 3.493 is absent in most manuscripts, including two early papyri (Π³ and *P. Köln* 40); it is probably an interpolation.

libation and conversation (24.283–307), prayer (24.308–13), omen (24.314–21), mounting the chariot (24.322), and driving off (24.323).

This awkwardness in Telemachus' departure scene has been variously explained. A. Hoekstra attributes the inconsistency to the effects of oral composition, regarding the scene as "a rather carelessly abbreviated version of a traditional theme of leave-taking."[34] D. Gunn regards the scene as an oral poet's poor rendering of a traditional theme, and he sees the poet's failure to go back and correct his slip as evidence for his view of an oral dictated text.[35] M. Edwards explains the awkwardness of the scene as a result of the poet's attempt to combine and compress into one episode more type-scenes than he could comfortably handle: type-scenes of gift giving, chariot departure, individual libation, greeting, and omen.[36] In the departure of Priam from Troy (*Il.* 24.228–323), and of Odysseus from Scheria (*Od.* 13.10–85), the successive type-scenes are given due weight and are gracefully interwoven. Here they are not, resulting in a certain amount of awkwardness.

The underlying assumption of Hoekstra, Gunn, and Edwards is that the awkwardness of this sequence was unintentional, resulting either from a momentary slip in performance, or from the poet's inability to handle his material skillfully. I agree with Edwards's explanation of the mechanics that produced this awkwardness, but in view of the pervasiveness of the theme of guest detention that we have been tracing throughout Telemachus' visit to Sparta, I suggest that the manipulation of the normal sequence of events here was a deliberate device used by the poet in order to represent, precisely by the chaotic juxtaposition of type-scenes, the frantic behavior of Menelaus, who is desperately trying to juggle gift giving, libation, leave-taking, and interpretation of the omen, in an attempt to delay the inevitable departure of his guest. This breach of convention on a formal level informs the corresponding breach of convention on a contextual level. The theme of detention is being reinforced one last time by rearranging the typical sequence so as to portray Menelaus clinging to his guests even as they depart. In adapting this view—that Homer demonstrates in this passage a better handle on the tools of his trade than the three oralists mentioned above concede—I am in general agreement with G.P. Rose's view that the poet had a purpose in altering the conventional and logical order of events, namely,

34. Hoekstra 1965, 117n.3.
35. Gunn 1970.
36. Edwards 1975.

to put a "final, convincing touch on an amusing tension that has developed between Telemachus' impetuous eagerness to return home and Menelaus' persistent failure to incorporate this in his mind."[37] But I am inclined to regard this "tension" with a little less humor.

---

37. Rose 1971.

Chapter 5

The Phaeacians (*Od.* 5.388–13.187)

Ὦ μοι ἐγώ, τέων αὖτε βροτῶν ἐς γαῖαν ἱκάνω;
ἦ ῥ' οἵ γ' ὑβρισταί τε καὶ ἄγριοι οὐδὲ δίκαιοι,
ἦε φιλόξεινοι, καί σφιν νόος ἐστὶ θεουδής;

[Ah me, what mortals' land have I come to this time?
Are they violent and savage and unjust,
or are they kind to strangers, and their mind god-fearing?]
—(*Od.* 6.119–21)

Scheria, the land of the Phaeacians, provides for Odysseus a transition between the fantastic world of his wanderings and the real world of Ithaca; it is both a geographical and a psychological boundary between the two worlds. The gods have determined that once he reaches Scheria he will have escaped the wrath of Poseidon; he will be honored as a god among the Phaeacians, who will bestow on him abundant gifts and ensure his safe return home; in short, he will have escaped death and accomplished his "return" (νόστος 5.29–42, 286–90, 339–50, 382–87). In Scheria, he is entertained lavishly: he is bathed, clothed, seated in the place of honor, feasted, entertained by the songs of the bard and the spectacle of the dance, loaded down with guest-gifts, and personally escorted home. It would seem that after ten years of struggle he has at last reached an oasis of tranquility from which his return home is finally secure. As one scholar has described the situation:

In the kindliness of Odysseus' reception by the Phaeacians, the joyful vitality and curiosity he finds among them, their assurance of his return, and their generous giving of gifts, they appear as a neutralization of the dangers he has met in the outlandish world between the Ciconians and Scheria. . . . They stand between Odysseus' great exertions on both sides of reality and provide a calm vantage point in the midst of his grim efforts. The calm and perfect safety Odysseus

101

finds among the Phaeacians are prefigured in the complete shelter from the wind, sun, and rain provided by the olive thicket. . . . He has reached a haven where uncertainty and hostility are suspended.[1]

But is this an accurate description of the scenario painted by Homer? I find the situation encountered by Odysseus in Scheria and the hospitality granted him by the Phaeacians much more ambiguous. The text of the *Odyssey* itself appears to present contrary views of the hospitality of the Phaeacians. Their attitude toward strangers appears ambivalent, and their behavior is often inexplicable.

The Hospitality of the Phaeacians

On the one hand, the Phaeacian episode appears to be a paradigm of proper hospitality. Even before Odysseus reaches Scheria, Zeus tells Hermes that Odysseus will enjoy good hospitality while among the Phaeacians and a safe return home thereafter (5.36–42). The hospitality Odysseus will receive on his arrival at the Phaeacian palace is indeed prefigured by his safe arrival on the Phaeacian land, which is a welcome sight to the storm-tossed Odysseus at the moment of his greatest peril (5.398). The natural elements of the land provide the shipwrecked sailor, naked and helpless, with safety and hospitality: the river, to whom Odysseus prays as suppliant, rescues him from the sea (5.445–53); he greets the land with a kiss (5.463); the woods and shrubs shelter him from the wind, sun, and rain (5.475–82); the abundance of leaves provides a generous bed on which he finds respite from his hard labors and falls asleep (5.482–6.2).

When Odysseus awakens in this strange land, he asks himself (6.120–21 = 9.175–76; 13.201–2):

ἦ ῥ’ οἵ γ’ ὑβρισταί τε καὶ ἄγριοι οὐδὲ δίκαιοι,
ἦε φιλόξεινοι, καί σφιν νόος ἐστὶ θεουδής;

[Are these men violent and savage and unjust,
or are they kind to strangers, and their mind god-fearing?]

But since he awakens to the shouts of young girls at play along the

---

1. Segal 1962, 22, 23, 59n.10.

beach (6.115–25), there appears to be little danger that, here in his first encounter with humans since he lost his crew eight years earlier (6.125), he will encounter the violence and savagery to which he has become accustomed. In response to his supplication, Nausicaa receives him courteously and hospitably with kind words of greeting:

> But now, since it is to our city and land that you have come, you will lack neither clothing nor anything else which is fitting for the much-enduring suppliant (6.191–93). . . . But since this is a miserable wanderer who has come here, we must attend to him, for all strangers and beggars are from Zeus (6.206–8).

Nausicaa proceeds to provide for the stranger the basic elements of hospitality: a bath in the river, fresh clothing, food, and drink. These rather simple provisions on the beach prefigure, just as Odysseus' initial arrival on the land did, the much more elaborate provisions that await in the palace.

The hospitality provided Odysseus in the palace spans the entire spectrum of the standard hospitality scene (see Appendix): the elaborate description of the palace on Odysseus' arrival, with its glittering gold, silver, and bronze, which recalls the splendor of Menelaus' palace in Sparta (IIIa; 7.81–135: 7.84 = 4.45; 7.85 ≈ 4.46; 7.134 ≈ 4.47); the seating of the guest in the place of honor next to the king (VIII; 7.168–71); the preparation and serving of the feast (IXa; 7.172–76); the interrogation of the guest (XIa; 7.237–39) and the subsequent exchange of stories (XII; 7.240–97); the provision of a bed for the night (XVII; 7.335–47); the reiteration of feasts (IX), songs and entertainment (XIII), and a bath (XVIII) on the next day (8.1–586); the reiterated offer of ever-increasing guest-gifts (XX; 8.389–432; 11.336–61; 13.7–22); and finally the safe escort (πομπή) to Odysseus' home in Ithaca, even in the face of certain punishment by Poseidon (XXV; 8.564–71; 13.172–78). The Phaeacians scrupulously live out Alcinous' boast to his guest (8.248–49):

αἰεὶ δ' ἡμῖν δαίς τε φίλη κίθαρίς τε χοροί τε
εἵματά τ' ἐξημοιβὰ λοετρά τε θερμὰ καὶ εὐναί.

[Always dear to us are the feast, the lyre, dances, changes of clothing, warm baths, and beds.]

The Phaeacians, it would seem, are specialists in all aspects of good hospitality. It is no wonder that a long line of commentators, beginning in antiquity, has ascribed to them the title "most kind to strangers."[2]

The Inhospitality of the Phaeacians

It comes as somewhat of a surprise, then, that, even before Odysseus reaches the palace, he is warned twice, once by Nausicaa and once by Athena in the guise of a young Phaeacian girl, to be prepared for a less than kind reception by the Phaeacians. A hint of potential hostility by the Phaeacians is first observed in Nausicaa's request that Odysseus not follow her all the way home, lest the townspeople, who are "very overbearing" (μάλα ὑπερφίαλοι 6.274)—a description often associated with the suitors in Ithaca (twenty-one times)—rebuke her for bringing a stranger home (6.273–84). By itself, Nausicaa's concern might be attributed solely to the embarrassment of a young girl at the thought of taking a man home with her, but this does not account for Athena's added precaution of covering Odysseus with a mist, "lest," as the narrator tells us, "one of the high-spirited Phaeacians, accosting him, insult him and ask who he is"[3] (7.14–17; κερτομέοι implies hostility; again it is often associated with the suitors in Ithaca: 16.87; 18.350; 20.263). Finally, Athena, disguised as a young girl, appears to Odysseus and warns him to keep quiet and not look anyone in the eye or ask anyone anything (7.30–31), since the Phaeacians have little tolerance for strangers (7.32–33):

οὐ γὰρ ξείνους οἵδε μάλ᾽ ἀνθρώπους ἀνέχονται,
οὐδ᾽ ἀγαπαζόμενοι φιλέουσ᾽ ὅς κ᾽ ἄλλοθεν ἔλθῃ.

[For they do not at all tolerate strangers,
nor are they fond of welcoming those from abroad.]

This ambivalence of the Phaeacians toward strangers is puzzling. If we pay any attention at all to these warnings, we cannot easily remark

---

2. Scholia to 7.32: φιλοξενώτατοι; Heraclides Ponticus, quoted in scholia to 13.119: φιλοξενία; Dio Chrysostom *Orat.* 7.90: φιλανθρωπία.

3. It is a serious indiscretion to ask a stranger's name before feeding him (cf. 1.123–24; 3.69–70; 4.60–62; 14.45–47; 16.54–59; *Il.* 6.171–77; 9.221–24; 18.385–87; *H.Dem.* 206–12). The Cyclops Polyphemus, who is the paradigm of improper conduct, does exactly that (9.252–55).

that "Odysseus has reached a haven where uncertainty and hostility are suspended."[4] In fact, uncertainty abounds, and the potential for hostility appears very real. Perhaps Scheria is not a safe haven for Odysseus. Perhaps there lurk here dangers as potent as those posed by the Cyclopes and the Laestrygonians. Perhaps Odysseus will experience here temptations as seductive as those of Circe and Calypso. A closer analysis of the text with a view to the deviations of the Phaeacians from normal hospitable behavior may shed some light on these ambiguities.[5]

Though the hospitality offered by the Phaeacians is elaborate, as a group they commit an extraordinary number of faux pas in the course of their treatment of Odysseus. Why does Nausicaa, the object of Odysseus' initial supplication, fail to lead him to the palace, a failure for which Alcinous himself blames her (7.299–301)?[6] What explanation is there for Arete's and Alcinous' failure to greet promptly the stranger, who for a long time (cf. ὀψέ 7.155) sits in a position of supplication in the ashes at the hearth, an indiscretion for which Echeneus must reprimand them (7.153–66)? Is there any significance to Alcinous' probing into Odysseus' identity even before he is finished eating (7.186–206), an impropriety that appears to arouse Odysseus' indignation (7.208–25)?[7] What accounts for the indiscretion of the king's son Laodamas in challenging a guest to participate in athletic contests (8.145–51), a challenge Odysseus regards as a cruel taunt and an imposition on himself as guest and suppliant (8.153–57)?[8] Why does Alcinous fail to shield his guest

---

4. Segal 1962, 22, 23, 59n.10.

5. This is an analysis that Homer's audience, both ancient and modern, is prepared to do after being educated in the mechanisms of *xenia* by the three preceding hospitality scenes of the Telemachy. In the analysis that follows, I am indebted to Rose (1969b), who marshals from the text the evidence for Phaeacian inhospitality. Though I find some of Rose's examples tendentious—as does De Vries (1977)—this does not invalidate his challenge to the commonly accepted view of Scheria as a realm of safety and hospitality.

6. It is a Homeric convention for the one who is encountered first by a guest, often the child of the king, to take upon himself the guest's welfare: cf. Telemachus (1.113–35), Pisistratus (3.36–39), and the young Achilles (*Il.* 11.777–79).

7. Arete, by contrast, waits until after Odysseus is finished eating and the tables are cleared to question him (7.230–39).

8. Gould (1973, 95) sums up the status of a suppliant, and by extension of a guest, as follows: "Supplication involves a form of self-abasement which constitutes an inversion of the normal patterns of behaviour. A normal face to face encounter between two men who are not φίλοι involves, in ancient Greek society, a transaction of challenge and counter-challenge in a context of competing claims to τιμή. The ritual of supplication, on the other hand, puts the new arrival 'out of play' in terms of the normal 'game' of competition, precisely because the suppliant's behavior is an inversion of normal expected behavior.

from the rudeness and violence of Euryalus, who publicly abuses and belittles Odysseus (8.158–64), angering him and leading to a dangerous confrontation (8.165–233)? Is it significant that the Phaeacians bungle in the entertainment of their guest: the songs of Demodocus, intended for his pleasure, instead twice bring him to tears (8.83–95, 521–34), and the exhibition of contests, again intended for his enjoyment, leads instead to harsh words and discomfort on both sides? And, finally, why must such extreme measures be taken to guard Odysseus' gifts from theft by his Phaeacian crew (8.443–48)? In light of these apparent indiscretions, one perhaps ought to go back and reconsider Odysseus' question on arrival in this strange land (6.120–21):

ἦ ῥ' οἵ γ' ὑβρισταί τε καὶ ἄγριοι οὐδὲ δίκαιοι,
ἦε φιλόξεινοι, καί σφιν νόος ἐστὶ θεουδής;

[Are these men violent and savage and unjust,
or are they kind to strangers, and their mind god-fearing?]

In addition to these apparent indiscretions, which create an ambiguity as to whether these Phaeacians are hospitable (φιλόξεινοι) or inhospitable (ἄξενοι), there arise a number of oddities in this hospitality scene in general. What is the motivation for the general secrecy surrounding Odysseus' arrival at the palace (7.30–42)? Why do the Phaeacians allow their guest to remain incognito for so long, even letting him go to bed for the night unidentified? Why is Arete's importance as an object of supplication for Odysseus so elaborately built up (6.303–15; 7.53–77), only to have her play such an insignificant role in the reception and entertainment of the guest? Why is Alcinous so eager to offer his daughter and part of his kingdom to an entirely unknown stranger (7.311–15)? What accounts for the unprecedented and peculiar nature of the Phaea-cians' guest-gifts to Odysseus—a collection of contributions from the nobility (8.387–95; 11.336–53; 13.7–23)? How is one to explain Odysseus' distribution of the chine, the portion of honor, to Demodocus and his request for a particular song (8.474–98), a rather presumptuous over-

---

Before the game of challenge and counter-challenge can commence the suppliant 'surrenders': the match is now a 'walk-over' and the other 'competitor' must now play according to a new set of rules."

stepping of his role as guest, as he takes on himself the duties and privileges of his host, the king?[9]

Responses to the Ambiguity of the Phaeacians' Hospitality

The *Odyssey* presents two different conceptions of the Phaeacians, one in which they are the saviors of shipwrecked sailors, to whom they afford hospitality and a safe return home, and another in which they are socially inept, or even stubbornly asocial, isolated as they are from other men, and therefore wary of, and even hostile to, strangers. This ambiguity has troubled readers of the *Odyssey* since antiquity, and many ingenious attempts have been made to reconcile the two conceptions.

Some ancient commentators attempted to reconcile the difference by drawing a distinction between the rudeness (ἀηδής) of the Phaeacian commoners, "the nautical crowd" (ὁ ναυτικὸς ὄχλος), and the hospitality (φιλόξενοι) of the royalty (βασιλεῖς).[10] Others record similarly that the leaders (οἱ ἄρχοντες) were philanthropic (φιλάνθρωποι), unlike their subjects.[11] Another remarks on the inhospitality (κακοξενία) of the commoners (δῆμος) and the hospitality (φιλοξενία) of the nobility (ἄριστοι).[12] But such a distinction is not clearly made in the *Odyssey;* on the contrary, most of the indignities suffered by Odysseus occur at the hands of the king and queen and the Phaeacian nobles.

A few discrepancies and oddities in the behavior of the Phaeacians toward their guest have been ingeniously explained by the analysts. In order to account for Arete's failure to respond promptly to Odysseus' supplication, W. Schadewaldt took 7.159–238, the interval during which Echeneus reprimands the king for his treatment of the stranger and Alcinous seats and offers food to Odysseus and makes a speech to the assembled Phaeacian nobles, as an expansion by "poet B," whose contribution to the poem consisted largely of scenes of eating, drinking, and conversing.[13] In order to account for Odysseus' rather uncomfortable and extended state of incognito, brought about by his failure to identify

---

9. Normally the host and ruler of the house grants the honored portion of chine (4.65–66; 14.437; *Il.* 7.371–72; 9.706) and orders a song to be sung (1.151–54, 337–44; 8.43–45, 98–99, 254–55, 537; 22.330–33, 345–53; 23.133–36).
10. Scholia to 7.32.
11. Scholia to 7.16.
12. Eustathius 1566, 7–9.
13. Schadewaldt 1959; cf. von der Mühll 1940, 718–19.

himself when questioned by Arete (7.237–39), A. Kirchhoff concluded that in the original poem Odysseus did in fact identify himself immediately, introducing the Apologoi in response to Arete's question.[14] Hence, in Kirchhoff's view, all of book 7 following verse 7.243 should be deleted. In a less radical excision, E. Schwartz attributed 7.298–316, Alcinous' rather overhasty offer of his daughter to the stranger, to the ubiquitous "poet B."[15] In order to account for Arete's failure to live up to the expectations created of her as an object of supplication by Nausicaa's and Athena's speeches to Odysseus, R. Merkelbach concluded that here again we are faced with interference by "poet B."[16] In general, this approach addresses very few of the problems regarding the ambiguity of the Phaeacians' hospitality, and even those it does attempt to answer remain unsolved by its methods. In the face of new discoveries about the nature of oral poetry and the genesis of the Homeric text generally, this naive approach to Homer, based as it is on an assumption of strict verisimilitude in poetry, has proven unproductive.

M. Finley, very briefly, and H. Kakridis, in more detail, put forward another explanation for the apparent ambivalence of the Phaeacians toward Odysseus—for the fact that their initial fear and suspicion of Odysseus give way to a kind and luxurious welcome. In their view, the Phaeacians' hospitality is simply a model of the basic ambivalence of the heroic world toward strangers.[17] The term ξεῖνος has a broad semantic range, from "a potentially hostile stranger who is outside one's own group" (i.e., a non-φίλος) to "a friend from a foreign country who is to be treated as an insider" (i.e., a φίλος). The Phaeacians, as might be expected in a world where there is so much anxiety about newly arrived strangers, are simply moving slowly from one pole to the other within this semantic range.

Indeed it is revealing to trace Odysseus' gradual incorporation into Phaeacian society. From the level of a lowly suppliant (ἱκέτης) sitting in the ashes at the hearth (7.139–54), he is raised to the level of guest (ξεῖνος), when Alcinous, after an initial pause, takes him by the hand, raises him up, and seats him at the place of honor next to himself—the seat previously occupied by Alcinous' son (7.167–71). The ritual handwashing, the serving of food and drink, and the libation that follow symbolically reinforce Odysseus' incorporation into the social group

14. Kirchhoff 1879, 275–91.
15. Schwartz 1924, 23.
16. Merkelbach 1951, 161.
17. Finley [1965] 1978, 116–17; H. Kakridis 1963, 87–105.

(7.172-85).[18] This incorporation quickly culminates in Alcinous' rather hasty invitation to Odysseus to marry his daughter and become his son-in-law (7.311-15), an invitation to move from the status of an outsider (ξεῖνος) to an insider (φίλος). Though Odysseus refuses the offer, he is henceforth treated as an insider (φίλος), increasing in heroic stature as he dominates the athletic contests (8.186-233) and even takes over the king's role and presides over the feast (8.469-98).

Odysseus, then, moves from one pole to the other within the semantic range of the term ξεῖνος—though it could be argued that this is due rather to his own heroic abilities than to Phaeacian charity. Yet it seems unproductive, and even incorrect, to define the Phaeacians' hospitality, as Finley and Kakridis do, simply as a model of the normal ambivalence of the Greeks toward strangers. Such ambivalence is, after all, not the norm in the *Odyssey*: none of the three earlier episodes of good hospitality (Ithaca, Pylos, Sparta) is characterized by the great number of indiscretions and oddities that are encountered in the Phaeacian episode. Further, the Phaeacians do not simply move from one pole of fear and suspicion to the other pole of lavish entertainment; rather, they oscillate back and forth between the two poles, some of the most serious indiscretions occurring toward the end of the episode. The Phaeacians, therefore, appear to be rather more exceptional than normal.

A more far-reaching and productive approach to the problems posed by the Phaeacian ambivalence toward strangers has been offered by those who have viewed the discrepancies in the behavior of the Phaeacians as resulting from a combining of two or more traditions. Of the many suggestions offered as to the nature of these traditions, one in particular appears to explain many of the inconcinnities in the Phaeacians' behavior toward their guest: J. van Leeuwen, noting that in the Phaeacian episode, Odysseus—who is in our version of the *Odyssey* a married man seeking a return to his wife—takes on the role of a wooer of the king's daughter, has suggested that underlying our inherited version was an "Odyssey" in which Odysseus was actually a suitor for Nausicaa's hand, that he was tested as a rival suitor by the Phaeacians, and that he won and eventually married the princess.[19] Van Leeuwen traces the source of this earlier version back to the tale of Jason and Medea.[20] Indeed the sim-

---

18. For an analysis of this scene, see Gould 1973, 78-79.

19. Van Leeuwen 1911, 19-30. For an addendum in support of van Leeuwen's article, see Paton 1912.

20. The idea that an Argonautic tradition influenced the *Odyssey* is as old as Homer himself (*Od.* 12.61-72). Homeric scholars have for over a century ascribed various parts

ilarities between Nausicaa and Medea are remarkable: both are unmarried princesses who live in fabulous lands at the edge of the civilized world; both come to the aid of a newly arrived Greek hero who must overcome many obstacles in that land; both become romantically involved with the stranger (though Nausicaa is only potentially a bride). Yet in spite of all these similarities, it is a very tricky matter to attempt to trace the direction of influence between two preliterate traditions—during the oral transmission of the Odyssean and Argonautic traditions, the two probably interacted, with influence going in both directions—and it is an equally tricky matter to reconstruct hypothetical earlier versions of the *Odyssey*.

It is indisputable, though, that the *Odyssey* as we know it contains an amalgam of older folktales, and that familiarity with these folktales often helps disentangle otherwise irresolvable problems in the inherited text. In a modification of van Leeuwen's views, W.J. Woodhouse suggested that underlying our episode of Odysseus among the Phaeacians is a common folktale about a castaway who comes on the scene incognito in a wretched guise and is revealed as a prince when he defeats all rivals to the hand of the king's daughter.[21] This motif is clearly discernible in the Phaeacian episode. It begins explicitly with Athena's advice to Nausicaa to wash her clothes, since she is being wooed by all the Phaeacians, and thus her wedding is close at hand (6.25–40). Nausicaa herself realizes the imminence of her marriage, as does her father (6.66–67). Therefore, when a shipwrecked and naked stranger accosts her as she plays with her handmaidens on the beach, the momentum of the tale is ostensibly moving toward the marriage of the couple.[22] In Odysseus' first speech to Nausicaa, he compliments her beauty and exclaims that whoever leads

---

of the *Odyssey* to this tradition: cf. especially Kirchhoff 1879, 287–90; Meuli 1921. For a more recent articulation of this view, which is tempered by the realization that all these traditions experienced a long transmission in oral form, see Crane 1988, 135–66.

21. Woodhouse 1930, 54–65.

22. Two other instances of this motif in the *Odyssey* have an erotic undercurrent: Odysseus' men's meeting with the Laestrygonian princess, who is drawing water from a well (10.103–11), and the Phoenician traders' meeting with the Sidonian slave girl, who is washing clothes at the beach (15.415–29). It is a universal folktale motif. Cf., for example, the remarkably similar story of the marriage of Isaac and Rebekah: an unknown stranger (Isaac's servant) accosts the maiden Rebekah while she is drawing water at the village well; she offers him water and directs him to her father's house, where her marriage to Isaac is arranged (Gen. 24.10–61). For other attestations of the folktale motif of a hero finding a maiden at a fountain, well, or river, see Thompson 1955–58, N715.1.

her away as wife will be a lucky man indeed (6.158–59). Then he pronounces a blessing on her:

> May the gods grant you whatever you desire in your heart; may they grant you a husband and a home and noble harmony of mind. For there is nothing better than when a husband and wife have a home, harmonizing in their thoughts. (6.180–84)

Though the briny and weather-beaten stranger does not impress Nausicaa at first sight, Athena soon endows Odysseus with a radiant grace and good looks, inspiring Nausicaa to whisper to her handmaidens: "If only such a man as he would be called my husband, dwelling here, and it would please him to remain here" (6.244–45). The princess even anticipates the jealousy with which the Phaeacians will greet this rival suitor. She warns Odysseus to follow her to the palace at a distance, lest some commoner see them together and say:

> Who is this large and handsome stranger who follows Nausicaa? Where did she find him? Now he will be her husband. . . . It is better that she has gone out and found a husband from elsewhere, for she dishonors the Phaeacians throughout the town, who woo her many and noble. (6.276–77, 282–84)[23]

Of common mind is Nausicaa's father, who, even before the stranger has identified himself, offers him his daughter and a share of his kingdom: "Oh that you, remaining here, would take my daughter and be called my son-in-law. I would give you a home and possessions, if willingly you were to remain" (7.313–15).[24]

In the Phaeacian episode, we also encounter many less clear vestiges of an underlying motif of a strange suitor to the hand of the princess.

---

23. Woodhouse (1930, 57–58) analyzes Nausicaa's entire speech (6.255–315), noting how her mind runs on the thought of marriage and how she hints broadly of her admiration for Odysseus, her availability for marriage, and her noble background and widespread desirability.

24. "Alcinous' prayer is 'bizarre' (ἄτοπος)," quotes a scholium to 7.311, "since Alcinous does not know who he is and without testing him prays to receive him as companion and make him his son-in-law." According to another scholium on the same passage, Aristarchus too expressed amazement at Alcinous' behavior and doubted the verses 7.311–16 were genuine.

The general secrecy surrounding Odysseus' arrival at the palace and his extended state of incognito, something not adequately motivated by the story in its inherited form, is explicable when understood as the normal situation for the unknown stranger in the folktale. Athena's warning that the Phaeacians have no tolerance for strangers (7.32–33) is understandable if Odysseus is seen as a potential rival for the hand of the princess, hence a threat to the local suitors.[25] Arete's extraordinary status can perhaps partially be attributed to her role as the potential bride's mother in the folktale.

The entire scene of the contests, too, can be illuminated in the light of this underlying folktale. It is entirely unmotivated in a scene of simple hospitality, as in our inherited text, that a guest be required to "accomplish many feats with which the Phaeacians test him" (8.22–23), and that he be challenged, especially by the king's son, who is his host, to take part in contests (8.145–51).[26] It is a serious breach of proper hospitality that a Phaeacian noble, Euryalus, should taunt the guest, and that Alcinous should fail to shield his guest from this rude behavior (8.158–64). But if we understand this scene as a residue of the underlying folktale of a strange suitor to the hand of the princess, the Phaeacians' behavior becomes explicable. In the folktale, the contest is the arena for the suitors—the "young and noble aristocrats" in our tale (8.110; cf. 6.284)—to vie for the hand of the princess. Euryalus in the underlying tale is a local suitor, who quite naturally speaks slightingly of a rival suitor's pedigree: "You are not an athlete but a merchant"; that is, "you are not an aristocrat, hence not a legitimate contender for the hand of the princess" (8.158–64). But Odysseus' subsequent throw with the discus (8.186–98) proves that he is in fact an athlete, and it wins for him not only the contest but, at least in the underlying motif, the hand of the princess.

What follows in our inherited text is the natural sequel to the deter-

---

25. Pitt-Rivers ([1967] 1977a, 106–7) mentions a modern analogy to this behavior of the Phaeacians. In rural villages of Spain, where extraordinary hospitality is the norm, there is one class of strangers toward whom hostility is shown: the young man who comes courting a local girl. He is either driven away by stoning or ducked into the village fountain. But if he survives this ordeal and perseveres with his suit, he is allowed to do so unmolested.

26. The only other incidents in Homer of guests participating in contests with their hosts are Tydeus' contest with the Cadmeans upon his notoriously hostile visit (*Il.* 4.385–400; 5.800–808) and Odysseus' own contest with his nominal hosts, the suitors, upon his arrival home. Guests, like suppliants, should be exempt from participation in agonistic relationships; they are "out of play" in terms of the normal "game" of competition; so Gould 1973, 95.

mination of the winning suitor in the folktale. The singing, dancing, acrobatics, and especially the song of Ares and Aphrodite, a marriage hymn of sorts (8.429), are more appropriate to the setting of a wedding feast than to a hospitality scene (8.250–384); the closest parallel in the *Odyssey* is the scene in Sparta (4.1–19), which is also a wedding feast. Odysseus himself presides over the feast, distributing the choice portion of the meat to the bard and asking him to sing a particular song (8.470–98). This is an odd way for a guest to conduct himself, but Odysseus' taking on himself the duties of the host is perfectly understandable in the light of the underlying folktale: he is merely presiding at his own wedding feast.

Finally, the peculiar nature of the Phaeacians' guest-gifts, a collection of treasure from the nobles of the land (8.387–95)—unprecedented in other scenes of hospitality—is well adapted to a tale in which these nobles would have been rival suitors. These gifts are closely associated with the contests, and Odysseus may be said to have won them by virtue of his discus-throw. This reflects the underlying folktale, in which the gifts were the bride-prices of suitors competing for the hand of the princess. It is compatible with the folktale that all this treasure is laid at the feet of the queen (8.417–20), the bride's mother, who shows extreme concern for its safety, since it is her daughter's bride-price. She packs it away carefully in a chest and has the successful suitor tie it with a special knot (8.438–48). The treasure is later placed on a ship, which lies at anchor in the harbor, ready to take the newly married couple to the groom's home (13.66–76).

In sum, this theory of an underlying folktale about a strange suitor to the hand of the princess unravels many of the problems in the Phaeacian episode and illuminates much that was previously obscure. It accounts for most of the oddities in the Phaeacians' behavior toward their guest and explains the accumulation of faux pas in the course of their entertainment of the stranger.

However, this theory of an underlying folktale could be subverted, at least in part, by a different, though not mutually exclusive, theory, which accounts for the many inexplicable elements in the Phaeacian episode by regarding it as somehow patterned on the episode of Odysseus' arrival in Ithaca.[27] Nausicaa's warning to Odysseus that the Phaeacians are "very overbearing" (μάλα ὑπερφίαλοι 6.274) and will blame her for preferring

---

27. Lang (1969) presents this theory in its clearest and most succinct, and as far as I am aware in its earliest, form.

a newly arrived stranger to the "many and noble" (πολέες τε καὶ ἐσθλοί 6.284) Phaeacian suitors echoes the situation in Ithaca, where Penelope is beset by "many and noble" (πολέες τε καὶ ἐσθλοί 22.204) suitors who are notoriously "overbearing" (ὑπερφίαλοι)—a word commonly associated with the Ithacan suitors (twenty-one times). Athena's warning to Odysseus that the Phaeacians do not tolerate strangers (7.32–33), and that some Phaeacian will accost him on the road and "insult him" (κερτομέοι 7.17), echoes the general treatment of Odysseus by the suitors in Ithaca (κερτομέωσιν 16.87; cf. 18.350; 20.263), specifically by Melanthius, who accosts Odysseus on the road and taunts him (17.212–32; cf. κερτομίοισι 20.177). The secrecy surrounding Odysseus' arrival at the Phaeacian palace—Athena covers him with a mist (7.14–15) and tells him to be quiet and not look anyone in the eye (7.30–31)—echoes Athena's transformation of Odysseus in Ithaca into a miserable beggar (13.429–38; 16.454–59; 17.201–3). But while this initial secrecy and Odysseus' extended state of incognito make perfect sense in Ithaca, where the suitors pose a danger to the returning master of the house, they remain unmotivated, indeed somewhat awkward, in Scheria, where Odysseus is simply a shipwrecked sailor seeking an escort home.

Since the secrecy motif is used, it is necessary to have a guide for Odysseus; hence, Nausicaa is modeled on Telemachus. The similarities in their roles are notable: both are children of ruling families in unusually female-oriented environments; both are on the brink of adulthood; Athena sends a dream to both, instigating their meetings with Odysseus (6.13–40; 15.1–42); Odysseus appears to both as a suppliant and in their presence is transformed into a godlike form by Athena (6.229–45; 16.172–85); both give clothing to Odysseus (6.214; 16.79); both give an account of the situation in the palace (6.303–15; 16.241–57); and both precede him into town (6.295–99; 17.1–25).[28]

Perhaps Arete's unusual importance in the Phaeacian episode, often explained as a vestige of a primitive matriarchal society[29] or as a reflection of the special role of women in ritual supplication,[30] can more economically and plausibly be attributed to her debt to Penelope as a model: both episodes present a picture of a helpless suppliant addressing a

---

28. Belmont (1967) emphasizes the artistic motivation for such doublets but does not comment on the clues the doublet provides to determining the genesis of the poem.

29. For a recent restatement of this popular nineteenth-century view, see Hirvonen 1968, esp. 105–11. But see Finley's objections to this view ([1965] 1978, 103–4).

30. Pitt-Rivers [1970] 1977b; Bremmer 1980.

powerful queen as the two sit by a fire (6.303–12; 7.139–54; 17.553–73; 19.55–64, 97–105, 505–8). Conversely, Alcinous' rather ineffective and even comical role would then be due to the absence of a strong male ruler in Ithaca. Penelope also seems to color the character of Nausicaa, both characters being objects of marriage/remarriage to this newly arrived stranger. Hence the description of Athena's beautification of Odysseus in the presence of Nausicaa echoes verbatim, simile and all, the description of Athena's beautification of Odysseus in the presence of Penelope (6.230–35 = 23.157–62). And the description of Nausicaa standing at the door of the *megaron*, looking at Odysseus as he rises from his bath, evokes the description of Penelope when she enters the *megaron* in Ithaca (8.458 = 1.333; 16.415; 18.209; 21.64). All these scenes have an erotic undercurrent.

Two more specific echoes deserve passing consideration. The description of Odysseus' plight in Scheria often evokes his situation in Ithaca: his generally miserable condition and particularly his specific complaints to Alcinous about the shamelessness of his belly seem more appropriate to his role as a beggar in Ithaca than to his role as an honored guest in Scheria (7.208–25; 17.468–76). Another specific echo, though a rather faint and contorted one, is the importance of an item of clothing as a token of identity in the scenes that lead up to Odysseus' recognition in both episodes (7.233–39; 19.215–48).

Perhaps the most compelling evidence that the Phaeacian episode is patterned on the Ithacan is the awkwardness of the scene in which the Phaeacians make trial of Odysseus in contests. The rudeness of Euryalus' taunt and Odysseus' participation in the contests are completely unmotivated in what should be a hospitality scene. But Euryalus' remarks closely echo those of Antinous and Eurymachus in Ithaca (8.159–64; 21.288–311, 321–29), and Odysseus' unexpected show of strength in the discus and his boast to the Phaeacians that he is second to none except Philoctetes in the bow (8.215–28) is an eerie evocation of the contest of the bow, and the subsequent slaughter of the suitors, in Ithaca. In Scheria, Odysseus boasts that he would be first to strike his man in a crowd of enemies (8.216–17); this is exactly what happens in Ithaca, where Odysseus steers his first arrow through the crowd of enemies into the throat of Antinous (22.1–16).

Finally, the festivities in Scheria following the contests echo the events in Ithaca following the contest of the bow and the slaughter of the suitors. Just as the "wedding" festivities of song and dance follow the contests in Scheria (8.250–380), so a "wedding" song and dance follow the contest in Ithaca (23.142–45). Just as Odysseus presides over the "wedding" feast in Scheria (8.469–98), so he, the master returned home at last, presides over the "wedding" in Ithaca (23.129–51). Demodocus' "wedding hymn" in Scheria (8.266–366), in which Hephaestus, Aphrodite's legitimate husband, returns home to find Ares sleeping with his wife, echoes the real story in Ithaca of a legitimate husband's return home to his much-beleaguered wife.[31]

Methodological Considerations

In sum, it does not seem implausible that the Ithacan episode, which is after all the central episode of the *Odyssey*, should have influenced the Phaeacian episode. This is a theory that has, in some form or another, achieved fairly wide acceptance.[32] Yet this theory poses many potential difficulties: How is one to determine with certainty in which direction the influence has gone? How can one be sure that the two episodes are not independently patterned on a third episode or on a folktale external to Homer's epics? How far can one take this method in analyzing details of an episode? For example, are the golden dogs outside the door of Alcinous' palace modeled on the dog Argus in Ithaca?[33] Is Nausicaa's nurse Eurymedusa modeled on Telemachus' nurse Eurycleia?[34] Clearly this method is open to abuse. Hence, some scholars, such as Fenik and Hainsworth,[35] while noting the similarities between these two scenes as well as between other scenes, have minimized the influence between one and the other, regarding both as allomorphs of a general narrative pattern or theme.

---

31. Rose (1969a) traces seventeen parallel motifs between the song of Ares and Aphrodite and Odysseus' return home to Ithaca.

32. Fenik occasionally comes close to this view; see esp. 1974, 7–60. Austin (1975, 179–238) sees the reunion of Odysseus and Penelope as the most important scene in the *Odyssey*, so pivotal that it generates a family of allomorphs: Arete in Scheria, Helen in Sparta. Krischer (1985) rejects Woodhouse's view of an underlying folktale in favor of this theory—unnecessarily in my opinion, since the two theories are not mutually exclusive.

33. So Lang 1969, 164.

34. Belmont (1967, 7–8) notes their similarity in name, function, and background. One may just as reasonably propose that the Phaeacian nobleman Euryalus is modeled on the Ithacan suitor Eurymachus.

35. See Fenik's criticism of Lang in Fenik 1974, 55n.76; Hainsworth in Heubeck, West, and Hainsworth 1988, 290–91: "It is unnecessary and probably misleading to suggest that either of these episodes is modelled on the other." This also appears to be Belmont's view (1967, 1–9), though he never states it as such.

My view is that we can productively use this theory of one scene influencing another, though we should do so with great caution, since Homer provides ample evidence of general narrative patterns, themes, and character types being applied independently to two or more particular instances. The narrative pattern of a typical hospitality scene, for example, is reiterated in a similar, though never strictly identical, form throughout the epic. Favorite themes appear repeatedly: the unknown or disguised stranger, grief over a missing family member or friend, and the ubiquitous presence of a dog at the door. Character doublets are also common: Eurycleia/Eurynome, Circe/Calypso, Eumaeus/Philoetius. Indeed these types of repetitions are as pervasive on the narrative level as repeated epithets, formulae, and verses are on a dictional level; they are a fundamental feature of the Homeric style, evidently derived from its oral background. The appearance of a repetition, then, should not compel us to ask which of two instances is the model. Nor should it send us off in a frantic search for the original in an earlier version of the "Odyssey" or in an early folktale. The search for a model for every repetition is a vain enterprise, and even when a suitable model is available, comparison of the two is often unproductive.

Yet repetitions can sometimes be profitably analyzed by trying to identify a model when a narrative pattern is exceptionally awkward, when a theme is particularly inappropriate to the situation, or when a character is remarkably one-dimensional and obviously derivative. Sometimes that model is external to Homer. Just as one may, on a dictional level, account for a metrical irregularity in a formula by re-creating its pre-Homeric form—for example, the ι of ἀμφιβρότης and the first α of ἀνδροτῆτα both fail to be lengthened by position in the formulae ἀσπίδος ἀμφιβρότης and ἀνδροτῆτα καὶ ἥβην, pointing back to a pre-Mycenaean origin for these formulae (i.e., when syllabic ṛ still existed)[36]—so may one, on a narrative level, search for pre-Homeric models for a narrative pattern, a theme, or a character type: for example, the Neoanalytic view that the "Patrocleia" is modeled on a pre-Homeric "Memnonis."[37] Van Leeuwen and Woodhouse have done this by explaining the

---

36. Cf. the metrical irregularities in the formulae: Ἐνυαλίῳ ἀνδρειφόντῃ, Νὺξ ἀμβρότη, δειλοῖσι βροτοῖσι, and κατὰ κλισμούς τε θρόνους τε. For a recent summary of the evidence for a pre-Linear B origin of some features of the epic language, see M.L. West 1988, 156–59.

37. This is most persuasively argued by Kullmann (1960, 303–35) and Schadewaldt (1965, 155–202).

oddities of the Phaeacian episode as derived from an earlier version of the "Odyssey" or from an early folktale about a strange suitor to the hand of a princess.

But sometimes one need look no further than the Homeric corpus itself for the model of a repetition. Just as on a dictional level a formula may be derivative—"with stout hand" (χειρὶ παχείῃ), appropriate in the *Iliad*'s predominately martial context, is somewhat uncomfortably applied to Penelope (21.6)—so on a narrative level a narrative pattern, a theme, or a character type may be derivative. Thus the narrative sequence in which a wounded warrior is carried "groaning heavily" (βαρέα στενάχοντα) from the field by his comrades (8.334; 13.538) is inappropriately applied to Hypsenor (13.423), who is apparently already dead (13.411); the theme of secrecy and incognito, which is so pervasive throughout the *Odyssey*, is somewhat bathetically extended to Odysseus' reunion with his father; and the somewhat one-dimensional and colorless Calypso is apparently modeled on Circe, her more interesting and fully elaborated doublet. This is essentially the view of Lang, Austin, and Krischer,[38] who see the narrative pattern of Odysseus' arrival home in Ithaca, the motif of his disguise, and the theme of his vengeance on the suitors and (re)marriage to the queen as a model that is somewhat inappropriately applied to the Phaeacian episode.

In my view, the two theories are not mutually exclusive. Indeed they are merely two perspectives on the same material: a diachronic perspective, which views each particular scene against its backdrop of inherited tradition; and a synchronic perspective, which views the interaction of two scenes with each other within an individual performance of the *Odyssey*. Hence, from a synchronic perspective, the Phaeacian episode does appear to interact with, and perhaps to be modeled on, the Ithacan episode. But since, from a diachronic perspective, the Ithacan episode itself is clearly a version of the old folktale motif—an unknown stranger arrives in a sorry state, proves to be a prince (king) by defeating all the rivals to the hand of the princess (queen), and thereafter marries (remarries) her—is not the Phaeacian episode derived, though perhaps less directly, from that very folktale? Are not both theories equally applicable, the folktale motif being ingrained in the poet's mind as a form that generally molds his tale, the importance and centrality of the Ithacan episode generating a family of more specific allomorphs, such as the Phaeacian episode?

---

38. Lang 1969, 159–68; Austin 1975, 179–238; Krischer 1985, 9–21.

The Aesthetics of the Phaeacian Episode

Having determined that the Phaeacian episode is the product of a com-
bining of motifs—that of an idyllic paradise, whose inhabitants succor
a shipwrecked sailor and grant him conveyance home, with that of an
arrival of an unknown suitor to the hand of a princess—one may ask
whether this combination of motifs is successful or not from an aesthetic
point of view. One may evaluate, on a dictional level, whether formulae,
epithets, or type-scenes that have been taken from one context and placed
in another are aptly or ineptly adapted to their new context—Penelope's
handling of a door key with her "stout hand" (χειρὶ παχείῃ 21.6),
Aegisthus' epithet "blameless" (ἀμύμων 1.29), and Eumaeus' chopping
of firewood with "pitiless bronze" (νηλέϊ χαλκῷ 14.418) may strike a
literate audience as ineptly adapted formulae. So one may ask, on a
narrative level, whether a motif or theme incorporated into a scene from
elsewhere is successfully adapted or not—critics often object to the theme
of secrecy and incognito extended to the scene of Odysseus' reunion
with his father (24.214–348). Is the Phaeacian episode a clumsy amalgam
of motifs by an inept bard, an accidental mishandling of traditional
material and techniques, an unfortunate victim of intrusive foreign ele-
ments? Or is it an artistic and purposeful joining of motifs, which
contributes to large-scale thematic development and enhances and enliv-
ens the narrative?

My view is that while a few awkward situations result from the com-
bination of motifs—for example, Alcinous' absurdly hasty offer of his
daughter to a perfect stranger, and the equally hasty and abrupt dismissal
of Nausicaa from the scene once her usefulness is over—the overall effect
is to transform the Phaeacian episode, which could have been a rather
boring and methodical hospitality scene, into one of the most intriguing
episodes of the *Odyssey*. Scheria could have been simply a transition
point in the epic, a place of respite for Odysseus between the harrowing
adventures of the Apologoi and his ominous arrival in Ithaca. The Phaea-
cians could have been simply the hospitable providers of conveyance
home for Odysseus. But by incorporating the motif of the unknown
suitor to the hand of the princess into the episode, the poet has added
considerable intrigue to the narrative and has adeptly connected the
episode thematically to what has preceded in the Apologoi and to what
is to come in Ithaca.

Just as Circe and Calypso have posed obstacles to Odysseus' return
in the past, tempting him to remain with them and become their husband

rather than seek a reunion with Penelope (e.g., 9.29-32),[39] so Nausicaa poses a potential obstacle to Odysseus' return: he is tempted to marry her and remain in Scheria (αὐτόθι μίμνειν 6.245; αὖθι μένων 7.314). Though Odysseus' ultimate return home to Penelope is never really in doubt, the audience of the tale is able to suspend this knowledge and enjoy Nausicaa's performance in Odysseus' last temptation. The entire episode is colored and enlivened by the possibility that Odysseus will never leave Scheria; even up to the time of his departure, he is to be found staring impatiently at the sun, wishing for it to set and longing for his return home (13.28-35), a scene hauntingly reminiscent of our first view of Odysseus, still in Calypso's grasp on Ogygia, staring longingly over the sea (5.81-85). Thus Scheria, far from being "a haven where uncertainty and hostility are suspended,"[40] may be described better as the last obstacle to Odysseus' return; like the other islands of his wanderings, Scheria is potentially obstructive and therefore potentially dangerous.

The Phaeacian episode is also adeptly connected, by the incorporation of the motif of the unknown suitor for the hand of the princess, to what follows in Ithaca. Many details of the Phaeacian episode anticipate what is to occur in the second half of the *Odyssey*: Nausicaa's and Athena's warnings about overbearing Phaeacians who will taunt Odysseus anticipate the behavior of the suitors in Ithaca; the secrecy surrounding Odysseus' arrival at the palace in Scheria anticipates his disguise as a beggar in Ithaca; Odysseus' unexpected show of strength in the Phaeacian contests anticipates his participation in the contest of the bow in Ithaca; Demodocus' song about the unforeseen return home of a legitimate husband to his courted wife anticipates Odysseus' long-awaited return home to his beleaguered wife; and, in general, the underlying motif of the newly arrived stranger's marriage to Nausicaa anticipates Odysseus' (re)marriage to Penelope.

The combination of motifs in the Phaeacian episode, then, is not clumsy or accidental but artistic and purposeful; it is an aesthetically

---

39. Both temptresses are partly successful. Odysseus' long stay with Calypso and the narrator's remark that now, in Odysseus' seventh year in Ogygia, "the nymph *no longer* pleased him" (οὐκέτι 5.153) suggest that Odysseus was not always so unhappy with her. Odysseus happily stays with Circe for a full year before his companions approach him and plead with him to "remember his fatherland" (10.467-74).

40. Segal 1962, 22, 23, 59n.10.

pleasing device that artfully connects the Phaeacian episode thematically with Odysseus' previous adventures and at the same time anticipates the adventures that await him in Ithaca.

Chapter 6

Polyphemus (*Od.* 9.105-564)

οὐ γὰρ Κύκλωπες Διὸς αἰγιόχου ἀλέγουσιν.

[For the Cyclopes do not heed aegis-bearing Zeus.]
—(*Od.* 9.275)

Books 9–12 of the *Odyssey,* commonly referred to as the *Apologoi,* contain Odysseus' own account to his Phaeacian hosts of his wanderings from the time he left Troy up to his arrival in Ogygia. Though these stories are generically different from the material of the rest of the *Odyssey,* being derived from inherited folktales and deep-sea yarns, Homer has suppressed many of the fantastic elements of the inherited material and endowed many of these folktale characters with human qualities: Aeolus, the wind god, lives in a city; the Laestrygonians, man-eating ogres, hold assemblies in an agora; Circe, the witch, resides in a palace with servants to assist her. One of the most persistent human institutions found in the Apologoi, even among these folktale characters, is the ritual of *xenia.*

As in the first eight books of the *Odyssey,* hospitality continues to function as a leitmotif throughout the tales of Odysseus' wanderings. The reiterated tale about a wandering hero in an exotic land is naturally conducive to this theme of hospitality, so it is not surprising that many of the conventional elements of hospitality scenes, which have become so familiar in the first eight books of the *Odyssey,* continue to occur in the Apologoi in some form or another (see Appendix): the arrival of a stranger at an unknown land (II); the stranger's apprehension over whether the inhabitant(s) will be hostile or hospitable; the stranger's reception by the inhabitant(s) (VII), including the provision of food (IX), song (XIII), bath and fresh clothes (XVIII), bed (XVII), and guest-gifts (XX); and the question of whether the inhabitant(s) will provide conveyance (πομπή) to the stranger's next destination (XXV).

While the first eight books of the *Odyssey* have demonstrated the

123

proper function of these elements in normal scenes of human hospitality, the Apologoi by contrast portray the guest being abused by these very elements. Every hospitality scene of the Apologoi is tainted by deviations from, and perversions of, the elements of the normal hospitality type-scene (food, song, guest-gifts, bed, etc.): the food of the Lotus-eaters causes Odysseus' men to forget their homecoming (9.94–97); Circe offers the men a meal mixed with a drug that causes them to forget their homeland (10.234–36); among the Cyclopes and Laestrygonians, the guests, rather than being offered food, actually become the food of their hosts (9.288–93; 10.115–16); the song of the Sirens, like the food of the Lotus-eaters, causes those who hear it to forget their homecoming (12.41–46); the guest-gift of Polyphemus—the privilege of being eaten last (9.369–70)—is a cynical parody of the normal ritual; even the guest-gift of the hospitable Aeolus—the bag of winds (10.19–22)—ultimately drives Odysseus and his men away from their long-sought homeland (10.47–49); and the overly zealous hospitality of Odysseus' two female hosts, Circe and Calypso, and specifically the attraction of their beds (5.154–55; 9.29–32; 10.347, 467–74), delays the hero's timely arrival home. In short, Odysseus' hosts are either blatantly hostile and violent, bringing death and destruction, or overly zealous in their hospitality, jeopardizing his return home. There is no middle ground. Surely Menelaus, who expresses his indignation both at hosts who are overly hospitable and at ones who are overly hostile, would find much to disapprove of in the Apologoi (15.69–74):

νεμεσσῶμαι δὲ καὶ ἄλλῳ
ἀνδρὶ ξεινοδόκῳ, ὅς κ' ἔξοχα μὲν φιλέῃσιν,
ἔξοχα δ' ἐχθαίρῃσιν· ἀμείνω δ' αἴσιμα πάντα.
ἶσόν τοι κακόν ἐσθ', ὅς τ' οὐκ ἐθέλοντα νέεσθαι
ξεῖνον ἐποτρύνει καὶ ὃς ἐσσύμενον κατερύκει.
χρὴ ξεῖνον παρεόντα φιλεῖν, ἐθέλοντα δὲ πέμπειν.

[I would be indignant at another man
who, receiving guests, acted excessively hospitable
or excessively hostile; all things are better in due measure.
It is as blameworthy to urge a guest to leave who does not
want to as it is to detain a guest who is eager to leave.
One must grant hospitality to a guest who is present and grant
conveyance to a guest who wants to leave.]

I have chosen to concentrate my analysis of hospitality in the Apologoi on the Cyclopeia. In many ways it is the centerpiece of the Apologoi: it is a relatively long account—the first adventure to be told in detail— and it is thematically important, since the blinding of Polyphemus leads to the wrath of Poseidon and the subsequent ten-year wandering of Odysseus. Most important for my purposes, the theme of hospitality— or more precisely the parody of the theme of hospitality—is woven through this episode from beginning to end (see Appendix): Odysseus' expressed intention of testing the Cyclops' hospitality and acquiring guest-gifts (9.174–76, 228–29, 266–71); the impiety of the Cyclops toward Zeus, protector of guests (9.270–78); the typical request for, and presentation of, the guest's name (XI; 9.252–66, 355–67, 504–5); the preparation and consumption of feasts (IX; 9.288–97, 308–11, 341–44), followed by an after-dinner drink (X; 9.345–61); the provision of guest-gifts (XX; 9.355–56, 364–70, 517); the offer of conveyance to the next destination (XXV; 9.350, 518); the departure libation (XXII; 9.458–60); the formal speeches by guest and host upon departure (XXIII; 9.523–35); and the omen upon departure (XXIV; 9.550–55).

I have also chosen to concentrate on the Cyclopeia because this episode, more than any other, or perhaps just more clearly than any other, demonstrates Homer's innovation at every level of the narrative in his use of inherited material: the folktales that make up the story; the narrative patterns and type-scenes that are the scaffolding of the story; and the formulaic diction in which the story is told. On the level of the story itself, we are in the rare situation of being able to reconstruct the material that Homer inherited by comparing the over two hundred mostly independent attestations of this widely distributed folktale. By comparing the common elements of these folktales to Homer's version of the tale, we are able to recognize Homer's innovations to his inherited material. On the level of Homer's presentation of the story—and by "story" I mean content (i.e., "what is told"); by "presentation" I mean form (i.e., "how it is told": the narrative patterns, type-scenes, and formulaic diction in which the story is related)—we are equally well equipped to recognize Homer's innovations, for the structure and diction of the typical hospitality scene are perhaps more familiar to the audience of the *Odyssey* by this point in the epic than those of any other type-scene. The first four hospitality scenes of the *Odyssey*—Athena-Mentes in Ithaca, Telemachus in Pylos, Telemachus in Sparta, and Odysseus in Scheria—have thoroughly steeped the audience in the conventional elements of hospitality, and the audience is now prepared to recognize and appreciate deviations from these norms. Homer clearly relies on the previous experience of his audience in the Cyclopeia, creating what may usefully be termed a parody of a hospitality scene by employing the structure and diction of the normal hospitality scene but presenting them in altered and abnormal ways. Hence, breaches of literary convention on a formal level inform the breaches of social convention on the level of the story.

In this analysis of Homer's innovations in the Cyclopeia, I have found it particularly critical to distinguish between the two levels story and presentation. While innovations of an inherited story are common to all genres of literature, written and oral, innovations of a story's presentation are much more closely associated with oral poetry, and especially with the highly formalized epic art-language. If Homer's *Odyssey* had been entirely lost in transmission, and all we knew of it was a prose version, such as we have, for example, in Apollodorus' summary of the epic in his *Bibliotheca* (*Epitome* 7.1–33), we would still be able to distinguish Homer's innovations of his inherited material on the level of story, but his innovations on the level of the story's presentation—his rearrangement of type-scene elements and his alteration of conventional diction—would have been obliterated.

Story

That the theme of hospitality is woven through the entire episode of Homer's Cyclopeia is particularly remarkable because it plays no part in any other version of this widely distributed folktale, a tale attested in more than two hundred versions, from Iceland in the west to Russia in the east, from Lappland in the north to Africa in the south. These versions are largely independent of Homer's Cyclopeia and therefore provide clues as to what is inherited and what is innovative in Homer's version.[1]

It has long been recognized that Homer has combined at least two independent folktales in his version: (a) the story of a hero who blinds

---

1. For a review of scholarship on the issue of whether these folktales are derived from Homer or are independent representations of a folktale shared by Homer, see Glenn 1971, 135–44. Since Grimm's study (1857), the *communis opinio* has leaned heavily on the side of the independence of these folktales. The clearest evidence of their independence is the fact that, with just two possible exceptions, only Homer's Cyclopeia combines two separate motifs (types a and b below). If Homer's version was the original tale from which all the other versions were derived, it would be impossible to account for the clean dissection of the two motifs in these later versions.

a man-eating ogre, escapes with the help of the ogre's sheep, and, very often, is almost recaptured by the ogre with the help of a magic ring or ax; and (b) the story of a hero who injures an ogre or devil and avoids harm by giving his name as "Myself" (or very rarely as "Nobody").[2] It has been generally noted that Homer has characterized his hero as exceptionally resourceful (Odysseus' deception about the whereabouts of his men and his ruse to get the Cyclops drunk), and that he has characterized his ogre as exceptionally contemptuous of the gods—thus placing the opposition of Polyphemus and Odysseus into a theological context—but at the same time as somewhat pathetic (Polyphemus' conversation with his favorite ram). It has also been observed that, as is his usual procedure when working with inherited material, Homer has here suppressed or entirely obliterated many of the supernatural elements of the folktales, most notably the magic ring.[3]

Some of Homer's innovations appear to be designed to connect the Cyclopeia to the overarching themes of the *Odyssey*. Goat Island, off the coast of the land of the Cyclopes, has been invented in order to facilitate the adaption of the folktale to the theme of the seafaring wanderer, whose fleet must somehow be preserved for later adventures. Polyphemus is made to be the son of Poseidon in order to adapt the folktale to the overarching Odyssean theme of the curse. And the name "Nobody" (Οὖτις 9.366) has been substituted for the inherited "Myself"[4] in order to make possible the pun with "Wiliness" (μῆτις 9.405–14), which connects this scene thematically to Odysseus as the man of "many wiles" (πολύμητις *Od.* 68x) in the rest of the *Odyssey*.[5]

Homer has made even more extensive innovations of his inherited

---

2. Only two other versions combine the two folktales: (1) A Lapp version recorded by Poestion (1886, 122–26) and translated into English by J.G. Frazer (1921, 423–26); but the remarkably close resemblances to the Homeric version suggest that this is not an independent attestation; cf. Hackman 1904, 36; Page 1955, 18n.6; Glenn 1971, 138n.21, 143–44. (2) A Modern Greek version recorded by Valavánis (1884) and translated into English by Dawkins (1955, 19–21). Dawkins (1955, 14) argues that it is a genuine survival, independent of Homer. This is not impossible, but the independent synthesis of an otherwise unparalleled combination of folktales seems too remarkable a coincidence.

3. On Homer's suppression of supernatural elements generally, see Griffin 1977.

4. As noted above, the trick of the name is foreign to the Polyphemus-type folktale (type a). The only exceptions other than the *Odyssey* itself are the two versions mentioned in n. 2, which appear to be dependent on Homer. Of the ninety-seven attestations listed in Hackman (1904) of the folktale in which a trick name is used (type b), only one (Hackman #128) uses "Nobody" rather than "Myself."

5. On the pun itself, see Stanford 1939, 104–5; Podlecki 1961, 129–31; Austin 1972, 13–17. On the thematic connection of the pun to the rest of the *Odyssey*, see Schein 1970, 77–81.

material in order to connect the Cyclopeia to the theme of hospitality, a leitmotif in the rest of the *Odyssey*. As elsewhere in the epic, Homer presents a uniquely Greek, and uniquely Odyssean, version of the folktale by highlighting this theme of hospitality. Of the over two hundred versions of the folktale, only in Homer's version is the hero motivated to visit the ogre by his curiosity as to whether he is friendly to guests (9.173–76; cf. 6.120–21; 13.201–2) and by his desire to acquire guest-gifts (9.228–29, 266–71); in most versions of the folktale, the victims are innocent travelers who accidentally meet up with the ogre.[6] Only in Homer's version is the impiety of the ogre toward the gods—specifically toward Zeus, protector of guests in Homer—so explicitly articulated and so thematically important (9.266–78).[7] Only in Homer's version do the hero and the ogre exchange gifts: Odysseus deceptively gives Polyphemus a powerful wine, which inebriates him and facilitates his blinding (9.347–50);[8] as an equally deceptive countergift, Polyphemus grants Odysseus the privilege of being eaten last (9.369–70).[9] Finally, Odysseus' revelation of his real name upon departure (an inversion of the traditional name giving upon a guest's arrival) and the subsequent curse of Polyphemus (a parody of the conventional blessing upon a guest's departure) are not regular elements of the folktale.[10]

---

6. Alternatively the hero intentionally seeks out the ogre in order to kill him (J.G. Frazer #36), steal his treasure (J.G. Frazer #1, #20, #21), or rescue a maiden (Hackman #31, #41), the king's daughter (J.G. Frazer #14; Hackman #84), or his own wife (Hackman #15); see Glenn 1971, 151–52.

7. The motif of impiety toward the gods occurs in some Christian and Muslim versions (J.G. Frazer #21; Germain "a" and "d" in Germain 1954), but these are clearly late accretions to the original folktale; see Glenn 1971, 157–58.

It should be noted here that Homer is refashioning not only the widely distributed folktale of the man-eating ogre but the earlier Greek concept of who the Cyclopes were. When he included the folktale of the ogre in his story of Odysseus' return, Homer attached to it the name "Cyclops," but there is little evidence that the Greek Cyclopes were the barbarous, impious creatures of the *Odyssey*. According to Hesiod, the Cyclopes are personified storm elements—Arges, Brontes, Steropes—who supply Zeus with the thunderbolt and are master craftsmen (*Theog.* 139–46). Perhaps this explains the inconsistency of the description of the Cyclopes as carefree inhabitants of a golden-age paradise who trust in the immortals (9.107–11) with their description as contemptuous of the gods (9.273–78). See Mondi 1983.

8. The motif of getting an ogre drunk and overcoming him is common (see Thompson 1955–58, G.521), but it is not generally found in the folktale of the blinding of a man-eating ogre. Drunkenness plays a minor part in only two versions (J.G. Frazer #23, #26); see Glenn 1971, 161–62.

9. A delay in eating the hero does occur, though under different circumstances, in a few versions of the folktale (J.G. Frazer #6, #12—which, as mentioned above, appears to be derived from Homer—Hackman #114); see Glenn 1971, 163–64.

10. The hero gives his real name in only four versions (J.G. Frazer #33, #36; Hackman

It would appear, then, that Homer himself is the source of those elements of the Cyclopeia that pertain to the theme of hospitality. But Homer has not only added new elements that are absent in the inherited folktale; he has also made alterations in some of the inherited elements in order to accommodate them to the theme of hospitality. The trick of the name "Nobody" ("Myself" in the folktale) is presented in the context of a typical hospitality scene: Polyphemus asks for Odysseus' name "in order that he may give him guest-gifts" (9.356).[11] In a rather more daring manipulation of the traditional folktale, Homer has replaced the usual ending of the folktale—the ogre, in order to recapture the escaped hero, offers him a magic ring or ax,[12] which either forces the hero to return to the ogre or else guides the ogre to him by making him shout "Here I am"—with Polyphemus' presumably deceptive offer of guest-gifts and conveyance home if Odysseus will only come back (9.517-18).[13] The inherited detail of a hero who is magically forced to shout "Here I am" has left vestiges in Homer's version in Odysseus' reckless shouting at the Cyclops when he thinks that he is out of his throwing range. This element of shouting has been accommodated to the theme of hospitality. Odysseus' first shout contains his condemnation of Polyphemus' perverted hospitality (9.475-79):

Κύκλωψ, οὐκ ἄρ᾽ ἔμελλες ἀνάλκιδος ἀνδρὸς ἑταίρους
ἔδμεναι ἐν σπῆϊ γλαφυρῷ κρατερῆφι βίηφι.
καὶ λίην σέ γ᾽ ἔμελλε κιχήσεσθαι κακὰ ἔργα,
σχέτλι᾽, ἐπεὶ ξείνους οὐκ ἄζεο σῷ ἐνὶ οἴκῳ
ἐσθέμεναι· τῷ σε Ζεὺς τίσατο καὶ θεοὶ ἄλλοι.

[Cyclops, you were not destined to eat the companions of a
    strengthless man
in your hollow cave with your powerful might.

#110, #194); a curse by the ogre is unattested outside of Homer; see Glenn 1971, 174–77. On the thematic relationship between the name giving and the subsequent curse, see Brown 1966.

11. For a discussion of how the Οὖτις theme is interwoven with, and facilitated by, the guest-gift theme, see Podlecki 1961.

12. A ring is used in eighteen versions of the folktale, an ax in fifteen, a staff in two, a sword in two, and a white stone in one; see Glenn 1971, 177–79.

13. So Page 1955, 19n.15. Others have seen vestiges of the magic-ring ending of the folktale in other parts of the Homeric version: in the rocks that Polyphemus throws at Odysseus' ship (so Cook 1925, 989n.5, and Röhrich 1962, 65); and in the curse of Polyphemus (so Brown 1966, 201–2).

But it was destined that your evil deeds catch up with you,
wretch, since you did not shrink from eating guests in your
house. Therefore Zeus and the other gods have punished you.]

Odysseus' second shout contains, at last, his formal identification (*Od.*
9.502–5):

Κύκλωψ, αἴ κέν τίς σε καταθνητῶν ἀνθρώπων
ὀφθαλμοῦ εἴρηται ἀεικελίην ἀλαωτύν,
φάσθαι Ὀδυσσῆα πτολιπόρθιον ἐξαλαῶσαι,
υἱὸν Λαέρτεω, Ἰθάκῃ ἔνι οἰκί᾽ ἔχοντα.

[Cyclops, if anyone of mortal men asks you
about the unseemly blindness of your eye,
say that Odysseus, sacker of cities, blinded you,
the son of Laertes, who has a home in Ithaca.]

In sum, Homer has transformed the inherited folktale of the blinding
of a one-eyed ogre into a hospitality scene—or rather a parody of one—
by introducing many typical elements of hospitality: the acquisition of
gifts by a guest; the impiety of the host toward Zeus, protector of guests;
the exchange of gifts, albeit deceptive ones, between guest and host; the
revelation of the guest's name, lineage, and homeland, albeit revealed
at his departure rather than arrival; the element of the curse—replacing
the typical blessing—upon departure; and the appearance of an omen
upon departure.

Presentation

Homer's innovations of his inherited material have thus far been dis-
cussed strictly on the level of story. More interesting, perhaps, and
certainly more revealing of Homer's methods as an oral poet working
within the structures of the epic genre, are his innovations on the level
of the story's presentation: the conventional patterns, type-scenes, and
formulae through which the story is related. The perversions of the
normal human ritual of hospitality on the level of story—symbolized
most vividly by the ogre's feasting on his guests—have an analogue on
the level of presentation in the perversions of the type-scene elements
and formulae through which the story is told; that is, the refashioning

of what is conventional and inherited into something innovative and unique. A comparison of the presentation of the Cyclopeia with the conventional elements of a normal hospitality scene will demonstrate how the parody works on the level of form as well as on the level of content.

Using the typical patterns and diction of the normal arrival scene (see Appendix), Homer describes how Odysseus and his men arrive (ἀφικόμεθα) at the land of the Cyclopes (II; 9.181). There follows the typical description of the inhabitant's residence, in this case a cave (IIIa; 9.182–86), and the description of the activities of the inhabitant, in this case a description of what Polyphemus customarily does, since he is away (IIIb; 9.187–92). The familiar description of the activities of those who accompany the inhabitant is conspicuously absent, the text thereby drawing attention to Polyphemus' isolation (IIIc; 9.188–89). The arrival at the cave itself follows the same pattern, but with a more striking deviation from the norm. Odysseus and his men arrive (ἀφικόμεθα) at the cave (II; 9.216), but they do not find the inhabitant within (IIIb; οὐδέ μιν ἔνδον εὕρομεν 9.216–17). Such negations of typical elements of type-scenes are always significant in Homer: one may profitably compare the negation of the same typical element in Hector's visitation scene with Andromache (Il. 6.369–71) and Hermes' messenger scene with Calypso (Od. 5.50, 55, 81). In both cases the negation of the type-scene element is remarkable: Andromache is not found weaving at home, like Helen (Il. 3.125–28), or dallying in the bedroom, like Paris (Il. 6.321)—she is standing on the city wall lamenting (Il. 6.372–73); Odysseus is not found comfortably situated in Calypso's cave—he is sitting on the shore, weeping for his unattainable homecoming (Od. 5.81–84). The significance of the negation of this type-scene element in the Cyclopeia is magnified when one considers that this is the only Homeric hospitality scene in which the host is not found at home.[14]

The negation of this single element of the type-scene—that is, not finding the host at home—precludes the sequence of events that normally follows. Instead of standing at the threshold (V) and waiting for the host to catch sight of them, rise from his seat, approach them, take them by the hand, bid them welcome, and lead them into the house

---

14. Such negations of typical elements have been recognized as characteristic Homeric devices since antiquity: see the scholium to Il. 6.371 (ἐκκλίνων τὸ ὁμοειδές); Eustathius 647, 47. Arend (1933, 15–16, 33–34, 48–49, 51, 55, 62, 71, 90, 93, 100, 103) makes many perceptive comments about such Negierung des Typischen.

(VIIa, c, d, f, g, i), Odysseus and his men enter the cave uninvited and take a look around (9.218). There is no host to invite them to take part in sacrifice (XV), as Nestor does in Pylos (*Od.* 3.31–66), or to offer them seats and a meal (VIII, IX), so Odysseus and his men start a fire and perform a sacrifice themselves; then, making a meal of their host's cheeses (9.231–32), these "guests," in an ironic inversion of the norm, sit down within and wait for their "host" to arrive (9.232–33).

Polyphemus arrives home, drives his sheep into the cave, blocks the entrance to the cave with a huge rock, prepares his meal, starts a fire, and only then catches sight of his guests (9.251). On seeing them, he immediately asks (9.252–55):

> Ὦ ξεῖνοι, τίνες ἐστέ; πόθεν πλεῖθ᾽ ὑγρὰ κέλευθα;
> ἦ τι κατὰ πρῆξιν ἦ μαψιδίως ἀλάλησθε
> οἷά τε ληϊστῆρες ὑπεὶρ ἅλα, τοί τ᾽ ἀλόωνται
> ψυχὰς παρθέμενοι, κακὸν ἀλλοδαποῖσι φέροντες;

> [O strangers, who are you? From where do you sail the watery ways?
> Are you on some business, or do you wander aimlessly,
> like pirates, who wander over the sea,
> risking their lives, bringing evil to foreigners?]

There is nothing particularly remarkable about Polyphemus' question. It is not necessarily a hostile interrogation; the hospitable Nestor uses the same four-verse block in questioning Telemachus when he visits Pylos (3.71–74; cf. *H.Ap.* 452–55). It is not the content of the question but its position in the sequence of typical elements that make up the scene that is remarkable: Polyphemus is inquiring into his guests' identity on first sight (XIa), even before offering them a meal (IX). In the hospitality scene in Pylos, Nestor questions his guests only after offering them food (3.65–68), and he prefaces his question by saying (3.69–70):

> Νῦν δὴ κάλλιόν ἐστι μεταλλῆσαι καὶ ἐρέσθαι
> ξείνους, οἵ τινές εἰσιν, ἐπεὶ τάρπησαν ἐδωδῆς.

> [Now it is better to inquire and to ask
> strangers who they are, after they have taken delight in food.]

In the four scenes of hospitality preceding the Polyphemus episode (at Ithaca, Pylos, Sparta, and Scheria), the hosts scrupulously observe the custom that a guest should be fed before being interrogated. Polyphemus turns the conventional type-scene of hospitality on its head by interrogating his guests on first seeing them.

Odysseus' response—that they are Achaeans returning from Troy (9.259-66)—adequately answers the Cyclops' question. Notably absent, however, is any mention of Odysseus' name, lineage, and homeland. This is the usual place for a guest to identify himself (XIb; cf. 1.179-81; 3.79-85), but Homer chooses not to reveal his hero's name yet, both in order to make possible the later Οὖτις ("Nobody") trick and, in conjunction with the other inversions of the normal hospitality scene, in order to have Odysseus reveal his name, lineage, and homeland upon departure, at the end rather than at the beginning of the scene.

In the second half of his response to the Cyclops' questions—his supplication of Polyphemus—Odysseus lays claim to the rights of suppliants and guests, pointedly, but rather pathetically, advising the Cyclops that Zeus himself is the protector of suppliants and guests (VI; 9.266-71):

ἡμεῖς δ' αὖτε κιχανόμενοι τὰ σὰ γοῦνα
ἱκόμεθ', εἴ τι πόροις ξεινήϊον ἠὲ καὶ ἄλλως
δοίης δωτίνην, ἥ τε ξείνων θέμις ἐστίν.
ἀλλ' αἰδεῖο, φέριστε, θεούς· ἱκέται δέ τοί εἰμεν.
Ζεὺς δ' ἐπιτιμήτωρ ἱκετάων τε ξείνων τε,
ξείνιος, ὃς ξείνοισιν ἅμ' αἰδοίοισιν ὀπηδεῖ.

[We have arrived and come to your knees,
to see if perchance you may grant a guest-gift or otherwise
give a gift, which is the custom of guest-friends.
But revere the gods, mighty one. We are your suppliants.
And Zeus is the protector of suppliants and guests,
Zeus Xeinios, who attends to revered guests.]

This reference to Zeus as protector of suppliants and guests is an appeal to the cultural norms of Greek society.[15] What is not normal, however, is the Cyclops' response to Odysseus' supplication (9.273-78):

---

15. Cf. Nausicaa's reception of Odysseus, in which she mentions Zeus' interest in suppliants and guests (6.206-8).

νήπιός εἰς, ὦ ξεῖν᾿, ἢ τηλόθεν εἰλήλουθας,
ὅς με θεοὺς κέλεαι ἢ δειδίμεν ἢ ἀλέασθαι·
οὐ γὰρ Κύκλωπες Διὸς αἰγιόχου ἀλέγουσιν
οὐδὲ θεῶν μακάρων, ἐπεὶ ἦ πολὺ φέρτεροί εἰμεν.
οὐδ᾿ ἂν ἐγὼ Διὸς ἔχθος ἀλευάμενος πεφιδοίμην
οὔτε σεῦ οὔθ᾿ ἑτάρων, εἰ μὴ θυμός με κελεύοι.

[You are a fool, stranger, or you have come from afar;
you who bid me to fear or shrink from the gods.
For the Cyclopes do not heed aegis-bearing Zeus
nor the blessed gods, since we are much stronger.
And I would not, shrinking from the hatred of Zeus,
spare you or your companions unless my spirit should bid me.]

This response clearly places Polyphemus outside the bounds of normal heroic society. Odysseus can no longer expect his host to observe the Greek laws of hospitality. He has shown himself to be "violent, savage, and unjust" (ὑβρισταί τε καὶ ἄγριοι οὐδὲ δίκαιοι 9.175), certainly not "friendly to strangers" (φιλόξεινοι 9.176).

Polyphemus proceeds to commit the ultimate outrage against his guests. Instead of offering them a meal, he makes a meal of them: he snatches up two of Odysseus' men and devours them. This is surely the darkest form of parody. Its parodic value is apparent on the level of story. But even a prose version of the *Odyssey,* like Apollodorus', would retain this sense of parody on the level of story. More interesting about Homer, as an oral poet working within the epic genre, is his formal presentation of the story, that is, the structure and diction of Polyphemus' feasting scene; for the perversion of normal civilized behavior on the level of story is mirrored on the level of its formal presentation by the perversion of the structure and diction associated with a typical banqueting scene. Homer uses the structure and diction of the normal, peaceful, banqueting scene but alters it to describe Polyphemus' cannibalistic feast. The tension between the familiar conventional diction (the "norm") and Homer's innovations (his "deviations from that norm") accentuates the utter perversity of this scene.

The normal banqueting scene is very often described by a combination of verses (e.g., 1.149–50; Homer uses this combination 11x; cf. Hesiod fr. 112.4):

οἱ δ᾽ ἐπ᾽ ὀνείαθ᾽ ἑτοῖμα προκείμενα χεῖρας ἴαλλον.
αὐτὰρ ἐπεὶ πόσιος καὶ ἐδητύος ἐξ ἔρον ἔντο,

[They stretched forth their hands to the food that was spread
out ready.
But when they had cast off their desire for drink and food,]

Although Polyphemus' feasting scene (9.288–98) is modeled structurally on this skeleton of the normal banqueting scene, it has been expanded and altered to accentuate the gory details of this unique feast. The first verse of the conventional combination of verses is modified here to accommodate this unique context: the object of the feast is not normal food but rather Odysseus' companions (9.288):[16]

ἀλλ᾽ ὅ γ᾽ ἀναΐξας ἑτάροις ἐπὶ χεῖρας ἴαλλε

[But he leaped up and stretched forth his hands upon my
companions.]

Only after the insertion of two similes—a poetic device more often associated with scenes of war than of banqueting (the men are like puppies—9.289; Polyphemus like a lion—9.292)—and a description of the dire condition of Odysseus' men, symbolized by their entreaty to Zeus, protector of guests (9.294–95), is the feast scene brought to an end with an expanded and modified form of the second verse of the usual combination of verses (9.296–97):

αὐτὰρ ἐπεὶ Κύκλωψ μεγάλην ἐμπλήσατο νηδὺν
ἀνδρόμεα κρέ᾽ ἔδων καὶ ἐπ᾽ ἄκρητον γάλα πίνων,

[But when the Cyclops had filled his great belly,
eating human meat and drinking unmixed milk,]

Here, instead of the simple nouns *food* (ἐδητύος 1.150, etc.) and *drink* (πόσιος 1.150, etc.), Homer has enlivened the action by employing the

---

16. The correspondences between these verses have rarely been noted: cf. Eustathius 1630, 20; Arend 1933, 75; Belmont 1962, 169.

corresponding verb forms and by describing the grotesque nature of the food and drink.[17]

Moreover, the formula used in this scene to describe Polyphemus' preparation of his feast after tearing his victims limb from limb, ὁπλίσσατο δόρπον (9.291), appears to be drawn from the diction of normal meal-preparation scenes. Although the exact phrase ὁπλίσσατο δόρπον (9.291 = 2.20; 9.344) and its metrical equivalent ὁπλίσσατο δεῖπνον (9.311; 10.116) are employed in the surviving epos only to describe the cannibalistic feasts of the Cyclops and the Laestrygonians, many similar phrases are attested in normal meal-preparation scenes: δόρπον ἐφοπλίσσαντες (Il. 23.55); δόρπα τ᾽ ἐφοπλισόμεσθα (Il. 8.503; 9.66); δόρπον θ᾽ ὁπλισάμεσθα (Od. 4.429, 574; 12.292); δόρπον ἐπισταδὸν ὁπλίζοντο (Od. 16.453); δεῖπνον ἐφοπλίσσαι (Od. 19.419); δεῖπνον ἐφοπλίσσωσι (Od. 24.360).

Finally, it appears that the formula used in this scene to describe the brains of Polyphemus' unfortunate victims flowing to the ground, χαμάδις ῥέε, δεῦε δὲ γαῖαν (9.290), is a slight adaption of a formula commonly used in libation scenes, as when Achilles pours a libation of wine at the funeral of Patroclus: χαμάδις χέε, δεῦε δὲ γαῖαν (Il. 23.220).[18]

In sum, in this uniquely grotesque feasting scene, Homer has borrowed the structures and formulae normally employed in the context of peaceful and civilized banquet, meal-preparation, and libation scenes, altered them, and employed them in a unique context of barbarous cannibalism. He has taken the diction of peace and applied it to a scene of violence. This perversion on the level of presentation mirrors and accentuates the perversion of the situation in the story, creating parody of form as well as of content.

The post-feast activities found in normal hospitality scenes obviously have no place in the Cyclopeia: the questioning of the guests has already

17. On the correspondences between these verses, see Arend 1933, 75.

18. This correspondence is noted by Arend (1933, 75). But, since this formula occurs only twice in the surviving epos, one must necessarily be less confident than, for example, in the case of the often repeated χεῖρας ἴαλλον that the primary use of this formula is in the context of libation scenes. The primary context of this formula is obfuscated further by the use of segments of it to describe the falling of leaves (χαμάδις χέε Il. 6.147), the flowing of tears (χαμάδις ῥέε Il. 17.438), and the spilling of a dying soldier's blood on the ground (ῥέε, δεῦε δὲ γαῖαν Il. 13.655; 21.119). Yet I suspect that the primary use of the formula was in the context of libation (Il. 23.220; 7.480), as is hinted by the simile at Il. 3.300, where the primary sense of libation of wine is extended to the spilling of brains.

occurred (XIa); and songs and stories would be entirely out of place (XIII), as would the preparation of the guests' beds (XVII). But what replaces these typical elements, specifically the normal preparation of a bed for the guest, is notably parodic. Polyphemus, the "host," stretches out and falls asleep in the cave, while his "guests" remain awake (9.306 = 436):

ὣς τότε μὲν στενάχοντες ἐμείναμεν Ἠῶ δῖαν.

[So then groaning we awaited the divine dawn.]

This verse appears to be closely modeled on a formula normally employed in more comfortable situations (9.151; 12.7):[19]

ἔνθα δ᾽ ἀποβρίξαντες ἐμείναμεν Ἠῶ δῖαν.

[And then having fallen asleep we awaited the divine dawn.]

In harmony with the overarching sense of parody in the feasting scene, Homer has altered the usual formula for sleeping, actually inverting it into a formula for not sleeping, thus accentuating the plight of Odysseus and his men.

The following two days that Odysseus and his men spend with the Cyclops are filled with parodies of the normal hospitality scene. The feasting, libation, gift giving, and name giving of the normal hospitality scene are all presented in perverted forms. It may be said that, just as a new formula for sleeping—or more precisely for not sleeping—has been substituted for the normal one, so has an entirely new type-scene of meal preparation been composed as a substitute for the normal scene of meal preparation. In its normal form, the oft-repeated scene of meal preparation is (1.136-40 = 4.52-56; 7.172-76; [10.368-72]; 15.135-[39]; 17.91-95):

χέρνιβα δ᾽ ἀμφίπολος προχόῳ ἐπέχευε φέρουσα
καλῇ χρυσείῃ, ὑπὲρ ἀργυρέοιο λέβητος,
νίψασθαι· παρὰ δὲ ξεστὴν ἐτάνυσσε τράπεζαν.
σῖτον δ᾽ αἰδοίη ταμίη παρέθηκε φέρουσα,

---

19. On the correspondences between these verses, see Arend 1933, 100.

εἴδατα πόλλ᾽ ἐπιθεῖσα, χαριζομένη παρεόντων.

[A handmaid brought water and poured it from an ewer,
a beautiful, golden one, into a silver basin,
to wash with; and set out beside them a polished table.
A respected housekeeper brought bread and set it beside them,
adding many dishes, gracious with her provisions.]

In the Cyclopeia, Polyphemus' repeated preparation of his human feast is described twice almost verbatim, and these two descriptions are themselves consolidations of various formulae in Polyphemus' first feasting scene (9.308–11 ≈ 341–44; cf. 244–45, 250–51, 289, 291):

καὶ τότε πῦρ ἀνέκαιε καὶ ἤμελγε κλυτὰ μῆλα,
πάντα κατὰ μοῖραν, καὶ ὑπ᾽ ἔμβρυον ἧκεν ἑκάστῃ.
αὐτὰρ ἐπεὶ δὴ σπεῦσε πονησάμενος τὰ ἃ ἔργα,
σὺν δ᾽ ὅ γε δὴ αὖτε δύω μάρψας ὁπλίσσατο δεῖπνον.

[And then he kindled a fire and milked his famous flocks,
everything in order, and he put a young one under each dam.
But when he had hastened to tend to his tasks,
he again snatched two men together and prepared his meal.]

The predictable rhythm of the normal type-scene of meal preparation has been replaced by a rhythm with an entirely different beat.

This cacophonous rhythm continues in a remarkable scene (9.345–70) in which three conventional elements of hospitality—the after-dinner drink (X), gift giving (XX), and name giving (XIb)—are all mixed together in a striking parody of the norm. In an unprecedented twist, Odysseus, the guest, provides a libation of wine for his host (9.349).[20] But it is offered to the Cyclops as a trick: this strong brew will inebriate him and facilitate his blinding. Polyphemus is so delighted by the wine that he asks Odysseus to tell him his name in order that he may give him a guest-gift (9.355–56).[21] But these two elements of hospitality become perversions of the norm too. In a deceitful exchange, Odysseus gives his name as "Nobody" (Οὖτις 9.366–67), a deception that will

---

20. On the uniqueness of this action, see Belmont 1962, 171n.118.
21. Cf. Scheria, where Odysseus gives his name to Alcinous in order that they might be guest-friends (8.550–56; 9.16–18).

later prevent Polyphemus' fellow Cyclopes from coming to his aid. Odysseus will withhold his real name until his departure. Polyphemus' cynical response is to offer Odysseus a deceptive guest-gift: the dubious privilege of being eaten last (9.369-70):[22]

Οὖτιν ἐγὼ πύματον ἔδομαι μετὰ οἷς ἑτάροισι,
τοὺς δ' ἄλλους πρόσθεν· τὸ δέ τοι ξεινήϊον ἔσται.

[I will eat Outis last of his companions,
and the others before him. This will be my guest-gift to you.]

As the later Greek literary critic Demetrius observed,[23] it is the very playfulness of Polyphemus—his gift to eat Odysseus last—that makes this scene so forceful and the Cyclops so repulsive. The utter perversion of the normal ritual of hospitality, which we have been tracing throughout this episode, reaches its climax here. Polyphemus has clearly shown himself to be violent, savage, and lawless (cf. 9.175, 215, 428). It is without reservation that Odysseus proceeds to plot his destruction.

In the blinding-scene that follows, Homer abandons altogether the diction of hospitality and peace—even the parody of it—and resorts to the diction of hostility and war, employing elements characteristic of Iliadic scenes of a warrior's *aristeia:* the arming of a hero (9.375-76); the exhortation to his men (9.376-77); the divinely inspired courage (9.381); and similes describing the violent action (9.384-88, 391-94).[24] Perhaps Odysseus' later taunts at his vanquished foe (9.502-5, 523-25) should also be seen in this light.

Odysseus regards his violence against the Cyclops as a justified response to the violations of hospitality that he and his men have suffered. He sees himself as a righteous avenger on one who has dishonored Zeus Xenios (9.475-79). Ironically the Cyclopes themselves inadvertently hit on this truth when they advise the blinded Polyphemus as follows (9.410-11):

εἰ μὲν δὴ μή τίς σε βιάζεται οἶον ἐόντα,
νοῦσόν γ' οὔ πως ἔστι Διὸς μεγάλου ἀλέασθαι,

---

22. Cf. Ctesippus' cynical guest-gift of an ox-hoof to Odysseus (20.288-302). In exchange Philoetius gives Ctesippus a "guest-gift" of a spear in the chest (22.285-91).

23. *On Style* 130 (cf. 152): "In (Homer's) jesting he is all the more fearful" (παίζων φοβερώτερός ἐστι).

24. Cf. Heubeck, in Heubeck, West, and Hainsworth 1989, 9.375-94n.

[If nobody is harming you, who are alone,
it is impossible to escape the disease of great Zeus.]

Polyphemus has offended Zeus Xenios and is suffering the bitter consequences.

The scene of Odysseus' departure from the land of the Cyclopes brings the parody of the normal elements of a hospitality scene to a close. When Odysseus thinks that he has successfully gotten beyond Polyphemus' throwing range, he finally identifies himself (9.504–5):

φάσθαι 'Οδυσσῆα πτολιπόρθιον ἐξαλαῶσαι,
υἱὸν Λαέρτεω, 'Ιθάκῃ ἔνι οἰκί' ἔχοντα.

[Say that Odysseus, sacker of cities, blinded you,
the son of Laertes, who has a home in Ithaca.]

His identification contains all the formal elements of the conventional identification: name, lineage, and homeland (XIb; cf. 9.19–21). It is remarkable, then, not for its content but for its position in the hospitality scene—upon the departure rather than the arrival of the guest. As such, it is a fitting parallel to Polyphemus' request for identification at the beginning of the scene (9.282–85); for, as noted there, it is not the content of Polyphemus' question but its position, immediately upon seeing his guests rather than after a meal, that is remarkable.

The conventional elements in a departure scene, guest-gifts (ξείνια XX) and conveyance (πομπή XXV), are also parodied. But it is only after Odysseus is out of reach that Polyphemus, in a vain attempt to lure him back, offers him guest-gifts and conveyance (9.517–19):

ἀλλ᾿ ἄγε δεῦρ᾿, 'Οδυσεῦ, ἵνα τοι πὰρ ξείνια θείω,
πομπήν τ᾿ ὀτρύνω δόμεναι κλυτὸν ἐννοσίγαιον·
τοῦ γὰρ ἐγὼ πάϊς εἰμί, πατὴρ δ᾿ ἐμὸς εὔχεται εἶναι.

[But come here, Odysseus, in order that I may provide you with
    guest-gifts
and urge the famed earth-shaker to give you conveyance;
for I am his son, and he claims to be my father.]

The deceptiveness of Polyphemus' offer is clear if one recalls that this is apparently Homer's substitution for the sequel in the inherited folktale, in which the ogre, in a vain attempt to recapture the escaped hero, offers him a magic ring or ax, which either draws the hero back or leads the ogre to the hero.

Finally, in place of the usual exchange of blessings upon the departure of a guest (XXIII), Homer substitutes in this scene an exchange of curses. First, Odysseus curses Polyphemus (9.523-24):

αἲ γὰρ δὴ ψυχῆς τε καὶ αἰῶνός σε δυναίμην
εὖνιν ποιήσας πέμψαι δόμον Ἄϊδος εἴσω.

[Would that I were able to make you bereft of soul and life
and send you to the home of Hades.]

This is a striking contrast to the blessing Odysseus pronounces on his Phaeacian hosts at his departure from Scheria (13.59-62):

Χαῖρέ μοι, ὦ βασίλεια, διαμπερές, εἰς ὅ κε γῆρας
ἔλθῃ καὶ θάνατος, τά τ᾽ ἐπ᾽ ἀνθρώποισι πέλονται.
αὐτὰρ ἐγὼ νέομαι· σὺ δὲ τέρπεο τῷδ᾽ ἐνὶ οἴκῳ
παισί τε καὶ λαοῖσι καὶ Ἀλκινόῳ βασιλῆϊ.

[May you constantly fare well, my queen, until old age
and death come, which are inevitable for men.
But I am going. Rejoice in your house
and children and people and in Alcinous your king.]

In return, Polyphemus invokes Poseidon and pronounces a curse on Odysseus (9.530-35):

δὸς μὴ Ὀδυσσῆα πτολίπορθον οἴκαδ᾽ ἱκέσθαι
[υἱὸν Λαέρτεω, Ἰθάκῃ ἔνι οἰκί᾽ ἔχοντα.]²⁵
ἀλλ᾽ εἴ οἱ μοῖρ᾽ ἐστὶ φίλους ἰδέειν καὶ ἱκέσθαι
οἶκον ἐϋκτίμενον καὶ ἐὴν ἐς πατρίδα γαῖαν,
ὀψὲ κακῶς ἔλθοι, ὀλέσας ἄπο πάντας ἑταίρους,
νηὸς ἐπ᾽ ἀλλοτρίης, εὗροι δ᾽ ἐν πήματα οἴκῳ.

---

25. Verse 9.531 is absent in all except two very late manuscripts (P³, P⁷); it is probably interpolated from 9.505.

[Grant that Odysseus, sacker of cities, not go homeward,
[the son of Laertes, who has a home in Ithaca.]
But if it is his fate to see his loved ones and come
to his well built home and to his fatherland,
may he arrive late and badly off, having lost all his companions,
upon a foreign ship, and may he find troubles at home.]

A comparison of this diction with the diction of conventional blessings shows Polyphemus' curse to be a negation of the normal blessing pronounced by a host upon a guest's departure (XXIII; Euryalus to Odysseus 8.410–11; Helen to Telemachus 15.128–29; cf. 15.111–12):

σοὶ δὲ θεοὶ ἄλοχον ἰδέειν καὶ πατρίδ᾽ ἱκέσθαι
δοῖεν, ἐπεὶ δὴ δηθὰ φίλων ἄπο πήματα πάσχεις.

[May the gods grant that you see your wife and come to your
    homeland,
since you have suffered woes away from your loved ones for a long
    time.]

σὺ δέ μοι χαίρων ἀφίκοιο
οἶκον ἐϋκτίμενον καὶ σὴν ἐς πατρίδα γαῖαν.

[May you fare well and return
to your well built home and to your fatherland.]

In retrospect, one can see that from his premature request for his guests' identity upon their arrival to his curse upon their departure Polyphemus has perverted the normal diction of the hospitality scene and generally turned the type-scene on its head. But perhaps Polyphemus is not alone in violating hospitality; for hospitality is a reciprocal relationship and requires a set behavior by both host and guest. Odysseus' and his men's behavior as guests can scarcely be considered exemplary. They have entered their host's house uninvited, helped themselves to his food, given him a deceptive gift of wine that inebriates him and enables them to blind him, stolen his sheep, and escaped to their ship.[26]

---

26. Belmont (1962, 168, 172) stresses the violations of Odysseus and his men as guests and points to this as the cause of Polyphemus' curse and the consequent ten-year wandering.

The reciprocal violations of hospitality by both host and guests are strikingly symbolized in this episode by the function of the threshold (οὐδός). The threshold, being the physical boundary between the outside, where the visitor is merely a stranger, and the inside, where he is a guest of the inhabitant, is a ritually symbolic place. It is where visitors normally stand and wait to be seen by the master of the house. In this episode, though, the threshold has been violated. Odysseus and his men have crossed it uninvited and invaded the habitation of the Cyclops (9.216–18). It is appropriate, then, that Polyphemus forcefully detains his guests within the cave by placing a huge rock on the threshold (9.240–43), as though to make inaccessible what had previously been too accessible. This motif of the violation of the threshold reaches its climax in the wish Polyphemus expresses to his ram (9.458–60):

τῷ κέ οἱ ἐγκέφαλός γε διὰ σπέος ἄλλυδις ἄλλη
θεινομένου ῥαίοιτο πρὸς οὔδεϊ, κὰδ δέ κ' ἐμὸν κῆρ
λωφήσειε κακῶν, τά μοι οὐτιδανὸς πόρεν Οὖτις.

[Then his brains, in all directions throughout the cave,
would be dashed on the threshold, once he has been struck, and
    my heart
would be relieved of the ills that worthless Outis brought me.]

Polyphemus' wish is a symbolically pregnant substitute for the normal libation upon a guest's departure (XXII).

Perhaps this perception of reciprocal violations by both guests and host explains a curious development in the story after Odysseus' departure. Odysseus and his men divide up the spoils from the Cyclops' cave, and Odysseus sacrifices his portion, Polyphemus' favorite ram, to Zeus (9.550–53). The sacrifice is intended to honor Zeus as protector of guests (cf. 9.270–71, 478–79), since he has helped Odysseus avenge the violation of hospitality by the Cyclops. But, quite remarkably, Odysseus receives an omen unfavorable to his voyage (XXIV): Zeus does not accept the sacrifice (ὁ δ' οὐκ ἐμπάζετο ἱρῶν 9.553). The stolen ram is symbolic of the violation of hospitality by the guests too, and in his function as Zeus Xenios, he cannot accept this perverted offering. Instead he devises destruction for Odysseus' men (9.554–55).

Chapter 7

Eumaeus the Swineherd (*Od.* 13.221–14.533; 15.301–494; 15.555–16.155; 16.452–17.25; 17.182–203)

ξεῖν', οὔ μοι θέμις ἔστ', οὐδ' εἰ κακίων σέθεν ἔλθοι,
ξεῖνον ἀτιμῆσαι· πρὸς γὰρ Διός εἰσιν ἅπαντες
ξεῖνοί τε πτωχοί τε· δόσις δ' ὀλίγη τε φίλη τε
γίγνεται ἡμετέρη· ἡ γὰρ δμώων δίκη ἐστὶν
αἰεὶ δειδιότων, ὅτ' ἐπικρατέωσιν ἄνακτες
οἱ νέοι.

[Stranger, it is not right, even if one worse off than you were to come,
for me to dishonor a stranger. For from Zeus are all
strangers and beggars. But humble and friendly
is our gift. For it is the way of slaves
always to fear, whenever masters hold power over them
who are young.]

                                    —(*Od.* 14.56–61)

When Odysseus finally reaches Ithaca, not recognizing his long-sought homeland, he ironically asks himself a question that has become something of a topos in the *Odyssey* (13.200–202; cf. 6.119–21; 9.174–76):

ὤ μοι ἐγώ, τέων αὖτε βροτῶν ἐς γαῖαν ἱκάνω;
ἦ ῥ' οἵ γ' ὑβρισταί τε καὶ ἄγριοι οὐδὲ δίκαιοι,
ἦε φιλόξεινοι καί σφιν νόος ἐστὶ θεουδής;

[Oh my! To the land of what mortals have I come this time?
Are they violent and savage and unjust,
or are they kind to strangers and have a god-fearing mind?]

As events unfold, both prove to be true. First Odysseus visits Eumaeus the swineherd, who shows him proper and generous, albeit humble, hospitality, and who proves to be a model of piety toward the gods; then he confronts the suitors, who have overstepped all boundaries of propriety and become paradigms of hubristic behavior. The scene of kind hospitality in Eumaeus' hut is a foil to the scene of cruel inhospitality in the palace, much as the warm reception by Telemachus of Athena, disguised as Mentes (1.103–324), was a foil to the cold indifference shown her by the suitors. The motif of the returned master is not unlike that of the disguised god, both involving the testing of loyalty and hospitality. Odysseus "makes trial" (πειρητίζων 14.459; 15.304) of the swineherd, who passes the test and receives his reward (21.213–16; cf. 14.624); the suitors, though well aware of the gods' habit of disguising themselves as visitors (17.483–87), fail to show the disguised Odysseus proper respect and receive their just deserts. As in Ovid's tale of Baucis and Philemon (*Met.* 8.611–724), the humble but generous host gets the reward, while those with the means to provide even extravagant hospitality prove inhospitable and are consequently punished.

One may justifiably question whether Odysseus' visit to Eumaeus' hut is really a scene of *xenia,* since in Homer's poetic cosmos, as in historical Greek society, *xenia* is a relationship between those of equal social status.[1] Here the visitor is a beggar and suppliant, not a proper *xenos,* as, for example, in the case of Telemachus in his travels to Pylos and Sparta. Complications and ambiguities arise from Odysseus' assumption of a disguise, a device that overturns and obfuscates all social distinctions and produces the rich ironies of a scene in which a master is given hospitality by his servant.

But whatever are the historical realities from which the theme of hospitality in Homer is derived, Odysseus' stay in Eumaeus' hut is manifestly a hospitality scene in terms of the pattern on which it is built and the diction in which it is expressed. We find here almost all the formal elements of the conventional hospitality type-scene (see Appendix): Odysseus happens upon a young man (actually Athena in disguise) on the beach, who directs him to Eumaeus' hut (I; 13.221–440); he finds (εὗρ') Eumaeus sitting at the entrance of his hut making leather sandals (IIIb; 14.5, 23–24); Eumaeus' residence is described in detail, using a typical structure (IIIa; 14.5–22);[2] Odysseus confronts dogs at the entrance

---

1. So Belmont 1962, 38–41, 156–59.

2. In this typical structure, a series of adjectives describing the house is followed by a relative clause acknowledging the builder (cf. *Od.* 24.205–7; *Il.* 18.369–71; 24.448–50); see Arend 1933, 36, 48.

(IV; 14.21–22, 29–32) and is forced to sit on the ground (V; 14.30–32); Eumaeus hastens to his guest and bids him enter (VIId; 14.33–45), leads him into his house (VIIi) and seats him (VIII; 14.48–51), and prepares a meal for him and invites him to eat (IXa; 14.72–81); at the conclusion of the meal (IXc; 14.109–11), the two drink wine (X) and exchange news and information (XII; 14.112–84); not until the meal is over does Eumaeus issue a formal request for his guest's identity (XIa; 14.185–90); Odysseus obliges his host by telling about his part in the expedition against Troy and its aftermath, the usual topic of choice between visitors and their hosts (XIb, XIII; 14.191–359); a second, more elaborate meal follows, preceded by a formal sacrifice (XV; 14.407–56), after which the guest again tells a tale of Troy (XIII; 14.462–506); finally, at the end of the day, a bed is provided for the guest (XVII; 14.518–24). Even the formal elements of guest-gifts (XX) and safe conduct (XXV; πομπή) are found in this scene, though in an appropriately humble form: Eumaeus' provision of a staff upon his guest's departure serves as his guest-gift, and his escort to the city serves as his πομπή (17.182–203); he delegates to Telemachus the responsibility for further provisions: clothes (15.338; 16.79 = 17.550), a sword and shoes (16.80), and safe conduct to wherever his guest wishes to go next (15.339 ≈ 16.81). In sum, of all the formal elements that comprise a typical hospitality scene, only one is conspicuously absent here: the provision of a bath for the guest (XVIII).

But Eumaeus' hospitality is not just a perfunctory fulfillment of obligations; it is highly proper, exceptionally generous, and intensely personal. Eumaeus' propriety is demonstrated by his explicit assurance to his guest that he will not interrogate him until he has been satiated with food and wine (14.45–47; cf. 1.123–24; 4.60–62). His generosity is signaled by his offer of the chine, the portion of honor, to his guest (14.437–38; cf. 4.65; 8.475; *Il.* 7.321; 9.207), and by his provision of a bed by the hearth for his guest, while he himself sleeps outside (14.518–33). The personal nature of his hospitality is accentuated throughout the scene: he offers a goatskin from his own bed as a seat for his guest (14.50–51), he shares wine from his own cup (14.112–13), and he offers his own cloak as a blanket (14.520–22). Odysseus rightly rejoices at the conduct of his faithful servant (χαῖρε δ' Ὀδυσσεύς 14.51, 526; χαῖρε δὲ θυμῷ 14.113; cf. κύδαινε δὲ θυμὸν ἄνακτος 14.438).

Yet this is not a typical hospitality scene, for it takes place not in the heroic setting of a king's palace but in the lowly hut of a swineherd.

Even in his initial welcome of his guest, Eumaeus apologizes for the meanness of his accommodations (14.58–59):

δόσις δ' ὀλίγη τε φίλη τε
γίγνεται ἡμετέρη·

                 [But humble and friendly
is our gift.]

Indeed the formal elements of this hospitality scene have been freely modified to reflect the humble circumstances of the swineherd. Many of Eumaeus' provisions are unprecedented in Homer: he provides a goatskin stretched over some brushwood as a seat (14.49–51) and skins of sheep and goats as a bed (14.518–19); the rustic κισσύβιον (14.78; 16.52) and σκύφος (14.112) replace the traditional κρητήρ and δέπας as mixing and drinking vessels (cf. e.g., *Il.* 3.295; 9.224); for the feast, he provides two young piglets (χοῖροι 14.73), again apologizing for offering only a "slave's portion" (τά τε δμώεσσι πάρεστι 14.80), while the fatted pigs are reserved for the suitors (14.81). In sharp contrast to palace scenes, with their entourage of heralds, handmaids, meat-carvers, stewards, and various attendants, Eumaeus has but a single servant, Mesaulius (14.449). Eumaeus performs almost all the duties of the host himself, welcoming and seating the guest (14.33–51), cooking and distributing the food (14.72–77), mixing and serving the wine (14.78–79), performing most of the sacrificial duties (14.418–38), making the bed (14.518–22), and conducting the guest to his next destination (17.182–203).

Perhaps the departures from tradition are most apparent in the highly ritualized sacrifice scene (14.418–38; contrast the typical sacrifices in 3.430–74; *Il.* 1.446–74; 2.402–33). The traditional ox or cow has been replaced by a pig, the sacrificial victim is clubbed with a piece of leftover firewood rather than slaughtered with an axe or knife, and it is dedicated at the hearth rather than at an altar. Many formal elements are omitted altogether: the ritual handwashing, the throwing of barley, the lifting of hands in prayer, the dedication of the thighbones, the pouring of wine on the burning sacrifice, and the tasting of the entrails. Even the objects of sacrifice, Hermes and the nymphs, are uniquely appropriate to this context, in view of Hermes' role as patron of herdsmen.

Formulae and Diction

The inherited epic art-language, as rich as it was in ornamental epithets and formulaic phrases with which to describe duels on the battlefield, sacrifices of hecatombs, royal feasts in the palace, and other such heroic events, appears to have been stricken by poverty when required to describe a nonheroic character or situation. Faced with a nonheroic character or situation, the poet sometimes resorted to the usual, heroic diction anyway, inevitably producing descriptions and collocations that strike a literate reader as contextually inappropriate: thus Odysseus' cowherd Philoetius is called "chief of men" (ὄρχαμος ἀνδρῶν 20.185, 254), the beggar Irus' mother is called "revered mother" (πότνια μήτηρ 18.5), and Antilochus' horses are called "swift-footed," even when they are slow and lose the race (ἵπποι ὠκύποδες *Il.* 23.303-4, cf. 310). At other times, the poet appears to abandon the inherited diction when describing a nonheroic character or situation: thus the long description of Thersites, that ugly and vulgar Achaean of dubious social status, is noticeably lacking in conventional diction (*Il.* 2.212-19).

In the nonheroic parts of the epic, we can expect to find the most extensive innovation and modification of the inherited diction and consequently the most extensive use of late linguistic forms. G.P. Shipp's analysis of Homeric diction demonstrates the concentration of late linguistic forms in similes, for example.[3] But, contra Shipp, these late forms are not to be attributed exclusively to the late development of the extended simile as a poetic device; surely the nonheroic context of many of these similes (fishing, cooking, reaping, etc.), for which there existed no rich corpus of preformulated diction, also contributed to the concentration therein of late linguistic forms. An illuminating illustration of the concentration of late linguistic forms in nonheroic, or in this case anti-heroic, parts of the epic may be observed in Eumaeus' criticism of the lifestyle of the traditional Iliadic warrior (14.85-86):

καὶ μὲν δυσμενέες καὶ ἀνάρσιοι, οἵ τ' ἐπὶ γαίης
ἀλλοτρίης βῶσιν καί σφι Ζεὺς ληΐδα δώῃ

[Even hostile and lawless men, who go against

---

3. Shipp 1972.

a foreign land, and to them Zeus grants booty]

In these two verses, remarkable for their enjambment (rare in Homer), there occurs a contracted form of the subjunctive in βῶσιν (a relatively late form), and the nu-mobile makes the preceding light syllable heavy by position in βῶσιν καί (an Attic-Ionic innovation).[4] These late linguistic forms provide external evidence for the lateness of this nonheroic sentiment.

The scene of Eumaeus' hospitality is set in a swineherd's hut rather than a king's palace. This nonheroic setting presented special challenges for a poet whose inherited diction was not primarily designed to describe such circumstances. Even a modern reader, if immersed in the mechanics of Homeric diction, will sense that the poet does not resort as happily or as readily to his preformulated, inherited diction in this scene as elsewhere in the epic. The poet goes about the business of narrating this unique scene in two ways.

First, Homer relies on the inherited traditional diction anyway. Sometimes this produces no notable inconcinnities; there is no difficulty, for example, in the swineherd's running "with swift feet" (ποσὶ κραιπνοῖσι 14.33), although the phrase is perhaps a bit more apt in the context of a running warrior (cf. *Il.* 6.505; 17.190; 21.247; 22.138; 23.749). Nor is it remarkable that he asks his guest's identity with the conventional phrase (14.187; cf. *Od.* 1.170; 10.325; 15.264; 19.105; 24.298):

τίς πόθεν εἰς ἀνδρῶν; πόθι τοι πόλις ἠδὲ τοκῆες;

[What men are you from? Where are your city and parents?]

But sometimes the poet's apparent disregard for the particular context of this scene results in descriptions and collocations that may strike the literate reader as rather inappropriate and awkward: Eumaeus is a "divine swineherd" (δῖος ὑφορβός 18x) and a "leader of men" (ὄρχαμος ἀνδρῶν 6x), who hopes for a "much-wooed wife" (πολυμνήστην 14.64) and cuts firewood with "pitiless bronze" (νηλέϊ χαλκῷ 14.418). These epithets result from the application of heroic diction to a nonheroic context.

Second, Homer modifies the inherited diction in various degrees to

---

4. Cf. Hoekstra, in Heubeck and Hoekstra 1989, 14.86n.

accommodate the humble circumstances of this particular scene. Often, in the absence of contextually appropriate preformulated diction, this entails the poet's resorting to his own linguistic vernacular. Consequently, these modifications often result in a concentration of late linguistic forms, indicating their derivative nature.

Conventional Diction

Sometimes the poet applies to a nonheroic scene inherited diction originally designed to describe heroic circumstances. A judgment as to the appropriateness or inappropriateness of the resulting collocations is of course a largely subjective matter. A preliterate audience may have been oblivious to phrases and collocations that strike a modern reader—who is oriented more toward a self-conscious, literary style—as contextually inappropriate.

The epithets applied to the swineherd are particularly notable. "Divine swineherd" (δῖος ὑφορβός 18x; cf. δῖ' Εὔμαιε 4x) is simply an example of the use of a generic epithet to fill out a certain part of the hexameter verse, usually the space between the bucolic diaeresis and verse-end (δῖος Ἀχιλλεύς, δῖος Ὀδυσσεύς, δῖος Ὀρέστης, etc.).[5] But the transference of this generic epithet, elsewhere used to describe heroes, to a nonheroic figure is striking. That the epithet is used to refer purposely and specifically to Eumaeus' noble birth (cf. 15.412–14) is doubtful, for Philoetius the cowherd and Eurycleia the nurse also receive this epithet (21.240; 20.147).

"Swineherd, leader of men" (συβώτης ὄρχαμος ἀνδρῶν 6x) is a similar use of a generic epithet to fill out a part of the hexameter verse, here the space between the trochaic caesura and verse-end (Πολίτης ὄρχαμος ἀνδρῶν; cf. Πεισίστρατος ὄρχαμος ἀνδρῶν, Ἄσιος ὄρχαμος ἀνδρῶν). Since antiquity, this epithet has been thought by some to refer to Eumaeus' noble birth or to his position of responsibility over other slaves.[6] But with a view to the mechanics of the verse, this epithet, like δῖος, appears to be another case of the transference of an epithet originally designed for heroes to a nonheroic character; its application also to Philoetius the cowherd (20.185, 254) makes untenable the view that its application to Eumaeus is purposeful.

The use of apostrophe to address the swineherd is a related phenom-

---

5. On δῖος as a generic epithet, see Parry 1971, 149–50.
6. So scholium to 14.22; Eustathius 1748, 1–3.

enon (Εὔμαιε συβῶτα 16x). The ancients attributed apostrophe, which is used in the *Iliad* to address Patroclus, Menelaus, Melanippus, Achilles, and Apollo, to the poet's striving for pathetic effect or to his special affection for the addressee.[7] This may be true, but in the case of Eumaeus, one may justifiably question whether pathos or affection is intended in all sixteen occurrences. Metrical and formulaic concerns seem to be at work as well. Since Homer did not inherit for Eumaeus, a nonheroic character, an extensive system of epithets in the various cases with which to describe him, as he did with other characters, he relied heavily on a vocative formula that filled the space between the hepthemimeral caesura and verse-end following a consonant (usually προσέφης 15x). Conceivably προσέφης Εὔμαιε συβῶτα was influenced by προσέφης Πατρόκλεες ἱππεῦ (*Il.* 3x), both vocative phrases referring to an animal with which the respective characters were associated.[8]

"Much-wooed" (πολυμνήστην 14.64), used of Eumaeus' prospective wife, is similar to δῖος and ὄρχαμος ἀνδρῶν, used of Eumaeus. The epithet, contextually appropriate in its application to the queen Penelope (4.770; 23.149), is somewhat jarring in its transference to a swineherd's wife.

"City-sacker" (πτολιπόρθῳ 14.447; cf. 18.356), used of Odysseus even in his disguise as a beggar, is less remarkable. It is a case of extending an epithet that is generally true and appropriate, to a particular context in which it is not—as in the case of Lycurgus, who is called "man-slaying" (ἀνδροφόνοιο *Il.* 6.134) even when he is attacking women, or as in the description of the moon as "brilliant" (φαεινήν *Il.* 8.555) even when the stars are shining around it. Aristarchus explained such contextual illogicalities by pointing to Homer's tendency to speak of things "not at the moment, but in general" (οὐ τότε ἀλλὰ καθόλου scholium to *Il.* 8.555), or "not at the moment, but by nature" (οὐ τότε ἀλλὰ φύσει scholium to *Od.* 6.74). This is in a slightly different category from δῖος, ὄρχαμος ἀνδρῶν, and πολυμνήστην.

The elaborate description of Eumaeus' house uses many formulaic phrases remarkable in a description of a swineherd's hut. It has an

---

7. Scholium to *Il.* 16.787 (τὸ ἐν αὐτῇ περιπαθές); cf. scholium to *Il.* 4.127a, Eustathius 453, 11; 1096, 49; 1750, 29. This view is followed by many commentators today: see Parry 1972; Block 1982; Kirk 1985, 4.127n; Russo 1985, 17.272n.

8. On metrical motivations for apostrophe, see Matthews 1980. On the apostrophe of Eumaeus as modeled on the apostrophe of the *Iliad,* see Hoekstra 1965, 138–40; Hoekstra, in Heubeck and Hoekstra 1989, 14.55n; Yamagata 1989, 91–103.

"entrance chamber" (ἐνὶ προδόμῳ 14.5); this phrase is used seven times of palaces in Homer, once of Achilles' shelter on the Trojan plain (*Il.* 24.673). "It has been built high, in a conspicuous place" (ὑψηλὴ δέδμητο, περισκέπτῳ ἐνὶ χώρῳ 14.6); compare the use of the identical verse to describe Telemachus' bedroom at the palace (1.426) and of περισκέπτῳ ἐνὶ χώρῳ to describe Circe's palace (10.211, 253). It is "beautiful and large" (καλή τε μεγάλη τε 14.7); elsewhere this combination is used only to describe women (13.289; 15.418; 16.158). It is built with "quarried stones" (ῥυτοῖσιν λάεσσι 14.10); this phrase occurs elsewhere only of the marvelous agora of the Phaeacians (6.267). Similar is the description of Telemachus "stepping over the stone threshold" of the swineherd's hut upon his arrival (ὑπέρβη λάϊνον οὐδόν 16.41); this phrase is used elsewhere only of the temple of Apollo and of Odysseus' palace (8.80; 19.30; 23.88). In sum, the description of Eumaeus' hut leaves one with a sense that the diction employed was not primarily designed for this type of scene.

Three inherited phrases are employed in a remarkable manner in Eumaeus' sacrifice scene (14.418–38). First, in preparation for the sacrifice, Eumaeus cuts firewood "with pitiless bronze" (νηλέϊ χαλκῷ 14.418), a transference of a formula more happily employed in the heroic contexts of wounded warriors or slaughtered animals (*Il.* 3.292; 4.348; 5.330; 12.427; 13.501, 553; 16.345, 561, 761; 17.376; 19.266; *Od.* 10.532; 11.545). Second, the pig sacrificed is described as a "five-year-old" (πενταετήρον 14.419), a formula more appropriately used of the heroic sacrifice of an ox or cow (19.420; *Il.* 2.413; 7.315). A five-year-old pig would be an entirely inappropriate sacrificial victim, and it would not make good eating either; earlier Odysseus and Eumaeus had eaten young "piglets" (χοίρων 14.73–82), but the most suitable age for the slaughter of a pig seems to be indicated by the "one-year-old pig" that comprises the later feast with Telemachus (σῦν ἐνιαύσιον 16.452–54).[9] Third, when the sacrificial victim dies in this scene, its spirit is said to leave it (τὸν δ' ἔλιπε ψυχή 14.426), a phrase usually employed in the context of a

---

9. Merrill Burbrink of The National Pork Producers Association tells me that modern-day, pen-fed pigs are best for roasting at 100–120 lbs. (3½–4 months; cf. the χοίρων of 14.73–82), and that their highest market price is at 230–50 lbs. (6 months; cf. the one-year-old pig at 16.452–54). A five-year-old pig is good for nothing but the sausage factory. Modern-day, stall-fed cows reach their highest market price much later, at 18–24 months, and a five-year-old cow, though perhaps tough, is still edible as a roast. In such countries as Australia and Brazil, where cattle are grazed rather than stall-fed, it is not unusual to roast 3- to 4-year-old cows.

fallen warrior (*Il.* 5.696; cf. 16.453; *Od.* 14.134; 18.91), but somewhat unhappily transferred to a pig.[10] Thus, in the sacrifice scene, as in the description of Eumaeus' hut and in the epithets applied to the swineherd, we see the poet transferring heroic diction to a nonheroic setting, here with rather unfortunate results.

Some have used the term *parody* of this phenomenon and have regarded the Eumaeus scene as something of a farce. D.B. Monro points to the description of Eumaeus' pigsties (14.13–16) as a parody of the description of Priam's palace (*Il.* 6.244–49), citing the shared use of the words πεντήκοντα and πλησίον ἀλλήλων; he points to the description of Eumaeus' five-year-old pig (πενταέτηρον 14.419) as a parody of Agamemnon's sacrifice of a five-year-old cow (πενταέτηρον *Il.* 2.403); and he cites the epithet "barking" (ὑλακόμωροι 14.29), used of Eumaeus' dogs, as a parody of the heroic epithets ἐγχεσίμωρος and ἰόμωρος. V. Bérard applies the term *parodie* to the depiction of Eumaeus as "leader of men" (ὄρχαμος ἀνδρῶν). D. Stewart defines the apostrophe of Eumaeus (Εὔμαιε συβῶτα) as a sort of proletarian parody of the Iliadic Πατρόκλεες ἱππεῦ. D. Belmont calls the whole scene of Eumaeus' hospitality "a gently humorous farce." F. Williams defines the entire scene as a parody of Homeric formal welcomes—the customary noble host and his attendants, as in Pylos and Sparta for example, being replaced here by the mock-royalty of the "noble" (δῖος) swineherd and his "attendants," the dogs.[11]

But parody, inasmuch as it is a self-conscious and intentional imitation for comic effect, does not seem an apt term for the scene of Eumaeus' hospitality. I do not perceive anything comical in the depiction of Eumaeus or his hospitality toward Odysseus. Homer portrays Eumaeus as loyal, generous, and pious; he is one of the most sympathetic characters of the *Odyssey,* not a mock-heroic object of humor. Moreover, if Milman Parry's work on the nature of traditional Homeric diction has taught us anything, it is that isolating *exemplum* from *imitatio,* the favorite pastime of nineteenth-century scholars, is not often profitable. Identical or similar phrases and verses in Homer are identical or similar not because one is modeled on the other but because they are independent attestations of a common reservoir of traditional diction. Hence, to say that a specific

---

10. Nowhere else in Homer is an animal endowed with a ψυχή, although a θυμός is said to leave a sacrificial victim at *Od.* 3.455, and the serpent Typhon has a θυμός at *H.Ap.* 361.

11. Monro 1901, 14.13–16n, 14.29n, 14.419n, cf. also 329, 331; Bérard 1930, 144–45; Stewart 1976, 95; Belmont 1962, 157; Williams 1986.

phrase in Homer is an imitation of, or a parody of, another specific phrase is to wrongly apply a form of literary criticism based on a concept of a fixed text to an orally generated, unfixed tradition. In my view, the notable inconcinnities in this scene, which have struck some as parodic, are not the product of self-conscious or intentional imitation but simply the result of rather loosely applying heroic diction to a nonheroic setting.

Modification

Sometimes Homer modifies the inherited traditional diction to accommodate the humble circumstances of a particular scene. Often these modifications entail the introduction of late linguistic forms drawn from the poet's own vernacular, a clear indication of the verses' derivative nature. A number of linguistic criteria could be applied to the epic diction, and to this scene specifically. One could note, for example, the high incidence of hapax legomena (words that occur only once in the surviving epic corpus). Indeed it is very high in this scene, but because of the small amount, a sample really, of the epic corpus that has survived, I do not find this a clear indication of date of composition. Innovations in morphology and syntax provide a much clearer picture. I have found four criteria especially useful: the employment of nu-mobile, the neglect of digamma, the incidence of irresolvable vowel contraction, and the appearance of the definite article.

We know from inscriptions that nu-mobile in the dative plural and in third-person verb forms was a marked characteristic of Attic-Ionic.[12] Nu-mobile is common enough in Homeric verse, but it is not profitable to consider verses in which nu-mobile is employed merely to obviate hiatus, for nu-mobile in this environment is no sure sign of the lateness of the verse; it could have been added to even a very ancient verse during a later stage, even during the post-Homeric transmission of the epic, since it does not disrupt the metrical scansion. It is worthwhile, though, to consider those verses in which nu-mobile makes a naturally light syllable heavy by position before a following consonant, for in those cases the nu-mobile is an organic part of the verse; if it is removed, the scansion is disrupted. Such verses could only have been composed during the latest period of the epic tradition, the Ionic period, not during the earlier Aeolic or Mainland stages.[13]

---

12. Buck [1955] 1973, 84.
13. Hoekstra 1965, 71–111; Janko 1982, 64–68.

In Ionic, digamma was lost at an early period. Observation of digamma in Homer—for example, where it is metrically necessary to make a preceding light syllable heavy by position—points to the relative antiquity of the verse. Conversely, neglect of digamma—for example, where a preceding light, closed syllable is maintained before a word that begins with prevocalic digamma—points to the relative lateness of the verse.[14] Thus, we can say with some confidence that the former verses had their origin in a period long before Homer, while the latter verses had their origin in a period close to Homer's own lifetime; some may be Homer's own creation.

Irresolvable vowel contraction is another linguistic element worth noting, since contraction of vowels became increasingly common with the disappearance of the intervocalic glide, sigma, and digamma. The o-stem genitive singular is an instructive case: we see in Homer the ancient -οιο, which goes back to Mycenaean; we see examples of contracted -ου that can be resolved into -οι' (with elision) or into -οο, a transitional form, or ο' (with elision); and we see examples of contracted -ου that cannot be resolved. Verses that contain this irresolvable -ου as an organic part of the verse must be of relatively late composition.[15]

The history of ὁ, ἡ, and τό, first demonstrative and relative pronouns and only much later evolving into the definite articles, places them in the category of linguistic criteria that may give a clue as to the relative date of composition of a verse. A passage in which ὁ, ἡ, and τό are frequently used as definite articles probably has a late date of composition.[16]

The clearest example of linguistic modification in the scene of Eumaeus' hospitality is in a verse describing the cooking of two piglets (14.75):

εὗσέ τε μίστυλλέν τε καὶ ἀμφ' ὀβελοῖσιν ἔπειρεν.

[He singed them and cut them up and pierced them with spits.]

This is a modification of a verse frequently used to describe the cooking of an ox or cow (*Il.* 1.465; 2.428; *Od.* 3.462; 12.365; but of a pig at 14.430):

---

14. Buck [1955] 1973, 46–52; Hoekstra 1965, 42–70; Parry 1971, 391–403; Chantraine 1973, 123–57; Janko 1982, 42–48.

15. Buck [1955] 1973, 36–37, 88; Janko 1982, 50–54.

16. Stummer 1886, 1–63; J.A. Scott [1921] 1965, 89–92.

μίστυλλόν τ' ἄρα τἆλλα καὶ ἀμφ' ὀβελοῖσιν ἔπειραν.

[They cut up the other pieces and pierced them with spits.][17]

Here the inherited verse has been modified to accommodate the cooking of pigs by adding the verb *singe* (εὗσε), a word used exclusively of pigs in Homer (*Il.* 9.468; 23.33; *Od.* 2.300; 14.426). The collocation of verbs joined by τε has resulted in the linguistically late nu-mobile's making position (μίστυλλέν τε), a clear indication of the verse's derivative nature.[18]

Another clear example of modification occurs in the description of the swineherd serving a meal to Odysseus and his recently arrived son (16.49–52):

τοῖσιν δ' αὖ κρειῶν πίνακας παρέθηκε συβώτης
ὀπταλέων, ἅ ῥα τῇ προτέρῃ ὑπέλειπον ἔδοντες,
σῖτον δ' ἐσσυμένως παρενήνεεν ἐν κανέοισιν,
ἐν δ' ἄρα κισσυβίῳ κίρνη μελιηδέα οἶνον·

[The swineherd placed platters of meat beside them,
roasted meat, which they had left over from eating before,
and he hastily heaped up bread in baskets,
and in an ivy bowl he mixed honey-sweet wine.]

This appears to be a modification of the more conventional description of the serving of a feast in a palace (1.141–43, 147; 1.141–42 = [4.57–58]):

δαιτρὸς δὲ κρειῶν πίνακας παρέθηκεν ἀείρας
παντοίων, παρὰ δέ σφι τίθει χρύσεια κύπελλα,
κῆρυξ δ' αὐτοῖσιν θάμ' ἐπῴχετο οἰνοχοεύων.
. . . .
σῖτον δὲ δμῳαὶ παρενήνεον ἐν κανέοισι

[A meat-carver lifted up and set out platters of meat

---

17. This, in turn, appears to be a modification of a very ancient verse (*Il.* 7.317; 24.623; *Od.* 19.422): μίστυλλόν τ' ἄρ' ἐπισταμένως πεῖράν τ' ὀβελοῖσιν; note the absence of augment, of nu-mobile to obviate hiatus, and of the post-Mycenaean particle καί here, in contrast to *Il.* 1.465, etc., which has augment, nu-mobile to obviate hiatus, καί, and a use of τά approaching its use as a definite article.

18. Hoekstra 1965, 62n.3.

of all kinds, and beside them he placed golden cups,
and a herald went back and forth pouring wine for them.
. . . .
And handmaids heaped up bread in baskets.]

In the humble circumstances of the swineherd's hut, Eumaeus takes on
the duties of meat-carver (δαιτρός), herald (κῆρυξ), and handmaids
(δμωαί); hence, the pronoun τοῖσιν (16.49) replaces δαιτρός (1.141), and
the adverb ἐσσυμένως (16.51) replaces δμωαί (1.147). "Roasted meats"
(ὀπταλέων 16.50), left over from a previous meal, replace the "meats
of all kinds" (παντοίων 1.142) of the palace scene; an "ivy bowl"
(κισσυβίῳ 16.52) replaces the "golden cups" (χρύσεια κύπελλα 1.142)
as a receptacle for wine. This replacement of δαιτρός by τοῖσιν has
resulted in the nu-mobile's making position (τοῖσιν δ'), and the assump-
tion of the duties of the δμωαί by Eumaeus himself, with the consequent
shift of the verb παρενήνεον to its singular form, has resulted in a nu-
mobile used to obviate hiatus (παρενήνεεν ἐν).[19] Again, these late lin-
guistic forms are clear indications of the derivative nature of these
modifications.

The description of Eumaeus' provision of a seat for Odysseus upon
his arrival is extensively modified (14.49–51):

εἷσεν δ᾽ εἰσαγαγών, ῥῶπας δ᾽ ὑπέχευε δασείας,
ἐστόρεσεν δ᾽ ἐπὶ δέρμα ἰονθάδος ἀγρίου αἰγός,
αὐτοῦ ἐνεύναιον, μέγα καὶ δασύ.

[He led him in and sat him down, and heaped thick brush
    underneath,
and stretched out on it the skin of a hairy, wild goat,
his own bedding, great and shaggy.]

This appears to be a loose adaption of a more conventional seating
scene. One may profitably compare (10.314–15 = 366–67):

---

19. Nu-mobile used to obviate hiatus is not a clear indication of late composition
because its removal does not affect the scansion and because we simply do not know much
about the regulation of hiatus in early epic verse. I suspect that hiatus was much more
common in the early period than the surviving epic corpus suggests. But in this verse, the
hiatus would be so jarring—παρενήνεε ἐν—that I cannot imagine that this verse was
composed before nu-mobile became a part of the linguistic vernacular.

εἷσε δέ μ᾽ εἰσαγαγοῦσα ἐπὶ θρόνου ἀργυροήλου,
καλοῦ δαιδαλέου· ὑπὸ δὲ θρῆνυς ποσὶν ἦεν·

[She led me in and sat me on a silver-studded throne,
beautiful and well-crafted; and under my feet was a footstool.]

or (1.130-31):

αὐτὴν δ᾽ ἐς θρόνον εἷσεν ἄγων, ὑπὸ λῖτα πετάσσας,
καλὸν δαιδάλεον· ὑπὸ δὲ θρῆνυς ποσὶν ἦεν.

[He led her in and sat her on a throne, having spread linen
    underneath,
beautiful and well-crafted; and under her feet was a footstool.]

But the description of Eumaeus' seat is not normal: δασύς as an adjective occurs only here in Homer; ἰονθάς is a hapax; ἐνεύναιος is attested elsewhere only once (*Od.* 16.35). The relative lateness of the modification is confirmed by the nu-mobile's making position twice (εἷσεν δ᾽, ἐστόρεσεν δ᾽).

The scene of Eumaeus' sacrifice and the subsequent feast (14.418-56) is built on the pattern of the conventional sacrifice and feasting scenes (cf. *Il.* 1.447-74; 2.402-33; *Od.* 3.418-74), and it employs some of the same formulaic diction (14.419, 422, 423, 427, 430-31, 437, 453-54), but extending to a sacrifice of a pig typical elements designed to describe the sacrifice of a cow required some remarkable modifications.

A simple modification is seen in the description of the slaughter of the pig (14.426):

τοὶ δὲ σφάξαν τε καὶ εὗσαν·

[They slaughtered and singed it.]

The usual phrase employed in the sacrifice of a cow or ox is (*Od.* 12.359 = *Il.* 1.459 = 2.422):

καὶ ἔσφαξαν καὶ ἔδειραν

[They slaughtered and flayed it.]

Clearly the verb εὖσαν was considered more appropriate in a pig sacrifice. A rather more complicated example is the modification of one of the most common typical elements of sacrifice scenes: the placing of raw pieces of flesh on the fat-encased thighbones (*Od.* 3.456–58; cf. 12.360–61; *Il.* 1.460–61; 2.423–24):

αἶψ' ἄρα μιν διέχευαν, ἄφαρ δ' ἐκ μηρία τάμνον
πάντα κατὰ μοῖραν, κατά τε κνίσῃ ἐκάλυψαν
δίπτυχα ποιήσαντες, ἐπ' αὐτῶν δ' ὠμοθέτησαν.

[Immediately they cut it up, and quickly they cut out the
    thighbones
all in due order, and they hid them in fat,
making a double fold, and on them they placed pieces of flesh.]

Compare the description of Eumaeus' sacrifice (14.427–28):

αἶψα δέ μιν διέχευαν· ὁ δ' ὠμοθετεῖτο συβώτης,
πάντων ἀρχόμενος μελέων, ἐς πίονα δημόν.

[Immediately they cut it up. The swineherd placed pieces of flesh,
beginning with all the limbs, on the rich fat.]

The description of cutting up the victim (αἶψα δέ μιν διέχευαν) is conventional (cf. 3.456; 19.421; *Il.* 7.316), but the usual cutting out of the thighbones is entirely omitted, perhaps because the ritual is for some reason inappropriate in the case of a pig.[20] Instead, Eumaeus sets pieces of raw flesh from various parts of the carcass onto some fat and throws it into the fire (14.431). This modification has produced the remarkable verb form ὠμοθετεῖτο (cf. ὠμοθέτησαν), which, in addition to being inexplicably imperfect and middle, has a linguistically late, irresolvable contraction.

Finally, it is worth noting that the special offering to Hermes and the nymphs, particularly apt here in view of Hermes' role as patron of herdsmen, is unprecedented in Homer (14.434–36):

---

20. The offering of the thighbones of various animals (bulls, cows, sheep, goats, kids, a ram) is common in Homer. But in spite of frequent descriptions of the sacrifice or cooking of pigs (*Il.* 9.208; 19.197, 250–75; 23.32–33; *Od.* 11.131; 14.72–77; 16.454; 17.181; 20.251; 23.278; 24.215), this ritual is never a part of them.

καὶ τὰ μὲν ἕπταχα πάντα διεμοιρᾶτο δαΐζων·
τὴν μὲν ἴαν νύμφῃσι καὶ ʽΕρμῇ, Μαιάδος υἱεῖ,
θῆκεν ἐπευξάμενος,

[Dividing it all into seven portions, he distributed it.
One portion to the nymphs and to Hermes, son of Maia,
he gave with a prayer.]

The lateness and unconventional nature of this offering is confirmed by
the concentration of three irresolvable contractions (διεμοιρᾶτο, ʽΕρμῇ,
and υἱεῖ).[21]

It appears, then, that while tales about swineherds were probably a
staple of prose folktales even long before Homer, they were not a part
of heroic poetry in dactylic hexameter verse form until the Ionic phase
of the epic tradition, and perhaps not until Homer incorporated the tale
of Eumaeus into his *Odyssey*. Homer clearly did not inherit a rich corpus
of preformulated diction for describing the circumstances of swineherds.
When he resorted to the inherited diction anyway, inconcinnities often
arose, since the diction was created for more heroic settings. When he
modified the inherited diction to accommodate it to the humble circum-
stances of a swineherd, this process often produced late linguistic forms
drawn from the poet's own vernacular; thereby the secondary and deriv-
ative nature of these modified verses is revealed.

Not surprisingly, in verses describing Eumaeus' hospitality, the inci-
dence of hapax legomena, both of vocabulary and of inflectional forms,
is exceptionally high, and many of these involve late linguistic forms
(irresolvable contraction in ὀλίγου 14.37, ἀντιθέου γὰρ ἄνακτος 14.40,
ὠμοθετεῖτο 14.427, διεμοιρᾶτο 14.434, ʽΕρμῇ 14.435, and βιότου 14.527;
neglect of digamma in χαμαιευνάδες ἐρχατόωντο 14.15 and ἀντιθέου
γὰρ ἄνακτος 14.40; the definite article in τὸ μέλαν δρυός 14.12, τὸν
ἄριστον 14.19, cf. 108, 414, οἱ τρεῖς 14.26, and οἱ νέοι 14.61).

Moreover, the concentration of late linguistic forms throughout this

---

21. Where υἱεῖ occurs elsewhere in Homer it can almost always be resolved to its
uncontracted form υἱέϊ, but not here at the end of the verse. As for ʽΕρμῇ, E-ma-a₂ (for
Hermahai) was the Mycenaean form; *ʽΕρμάᾳ would have been the Aeolic form; ʽΕρμέῃ
was the uncontracted Ionic form; the usual form in Homer, ʽΕρμείη, was a metrically
necessary compromise between the two—a cretic cannot be accommodated in epic verse;
the contracted form here, ʽΕρμῇ, was later Ionic and must have been from the poet's own
vernacular. This contracted form is generally used in the *Hymns*, and it is the only form
used in *H.Herm.* (31x); see Janko 1982, 133–34.

scene is remarkable. In the 117 verses (14.5–82, 418–56) that describe the essence of Eumaeus' hospitality toward Odysseus—Odysseus' arrival, the description of the house, Eumaeus' greeting, the seating of the guest, the preparation and serving of the first meal, the sacrifice, and the preparation, serving, and eating of the second meal—the following late forms occur: nu-mobile makes position 12 times; digamma is neglected 4 times (5 if ἀκτῇ at 14.429 is from ϝάγνυμι); irresolvable contraction occurs 11 times, 3 of which involve the late contraction of the genitive singular in -ου (12 and 4 if ἀκτῇ at 14.429 is from ϝάγνυμι); and ὁ, ἡ, and τό are used as definite articles 4 times, and in 7 more instances they come very close to their use as definite articles.

Admittedly, given the small sample (117 verses), it is hazardous to make generalizations based on a statistical comparisons with other samples of epic text; yet it may be illuminating to compare the frequency of these same late linguistic forms in a more heroic scene of hospitality than that of Eumaeus, in a description of a king's palace rather than a swineherd's hut, and in a more conventional scene of a sacrifice of a cow rather than a pig. As *comparanda*, I will use the scene of Telemachus' reception and entertainment of Athena-Mentes (1.103–50), the description of Priam's palace (*Il.* 6.242–50), and two Iliadic scenes of cow sacrifice (*Il.* 1.446–74; 2.402–33), a total of 118 verses. In this roughly equivalent number of verses, nu-mobile makes position 5 times (vs. 12); digamma is neglected 1 time (vs. 4; 5 if ἀκτῇ at 14.429 is from ϝάγνυμι); irresolvable contraction occurs 11 times, 3 of which are in the genitive singular -ου (about the same frequency as in the Eumaeus passages); and ὁ, ἡ, and τό are used as definite articles 3 times (vs. 4); while in 3 more instances (vs. 7) they come very close to their use as definite articles. The comparatively high frequency of nu-mobile's making position and of the neglect of digamma in the nonheroic Eumaeus passages seems worthy of note.

It may also be illuminating to compare the frequency of the late linguistic forms in the Eumaeus passages to their frequency in the *Iliad* and *Odyssey* as a whole. Nu-mobile makes position 559 times in the 15,693 verses of the *Iliad* (3.56%) and 451 times in the 12,110 verses of the *Odyssey* (3.72%); the frequency in the Eumaeus passages is nearly 3 times as high (12/117 = 10.23%). Digamma is neglected 312 times in the *Iliad* (1.99%) and 303 times in the *Odyssey* (2.10%); the frequency of neglect in the Eumaeus passages is substantially higher (4/117 = 3.42%; 5/117 = 4.27% if ἀκτῇ at 14.429 is from ϝάγνυμι). Irresolvable contraction in the genitive singular -ου occurs 375 times in the *Iliad* (2.40%) and 348 times in the *Odyssey* (2.87%); the frequency in the Eumaeus passages is roughly equivalent (3/117 = 2.56%; 4/117 = 3.42% if ἀκτῇ at 14.429 is from ϝάγνυμι). The use of ὁ, ἡ, and τό as definite articles occurs 218 times in the *Iliad* (1.39%) and 171 times in the *Odyssey* (1.41%); their frequency in the Eumaeus passages is much higher (4/117 = 3.42%).[22] Again, the comparatively higher frequency in the Eumaeus passages of nu-mobile's making position and of the neglect of digamma, as well as the occurrence of the definite article, is worthy of note. The relative frequency (per 100 verses) of late linguistic forms in the *Iliad,* the *Odyssey,* the selected heroic scenes (118 verses), and the Eumaeus scene (117 verses) may be observed schematically as follows:

Nu-mobile makes position

Iliad	3.56%
Odyssey	3.72%
Heroic Scenes	4.25%
Eumaeus Scene	10.23%

Digamma neglected

Iliad	1.99%
Odyssey	2.10%
Heroic Scenes	0.85%
Eumaeus Scene	4.27%

Irresolvable contraction in the genitive -ου

Iliad	2.40%
Odyssey	2.87%
Heroic Scenes	2.54%
Eumaeus Scene	3.42%

ὁ, ἡ, and τό as definite articles

Iliad	1.39%
Odyssey	1.41%

22. The statistics for neglect of digamma, contraction in the genitive singular -ου, and nu-mobile's making position in the epics as a whole are derived from Janko 1982, 201, 207–8, 217–18; those for the definite article in the epics as a whole are derived from Stummer 1886, 1–63. Stummer's figures are put in proper perspective by J.A. Scott [1921] 1965, 89–92.

Heroic Scenes   2.54%
Eumaeus Scene   3.42%

In sum, a typological and formulaic analysis of the scene of hospitality in Eumaeus' hut shows that, from a structural perspective, it is built on the pattern of the conventional scene of hospitality (see Appendix); it even employs many of the formulaic phrases in which the conventional elements of hospitality are normally expressed. However, because of the uniquely unheroic circumstances of this scene—a swineherd's hut rather than a palace, a sacrifice of a pig rather than a cow, etc.—some of these conventional elements and formulaic phrases have been heavily modified. A linguistic analysis of these modifications reveals a higher than normal concentration of late linguistic forms, pointing to the secondary and derivative nature of these verses; in the medium of heroic dactylic hexameter verse, there was apparently no tradition of swineherd poetry from which Homer could draw. But this does not in any way suggest that these verses were composed later than the rest of the *Odyssey*. It only confirms what one suspects intuitively when reading the Eumaeus scene for the first time—that faced with the need to adapt his inherited diction when describing a nonheroic setting, Homer relied more than usual on his own linguistic vernacular.

Chapter 8

Odysseus' Homecoming
(*Od*. 17.204–23.348)

ἀλλά τις ἀθανάτων κτεῖνε μνηστῆρας ἀγαυούς,
ὕβριν ἀγασσάμενος θυμαλγέα καὶ κακὰ ἔργα.
οὔ τινα γὰρ τίεσκον ἐπιχθονίων ἀνθρώπων,
οὐ κακὸν οὐδὲ μὲν ἐσθλόν, ὅτις σφέας εἰσαφίκοιτο·
τῷ δι' ἀτασθαλίας ἔπαθον κακόν·

[But one of the gods has killed the proud suitors,
angered at their heart-grieving violence and evil deeds.
For they honored no one of men on the earth,
neither an evil nor a good man, whoever approached them.
Therefore through their folly they have suffered evil.]
                                        —(*Od*. 23.63–67)

The final hospitality scene of the *Odyssey,* occupying the last third of
the epic (books 17–23), is Odysseus' arrival at his own home and his
reception by the suitors, who, though themselves guests in the house,
have taken on themselves the role of master.

One may object that this is not properly a hospitality scene, since
Odysseus is not actually a guest (ξεῖνος) in search of a reception at
someone else's house but a returning hero, a master (ἄναξ), who seeks
to test the loyalty of those in his own house. But while it may be true
that Odysseus is in reality the ἄναξ, his disguise as a ξεῖνος allows a
guest-host relationship to develop between him and the suitors. Odysseus'
vengeance against the suitors, then, is justified not only because they
have committed a personal affront by courting his wife, devouring his
possessions, and threatening his son but because they have shown their
disregard for, indeed perversion of, a fundamental institution of civilized
society by displaying abusive behavior toward him as a guest.

On the other hand, one may object that this is not properly a hos-
pitality scene because the relationship of *xenia* can only exist between

social equals, and Odysseus is not a ξεῖνος but a beggar (πτωχός).[1] But the distinction between ξεῖνος and πτωχός is a blurred one in any case, often depending solely on the vagaries of circumstance, and here the distinction is blurred further by the ambiguity of Odysseus' disguise. Odysseus seems to fluctuate between the two positions, depending on whether he is seen through the eyes of Melanthius, Antinous, and Eurymachus, or Eumaeus, Telemachus, and Penelope. The diction of this scene is divided when referring to Odysseus: ξεῖνος is the more frequent appellation (61x),[2] but πτωχός is not uncommon (12x).[3] The general ambiguity of the demarcation between these terms is suggested by Zeus' equally zealous patronage of both groups (14.56–58).[4]

The ambiguity of status and identity created by Odysseus' slow progression and elevation from anonymous beggar to respected guest to self-declared master is one of the most carefully developed themes in what has often been perceived as a rather long, drawn out denouement to the *Odyssey*. This slow progression over the course of seven books (17–23) from πτωχός to ξεῖνος to ἄναξ is powerfully and symbolically portrayed by the text's focus on physical objects associated with the rituals of *xenia*. Perhaps the clearest portrayal of Odysseus' progression can be observed in the use of various implements of hospitality: chairs, tables, and beds.

When Odysseus first arrives at the palace, he sits down on the threshold and leans against a pillar (17.339–41); in lieu of a table, he places the food provided by Telemachus on his "ugly satchel" (ἀεικελίης ἐπὶ πήρης 17.357). This is where Odysseus remains until his interview with Penelope, who, while seating herself on an ivory and silver armchair (κλισίη) with a footstool (θρῆνυς) for her feet (19.55–57), offers him the less distinguished stool (δίφρος 19.97, 101). But his false story—that he is of noble birth, the brother of Idomeneus, who was a ξεῖνος of Odysseus, and that he had himself once offered hospitality to Odysseus in Crete (19.172–202, 221–48)—convinces Penelope to regard him, who was previously

---

1. So Belmont 1962, 38–47.
2. 17.345, 350, 371, 382, 398, 478, 501, 508, 544, 553, 584, 586; 18.38, 61, 112, 122, 222, 223, 233, 327, 357; 19.27, 66, 94, 99, 104, 124, 215, 253, 309, 325, 333, 350, 351, 379, 509, 560, 589; 20.129, 166, 178, 191, 199, 236, 293, 295, 305, 324, 360, 374, 382; 21.288, 292, 313, 314, 334, 349, 424; 22.27; 23.28; 24.281.
3. 17.220, 337, 366, 377, 475; 18.41, 49, 403; 19.74; 21.292, 327; 24.157.
4. For a parallel ambiguity of demarcation between the terms ξεῖνος and ἱκέτης, see Gould 1973, 92. Although Odysseus is referred to as a ἱκέτης during his stay with Eumaeus (14.511; 16.67), this term is not used of him after he arrives at the palace.

merely an "object of pity" (ἐλεεινός 19.253), as an "insider" (φίλος 19.254) and an "object of honor" (αἰδοῖος 19.254). The beggar's false story has elicited reciprocal generosity from Penelope, whereby he is elevated in status from πτωχός to ξεῖνος; properly, she promises him the seat of honor beside Telemachus at the next day's feasting (i.e., presumably on a κλισμός or θρόνος 19.321–22). But this promise is never fulfilled; the humble δίφρος continues to be his seat throughout the period of his disguise as a πτωχός (19.506; 20.259—with a "lowly table" ὀλίγην τε τράπεζαν; 21.243, 420). It is not until after the slaughter of the suitors, when Odysseus has been bathed, anointed, clothed, and beautified by Athena, that he, now revealed as the ἄναξ of the house, finally takes his proper place on the θρόνος (23.153–65). The elevation in his physical position from οὐδός to δίφρος to θρόνος roughly corresponds to his elevation in status from πτωχός to ξεῖνος to ἄναξ.[5]

This elevation is also symbolized by the different types and locations of beds offered to Odysseus. As a πτωχός, Odysseus is abused by the maid Melantho, who rebukes him for loitering around the palace rather than sleeping at the smithy or at some other public lounging place for beggars (18.327–29). After Penelope acknowledges him as a ξεῖνος, she offers him a bed in the customary place for guests: in the portico (πρόδομος) at the periphery of the house (19.317–19, 598–99; 20.1). Once Odysseus has gained the upper hand against the suitors, his successful response to Penelope's trial of the marriage bed becomes his rite of passage to the bedroom (θάλαμος 23.295), the location of which in the "innermost part of the house" (μυχὸς δόμου cf. 3.402; 4.304; 7.346) is symbolic as well as functional. Odysseus' spatial progression from outside the house to the periphery of the house to the innermost chamber of the house corresponds exactly to his elevation from πτωχός to ξεῖνος to ἄναξ.

---

5. θρόνος at 21.434 may refer to Odysseus' chair; if so, the shift from δίφρος to θρόνος is extremely abrupt, and it comes symbolically at a critical juncture in the narrative—after the stringing of the bow. At 21.420 Odysseus strings the bow and shoots the arrow through the axes while sitting on a δίφρος, but at 21.434, when Telemachus, having armed himself, comes to the support of his father and stands near him, the chair (the same one?) is called a θρόνος. The trial of the bow has transformed Odysseus from beggar to master; hence the change in appellation for his chair. For this interpretation, see Houston 1975. But perhaps θρόνος at 21.434 is meant to refer to Telemachus' own chair rather than Odysseus'. In support of this view is Telemachus' position in the room when the fighting starts: he is apparently on the opposite side of the hall to Odysseus, for he kills Amphinomus, who is facing Odysseus, from behind, and only then joins his father (22.89–100).

Not all the references to physical objects of hospitality can be so neatly diagrammed to illustrate Odysseus' progression and elevation from πτωχός to ξεῖνος to ἄναξ. Whether Odysseus is to be considered primarily a πτωχός, a ξεῖνος, or an ἄναξ is often left ambiguous; he is ever in a state of transition. Yet Odysseus' homecoming can be profitably analyzed as a hospitality scene, for architecturally it is built on the structure of the conventional hospitality scene (see Appendix): a visitor meets someone at a well as he approaches the city (I); he arrives at the palace (II), which is described in detail (IIIa), along with the activities of those within (IIIb-c); he waits at the threshold of the palace for someone to notice him (V); he is met by a guard-dog at the door (IV); the master of the house provides him with a seat (VIII) and food (IX); after the feast, he is questioned about his identity (XIa); entertainment is provided (XIII); a bath and a fresh change of clothes are offered (XVIII); a bed is prepared (XVII); later, guest-gifts are presented (XX); finally, he is offered conveyance to his next destination (XXV). All these conventions are present in this scene, but in almost every instance, they occur with notable deviations from what is normal and proper in a hospitality scene. The suitors' breaches of convention on the level of form mirror their actual breaches of conduct and reflect the inversion of the normal social structure on Ithaca as a whole; host and guest have virtually exchanged positions, the visiting suitors taking the position of the master of the house, while the master is forced to visit his own home as a beggar.

Inversions of the Conventions of the Homeric Hospitality Scene

A motif common to folktale that has found its way into Greek epic is that of the newly arrived stranger meeting at a fountain, well, or river a maiden who is kind to him and directs him to the city or palace (I).[6] Three times in the *Odyssey* there occurs a male counterpart to this motif: Hermes, likening himself to a young man, meets Odysseus on his way to Circe's palace and instructs him about how to conduct himself there (10.274-306); Athena, in the form of a young man, is the first to meet the newly arrived Odysseus on Ithaca, and she instructs him about how to regain his wife and palace (13.221-440); and the son of Pheidon, king

---

6. Thompson 1955-58, N715.1. This motif occurs four times in the *Odyssey* (6.110-322; 7.18-81; 10.103-11; 15.415-29); a version of it also occurs in the *Hymn to Demeter* 98-183; see further chapter 1.

of the Thesprotians, comes to the aid of the shipwrecked Odysseus and leads him to his father's palace (14.314–20).[7]

A rather dim vestige of both these versions of the motif occurs upon Odysseus' approach to his own palace. En route to the palace, he comes to the beautiful spring of the nymphs (17.204–53), but instead of a princess or maiden, he is met by the abusive goatherd Melanthius, who regards him as a "vexatious beggar" and "defiler of feasts" (πτωχὸν ἀνιηρόν, δαιτῶν ἀπολυμαντῆρα 17.220) rather than as a ξεῖνος. Instead of directing him to the palace, Melanthius warns him to stay away, "lest his head and ribs be worn out by the footstools flung at him" (17.231–32). Thus, even before Odysseus arrives at the palace, he has had a foretaste of the inhospitable behavior that awaits him.

In an arrival scene, a visitor typically stands for a moment at the threshold of the palace and marvels at the surroundings (V); meanwhile the palace and the activities of those within are often described (IIIa–c). Typically the visitor waits for someone within, usually the master or the master's son, to catch sight of and welcome him (VIIa, c, d, f, g, i). This pattern recurs upon Odysseus' arrival at the palace, but with some notable transformations. As Odysseus and Eumaeus stand outside the palace doors, Odysseus himself describes in touching detail the home from which he has been long absent, and to which he returns not yet as a master but as a lowly beggar (17.264–68). As is often the situation, these visitors have arrived at a time of feasting and singing (17.269–71), but in this scene the feasting of the suitors is tantamount to pillaging, and the bard is made to sing under constraint (22.350–53). Eumaeus warns Odysseus of the danger: he must not tarry too long outside, "lest someone pelt him or strike him" (17.278–79). But Odysseus, well versed as he is in his role as beggar, assures Eumaeus that he is "familiar with blows and pelts" (17.283), and when he enters, he does not stand at the threshold as a visiting ξεῖνος would (V); he sits down on the threshold and leans against a doorpost, assuming the posture of a beggar (17.336–41).

A welcome for the visitor comes not from the master or the master's son within the house but from the old, flea-bitten dog Argus, who is lying on a pile of dung outside the door (17.291–327). The motif of the guard-dog at the door is common in arrival scenes (IV), and it has assumed a variety of forms in the *Odyssey* (7.91–94; 10.212–19; 14.21–

---

7. A version of this motif also occurs in the *Iliad* (24.334–467): Hermes, in the form of a young man, meets Priam on his way to recover Hector's body and escorts him to Achilles' camp; see further chapter 1.

22, 29–32; 16.4–10, 162–63; cf. chap. 1). Odysseus' reception by Argus, as the culmination of this progression of receptions by dogs at the door, is a particularly striking scene. The old, worn-out dog, neglected by the household, symbolizes his master, who will also suffer abuse and neglect in his own home. But at the same time, Argus, who alone of all Ithaca's inhabitants recognizes Odysseus spontaneously, offers a glimmer of hope that others too—such old and humble servants as Eurycleia, Eumaeus, Philoetius, and the anonymous barley-grinder—will acknowledge Odysseus as master.[8]

In a typical hospitality scene, the host greets the newly arrived visitor (VIIa, c, d, f, g), leads him into the hall (VIIi), provides a seat in the place of honor next to the master (VIII), and offers him a choice portion of the feast (IXa). These elements are present in this scene, but again in an inverted form. The suitors themselves, as in their earlier reception of Athena-Mentes (1.103–12), are oblivious to the stranger, and when they finally do acknowledge his presence, they do not provide him with a proper seat and a share of the food but use these very implements of hospitality—footstools (17.462; 18.394) and a hoof from the meat basket (20.299)—as weapons to hurl at him. Telemachus for his part plays along with Odysseus' disguise as a beggar by letting him remain seated on the floor, with an ugly satchel for a table, throughout most of this scene (17.339–41, 356–58). Not until his interview with Penelope is he offered even the humble δίφρος (19.97, 101), the customary stool for servants; this, along with a "lowly table" (ὀλίγην τε τράπεζαν 20.259), remains his seat until the slaughter of the suitors. As for the provision of food, the disguised master of the house, rather than being honored with the chine, which is his prerogative, is forced to resort to begging for scraps from the suitors (17.345–47, 365–66, etc.). Among the suitors, Antinous is notoriously niggardly; he will not even give a piece of bread, albeit from someone else's provisions (17.455–57).

---

8. Rose (1979) traces the references to dogs throughout the scene of Odysseus' homecoming, noting that each reference shows Odysseus' progressively greater control over the situation. At Eumaeus' hut, he is a helpless suppliant. At the door to the palace, he is recognized as master. A third dog is depicted on the brooch Odysseus wore when he left for Troy—the one the beggar describes to Penelope as a sign that he is telling the truth (19.228–31); this dog is strangling a fawn, surely a foreshadowing of what Odysseus, who is now identified with the dog, will do to the suitors. Corresponding to this is a fourth reference to a dog, this time in a simile, in which Odysseus, in anger at seeing the maid servants of the house going off to bed with the suitors, is described as a bitch barking at an unknown man, desirous to fight in order to protect her brood (20.14–16). Now Odysseus, rather than being the object of attack by watch dogs, is himself the watch dog; the helpless and threatened stranger has become the powerful and threatening master.

In the wake of the feasting, there typically follows the questioning of the visitor (XIa). But because of the dangerous situation in Ithaca, Odysseus cannot risk identifying himself. He lies in response to the suitors' indirect query (XIb; 17.368), saying that he is a slave of Dmetor (17.419–44), and in response to Penelope's proper and conventional request for his identity (19.105, 162–63), he replies reluctantly (19.116, 166–67), again with a falsehood, that he is Aethon from Crete (19.172–202).

The provision of entertainment for a visitor is a regular element in hospitality scenes (XIII). Usually this is in the form of a song by a bard or mutual storytelling by the host and guest. In Scheria, Odysseus is entertained by the spectacle of athletic games: running, wrestling, jumping, discus, and boxing (8.100–131). Here in Ithaca, Odysseus suffers an inversion of this typical element: he himself is forced to provide the entertainment, much to the glee of the suitors, by participating in a boxing match with Irus (18.1–111). The master is ironically lowered to the status of the local beggar's rival for the privilege of begging for scraps in his own home. Yet, seen from another perspective, this humbling contest foreshadows the defeat of the suitors at these very hands. Later, Telemachus perspicaciously prays that just as Irus was subdued so may the suitors be subdued (18.233–42).

Visitors are typically provided a bath (XVIII), administered by the handmaids or the lord's daughter, and a change of clothing, either immediately upon arrival or on the following day. A bath and change of clothing would destroy Odysseus' disguise, however, and would possibly lead to his recognition; therefore he refuses Penelope's offer of a washing from the handmaids and her promise of a proper bath and anointing on the next day (19.317–20), preferring instead a footwash from his old nurse, Eurycleia (19.343–48).[9] The provision of clothing is a theme reiterated throughout the scene.[10] It is first promised by Eumaeus (14.395–96; 15.337–39), then by Telemachus (16.78–79), then by Penelope (17.549–50, 556–57; 21.338–39), and finally by Eurycleia (22.487–89). But its provision is conditional upon the truth of the beggar's prediction that Odysseus

---

9. Odysseus' refusal to be washed by the handmaids here recalls his refusal to be washed by Nausicaa's handmaids at the river in Scheria (6.218–22). The prudent Odysseus is reluctant to expose himself in both potentially dangerous situations. The parallel refusals suggest that Odysseus is still in a no less perilous position, in fact is no more at home, in Ithaca than in Scheria. So Segal 1967, 329–32. For an entirely different view of the scene in Scheria—that Odysseus refuses a bath from the handmaids in order to help Nausicaa save face in view of their disobedience to her command to bathe him—see Jones 1989.

10. On the development of the theme of clothing in this scene, see Block 1985, 1–11.

will return (14.395-96; 17.549-50). Ironically, he does receive the clothing, along with a proper bath and anointing, but only after his self-revelation as Odysseus has proved the beggar's prediction true (23.153-55).

The provision of a bed on the portico is an indispensable element of a hospitality scene (XVII); its preparation is usually described in great detail. But in this scene, there is even some doubt as to whether the visitor will be accommodated; Melantho suggests that he go away and sleep at the smithy or at some other public place (18.327-29). Even when Penelope offers him a bed on the portico, with proper bedding and blankets (19.317-19, 598-99; 20.1), he refuses, as with her offer of a bath, choosing instead to lie on the raw hide of an ox with fleeces of sheep for blankets (19.337-42; 20.1-4, 138-42); Eurynome throws a cloak on top of him as he lies there (20.4, 143). This is a symbolically powerful image: Odysseus plots the death of the suitors while he lies between the skins of the cattle that they have wantonly slaughtered (20.3, cf. 1.108).

Another indispensable element of proper hospitality is the provision of a guest-gift (XX). In a brutal perversion and parody of this custom, the suitor Ctesippus offers as a guest-gift an ox-hoof from the meat basket, which he hurls at Odysseus (20.299-302).[11] This travesty of hospitality puts the suitors on the level of the uncivilized Cyclops, who offers an equally parodic guest-gift to Odysseus, the privilege of being eaten last (9.369-70). Like the Cyclops, Ctesippus is punished by means of a reciprocal guest-gift, a spear in the chest from the hand of the cowherd Philoetius (22.285-91).

The final duty of a proper host is to provide his guest safe conduct (πομπή) to his next destination (XXV). Penelope herself laments that in the absence of Odysseus there is no hope of πομπή for the beggar (19.312-16). The suitors would eagerly offer πομπή to Odysseus, but it is not the proper conveyance to the guest's desired destination, such as that for which the Phaeacians are deservedly praised (16.227-28; cf. 8.566 = 13.174); πομπή means something very different to the suitors: "to expel" the guest by force from the house (ἐκπέμψασθε θύραζε 20.361; δώματος ἐκπέμψῃσι 18.336) or to throw him into a ship and "send" him as a slave to Egypt, Cyprus, Sicily (17.448; πέμψωμεν 20.382-83), or, even worse, king Echetus (πέμψομεν 21.307-9), who is notorious for cutting off the noses, ears, and genitals of his victims (18.84-87).

---

11. This "gift" of an ox-hoof is perhaps intended to parody the typical offer of chine to an honored guest.

The Inverted Hospitality of the Suitors

The most blatant deviation from the conventional hospitality scene is the heavily ironic inversion of the guest-host relationship. The 108 suitors, who should in reality be the guests of the house, have overstepped all bounds of propriety and taken on themselves the role of master of the house, controlling access to the material wealth, lording it over the household servants, and taking responsibility for the reception of guests (or lack thereof).

The *Odyssey* is rich in vocabulary describing the transgressions and general moral bankruptcy of the suitors. They are described as "sinners" (ἀλεῖται 20.121), a word used by Homer only of the suitors and of Paris (*Il.* 3.28), another notorious violator of hospitality, who stole his host's wife while a guest in his house. They and their actions are described in terms that specify outrageous excess (ὕβρις, λώβη, ὑπερβασίη, ἀτάσθαλος, ὑπερφίαλος, ὑπερηνορέων, ὑπέρβιος) and shamelessness (ἀεικής, ἀναιδής, αἶσχος). They fear neither the righteous indignation of men (22.40; cf. 1.228; 2.64, 198-99) nor the punishment of the gods (14.82-84; 22.39; cf. 2.66-67, 201). Their veritable orgy of feasting and drinking is noticeably lacking in the religious dimension of sacrifice and libation: Amphinomus alone, the most virtuous of the suitors, initiates a proper libation (18.418-28); Antinous initiates a libation that astonishingly omits the most critical element, the formal libation to the gods (21.263-73), and his proposal of a sacrifice to Apollo is never accomplished (21.265-68). The suitors have appropriated what belongs to the gods; in their world, "to libate" (σπένδειν, λείβειν) and "to sacrifice" (ἱερεύειν) have come to mean merely "to drink" and "to feast."[12]

The suitors' lack of regard for both religious and secular institutions puts them on the same level of civilization as the savage Cyclops (cf., e.g., 9.215: ἄγριον, οὔτε δίκας εὖ εἰδότα οὔτε θέμιστας). The text itself draws a number of parallels between the two. Upon reaching Ithaca, Odysseus, failing to recognize his homeland, asks himself the same question he had asked in the land of the Cyclopes (13.200-202; cf. 6.119-21; 9.174-76):

ὤ μοι ἐγώ, τέων αὖτε βροτῶν ἐς γαῖαν ἱκάνω;
ἦ ῥ᾽ οἵ γ᾽ ὑβρισταί τε καὶ ἄγριοι οὐδὲ δίκαιοι,

---

12. For the absence of sacrifice among the suitors, see Vidal-Naquet 1970, 1291. For the text's manifestation of the suitors' omission of sacrifice and libation at a linguistic and structural level, see Saïd 1979, 32-41.

ἦε φιλόξεινοι καί σφιν νόος ἐστὶ θεουδής;

[Oh my! To the land of what mortals have I come this time?
Are they violent and savage and unjust,
or are they kind to strangers and have a god-fearing mind?]

Odysseus encounters someone "kind to strangers" (φιλόξεινος) in Eumaeus; then he confronts in the suitors men who are "violent, savage, and unjust" (ὑβρισταί τε καὶ ἄγριοι οὐδὲ δίκαιοι). The Cyclops is presented in these same terms (9.175).

In blatant disregard of Zeus, the patron of guests and suppliants, both the suitors and the Cyclops deny Odysseus the fundamental rights of a guest, regarding him rather as something to be sold abroad in the case of the suitors and something to be eaten in the case of the Cyclops. Both invert specific elements of hospitality: Ctesippus' offer of a cynical guest-gift, a pelting with an ox-hoof (20.296–300), parallels the cruel guest-gift of the Cyclops, the prerogative of being eaten last (9.369–70). Both are in turn reviled and punished for their improper guest-gifts (9.474–79; 22.285–91).[13] Both the suitors and the Cyclops are notorious for their attempts to hit Odysseus with objects (9.481–86, 537–42; 17.462–63; 18.394–97; 20.299–302). Both are also notorious for their acts of devouring, of Odysseus' house in the case of the suitors (βιβρώσκω 2.203; δαρδάπτω 14.92; 16.315; ἔδω 1.160, 375; 14.377, 417; 18.280; 21.332; ἐσθίω 4.318; κατέδω 17.378; φάγω 15.12)[14] and of Odysseus' men in the case of the Cyclops.

Odysseus' vengeance on both is parallel in its poetic justice. Antinous, the worst violator of hospitality, is killed with an arrow in the throat while he is drinking wine. There appears to be a trace here of the folktale motif on which the Cyclopeia is based: an ogre is made drunk with wine and killed.[15] The "human blood" (αἵματος ἀνδρομέοιο 22.19) that flows from Antinous' neck and defiles the food recalls the only other use of this adjective ἀνδρόμεος in the *Odyssey* to describe the Cyclops' human feast (9.297, 347, 374). In both cases, vengeance is wreaked on the violators of hospitality by means, appropriately enough, of a guest-gift:

---

13. The parallels between Ctesippus and Polyphemus have been generally noted; see Saïd 1979, 31–32; Levine 1984, 4. But the parallel can be drawn more largely to include the suitors as a group.

14. On the imagery of the suitors as devourers, see Bader 1976, 20; Saïd 1979, 10.

15. Thompson 1955–58, K871; Powell (1977, 45n.101) points out this parallel.

Odysseus kills the suitors with a bow that was a guest-gift from Iphitus (21.31–41); he incapacitates the Cyclops with some wine that was a guest-gift from Maron (9.196–211).

The transgressions of the suitors and their consequent punishment, then, recall those of the Cyclops. A clear connection between the two is made by Odysseus himself when, angered as he watches from the portico the rendezvous of his maidservants and the suitors, he reminds himself that he had endured worse things at the hands of the Cyclops (20.18–21):

τέτλαθι δή, κραδίη· καὶ κύντερον ἄλλο ποτ᾽ ἔτλης,
ἤματι τῷ ὅτε μοι μένος ἄσχετος ἤσθιε Κύκλωψ
ἰφθίμους ἑτάρους· σὺ δ᾽ ἐτόλμας, ὄφρα σε μῆτις
ἐξάγαγ᾽ ἐξ ἄντροιο ὀϊόμενον θανέεσθαι.

[Endure, my heart! You once endured something even more shameful
on that day when the Cyclops, with irresistable fury, was devouring my
mighty companions. But you endured, until your wiliness brought you, expecting to die, out of the cave.]

But while such savage behavior is to be expected of a one-eyed ogre, it is reprehensible of the suitors, for they are humans, who are supposed to participate in the fundamental institutions of civilization. But they do not. Just as they fail to give a proper portion of the feast to the gods in the form of libation and sacrifice, so they fail to observe the rituals of hospitality generally (οὔ τινα γὰρ τίεσκον... ὅτις σφέας εἰσαφίκοιτο 22.414–15; 23.65–66; ξείνους στυφελιζομένους 16.108; 20.318; ἀτέμβειν ξείνους 20.294–95; 21.312–13) and to respect the status of Odysseus as guest specifically (ὁ ξεῖνος τὸν πάντες ἀτίμων 23.28; ξεῖνον ἀεικισθήμεναι 18.222; μήτε τι τὸν ξεῖνον στυφελίζετε 18.416; 20.324).

The behavior of three of the most notorious violators of hospitality is particularly reprehensible because they owe a special debt of gratitude to the household of Odysseus. Antinous, Eurymachus, and Melantho all fail to reciprocate for past favors. Odysseus had protected Antinous' father when he came to Ithaca as a suppliant (16.424–30), he had nurtured Eurymachus on his own lap (16.442–44), and Penelope had reared

Melantho as though she were her own child (18.322–23). Their failure to reciprocate—an essential ingredient in a relationship of proper *xenia*—makes their abuse of Odysseus particularly heinous. They, along with another suitor, Ctesippus, are guilty of the most tangible manifestation of the violation of hospitality, a violation that becomes a fully developed motif in the denouement of the *Odyssey,* in their constant threat to pelt Odysseus, ironically with some implement normally associated with proper hospitality.

This motif first occurs in Eumaeus' hut, where Odysseus has a premonition that when he reaches the palace he will be "pelted with missiles" (βέλεσιν βάλλωσι 16.277). His premonition is validated by two warnings he receives even before entering the palace. First the goatherd Melanthius warns him at the nearby spring that if he goes to the house of Odysseus he will be pelted (βαλλομένοιο) on the head and ribs with many footstools (σφέλα 17.230–32). Then, upon approaching the palace, Eumaeus warns him not to tarry at the door, lest someone pelt (βάλῃ) him or drive him off (ἐλάσῃ), to which Odysseus reassures him that he knows all about blows (πληγέων) and pelts (βολάων 17.278–83).

These warnings are well founded: a series of three casts at the hands of the suitors awaits Odysseus in the palace. Antinous pelts him on the right shoulder with a footstool (θρῆνυν 17.462). Then Eurymachus throws a footstool (σφέλας 18.394) at him but hits the wine steward on the right hand instead. And finally Ctesippus hurls an ox-foot (βοὸς πόδα 20.299) at him but misses and hits the wall. This series of three incidents, spread over four books, has elicited much commentary.

The analysts, from Wilamowitz to Merkelbach, have held the latter two passages under suspicion. U. von Wilamowitz regarded Eurymachus' and Ctesippus' casts as poor imitations of Antinous' and attributed them to an interpolator. P. von der Mühll regarded Ctesippus' cast as a rather trivial imitation of Antinous' and Eurymachus' by the hand of a different poet ("B"). And R. Merkelbach attributed Antinous' and Eurymachus' casts to different hands ("A" and "R").[16]

But even in the heyday of analytical criticism, P. Cauer wondered if the subtle variations in the characterization of the three suitors should not be attributed to one and the same poet.[17] This has become the *communis opinio,* especially since the advent of oral criticism. W.B. Stanford

---

16. Von Wilamowitz-Moellendorff 1884, 28–48; von der Mühll 1940, 7, coll. 752; Merkelbach 1951, 78–82.

17. Cauer 1909, 490–91.

noted several subtle variations between the episodes. In the first, Odysseus provokes the attack; in the second, Eurymachus; in the third, there is no provocation. After the first cast, Telemachus keeps quiet; after the second, he protests; after the third, he protests more strongly. After the first cast, the suitors sympathize with Odysseus; after the second, they blame him; after the third, there is a discussion about the suitors' rights.[18] B. Fenik praises the artistry of the sequence, observing that as Telemachus' reaction grows more forceful in each episode, the effectiveness of the cast itself decreases.[19]

Indeed one positive result of this series of casts is its effect on Telemachus, who appears to mature as a man and as a host partly as a result of witnessing these abuses of his guest. After Antinous' cast, Telemachus remains silent, plotting evil for the suitors, but failing to defend his guest (17.489–91, 568). After Eurymachus' cast, he rebukes the suitors, albeit mildly, and bids them to leave the palace (18.406–7); he is then confirmed by Amphinomus as the rightful host of Odysseus (18.420–21). After Ctesippus' cast, he threatens him with death and orders the suitors to refrain from any further improper behavior, thus asserting his newfound manhood and mastery of the house (20.304–19).[20]

This sequence of episodes is a symbolic manifestation of the complete inversion of the ritual of hospitality by the suitors. The objects with which Odysseus is pelted are all closely associated with the feast, hence with the primary locus of hospitality: Antinous and Eurymachus throw footstools, Ctesippus a hoof from the meat basket. In a fourth episode, the maid Melantho threatens to pelt Odysseus with a "firebrand" (δαλῷ βεβλημένος 19.69), again an implement associated with hospitality by its connection to the fire and the hearth. The descriptions of the three casts by the suitors are articulated to stress the theme of inverted hospitality. The most blatant case is Ctesippus' ox-hoof, which is presented as a cynical guest-gift (ξείνιον 20.296). But Antinous' footstool too is described in terms of a gift (17.400, 404, 407–10, 415, 417): while the other suitors "give" (ἔδοσαν) the beggar food, Antinous "gives him over to pain" (ὀδύνῃσιν ἔδωκεν) by pelting him (17.503–4, 567).

---

18. Stanford 1958–59, 17.462ff.n.

19. Fenik 1974, 180–87. In quite another vein, Focke (1943, 346) noted that the number 3 is often associated with death in Homer (here the death of the suitors); Woodhouse (1930, 79) attributed this three-fold action, and the generally high frequency of such triplicates in the *Odyssey,* to the importance of the number 3 in folktale.

20. On Telemachus' increasing confidence as man and host, see Fenik 1974, 185–87; Murnaghan 1987, 105–6n.20.

Eurymachus' cast too stresses the theme of inverted hospitality: he misses Odysseus but hits the wine steward, whose pitcher falls clanging to the ground, while he groans and falls "backward into the dust" (ὕπτιος ἐν κονίῃσι 18.398). This formulaic phrase signifies on a formal level the inversion of peace and war that is implicit on the contextual level, for it is a formula more aptly employed of a dying soldier on the Iliadic battle field (*Il.* 4.522; 13.548; 15.434; 16.289) than of a wine steward at a feast within the confines of a *megaron*. The act of pelting a guest with the implements of hospitality has transformed a hospitality scene into a hostility scene, introducing strife into the feast, or as the suitors themselves describe it, ἔρις into the δαίς (18.403–4).[21]

Odysseus' Reciprocation

The poetic justice of Odysseus' reciprocation reemphasizes the theme of inverted hospitality. Just as Antinous pelted (βάλε 17.462) him on the right shoulder with a footstool, so he pelts (βάλεν 22.15) Antinous with an arrow through the throat. This is the fulfillment of the prayer that Penelope offered when she heard that Odysseus had been pelted (βλημένου 17.493) by Antinous in the *megaron* (17.494):

αἴθ᾿ οὕτως αὐτόν σε βάλοι κλυτότοξος ᾿Απόλλων.

[Thus may bow-famed Apollo pelt you yourself.]

Just as Eurymachus profaned the implements of the feast when he tried to pelt (βάλε 18.396) Odysseus—the footstool (σφέλας) that he throws, the wine steward (οἰνοχόος) who rolls groaning in the dust, and the pitcher (πρόχοος) of wine that falls clanging to the ground (18.394–98)—so he profanes implements of the feast when Odysseus pelts (βάλε 22.82) him with his arrow—he himself falls on a table (τράπεζα), knocking the food (εἴδατα) and his cup (δέπας) to the ground; then he too falls to the ground, kicking at his chair (θρόνος) with his feet (22.81–88). Just as Ctesippus gave Odysseus a cynical guest-gift (ξείνιον 20.296) of a pelting (βέλος 20.305) with an ox-hoof, so Philoetius, the cowherd

---

21. Bader (1976, 33–34) observes how the succession of casts with utensils has transformed the theme of hospitality into one of hostility. Saïd (1979, 31–32) notes that the use of utensils of the feast as weapons introduces warfare into the banquet, causing two opposite poles of the Homeric world to meet.

(ironic?),[22] gives Ctesippus a guest-gift (ξεινήϊον) of a pelting (βεβλήκει) in the chest with his spear (22.285-91).

This series of three exchanges warns that, just as proper guests and hosts expect reciprocity, so violators of hospitality should expect reciprocity; they should be prepared to be paid back in the same coin.[23] Just as the suitors have violated their guest by pelting him with implements of hospitality, so this guest exacts retribution from them through the medium of implements associated with hospitality. The imagery of the suitors' slaughter portrays Odysseus as a bard who with his lyre entertains the suitors at their final feast. This bard who provides entertainment with his lyre is in reality an avenger who brings slaughter with his bow.

The earlier allusions to the newly arrived stranger as a bard are somewhat faint, but they become increasingly stronger until the culmination of this theme in the scene of the stringing of the bow. The first allusion is Eumaeus' implication, in his response to Antinous' complaint that he has brought a useless beggar to the palace, that the stranger is some sort of public worker (δημιοεργός)—a prophet, a doctor, a carpenter, or a bard—for no one, he argues, would invite a useless beggar to a feast (17.382-87). The second allusion is Odysseus' claim that he is able to spread Antinous' fame (κλέος) throughout the land; this is the essential function of a bard (17.418). A third allusion occurs when Penelope inquires about the stranger: Eumaeus praises his storytelling ability (μυθεῖται, θέλγοιτο, ἔθελγε 17.514-21) and compares him to "a bard who has learned his craft from the gods" (ἀοιδὸν ... ὅς τε θεῶν ἒξ // ἀείδῃ δεδαώς 17.518-19). The culmination of this theme is Odysseus' stringing of the bow, which is described by a simile (21.406-9):

ὡς ὅτ' ἀνὴρ φόρμιγγος ἐπιστάμενος καὶ ἀοιδῆς
ῥηϊδίως ἐτάνυσσε νέῳ περὶ κόλλοπι χορδήν,
ἅψας ἀμφοτέρωθεν ἐϋστρεφὲς ἔντερον οἰός,
ὡς ἄρ' ἄτερ σπουδῆς τάνυσεν μέγα τόξον Ὀδυσσεύς.

[As when a man skilled in the lyre and in song
easily stretches a string over a new peg,
fastening on both sides the well-twisted gut of sheep,

---

22. So Woodhouse 1930, 175n.9; Stanford 1958-59, 22.285ff.n.
23. Eustathius (1926, 59-64) notes that Philoetius' cynical taunt of Ctesippus, τοῦτό τοι ἀντὶ ποδὸς ξεινήϊον, later became a maxim for returning evil for evil.

thus without effort did Odysseus stretch the great bow.]

Then Odysseus tests the string with his right hand (21.411):

ἡ δ' ὑπὸ καλὸν ἄεισε, χελιδόνι εἰκέλη αὐδήν.

[It sang beautifully, like the voice of a swallow.][24]

Odysseus, then, is the bard/avenger who entertains with his lyre/bow at the feast. The feast itself symbolizes the slaughter of the suitors; this too is an image that has been developed for some time and reaches its culmination in the scene of the stringing of the bow. These suitors, who have both metaphorically and literally devoured (βιβρώσκω 2.203; δαρδάπτω 14.92; 16.315; ἔδω 1.160, 375; 14.377, 417; 18.280; 21.332; ἐσθίω 4.318; κατέδω 17.378; φάγω 15.12) the house of Odysseus with their continuous orgy of feasting, now enjoy a final feast prepared for them by Odysseus himself. This final feast is well anticipated, first by the lone loyal maidservant who, on the dawn of the fateful day, prays to Zeus that the suitors may on this day have their final feast (20.112–19), then more dramatically by the macabre scene in which the suitors break out into hysterical laughter and begin to eat "meat dripping with blood" (αἱμοφόρυκτα κρέα 20.348). This bloody feast is a foretaste of their slaughter at the hands of Odysseus, when, as Theoclymenus prophecies, the hall will be sprinkled with their own blood (20.354).

The slaughter of the suitors is twice explicitly and once implicitly referred to as a feast prepared by Odysseus. As the suitors are preparing what is to be their final meal, the narrator makes the cynical comment (20.392–94):

δόρπου δ' οὐκ ἄν πως ἀχαρίστερον ἄλλο γένοιτο,
οἷον δὴ τάχ' ἔμελλε θεὰ καὶ καρτερὸς ἀνὴρ
θησέμεναι·

[No other meal could be more joyless

---

24. The association of Odysseus' bow with a lyre is perhaps a manifestation of a version of the universal "return tale" in which the returned master, disguised as a minstrel, identifies himself through a song accompanied on a stringed instrument. In a version of the contest of the bow in the Russian *byliny* of Dobrynja—Propp and Putilov 1958, 99— the hero Dobrynja's bow actually has a *gusli* (a stringed instrument) attached to it, on which he performs before shooting; see further Coote 1981.

than the one that the goddess and the strong man were soon
to set out.]

Then, as Antinous contemplates the possibility of stringing the bow,
the narrator remarks that Antinous himself will be the first "to taste"
(γεύεσθαι) of the arrow from the hands of Odysseus (21.96–100). Finally,
in the culmination of this theme, when Odysseus has strung the bow and
successfully shot through the axes, he declares (21.428–30):

νῦν δ᾽ ὥρη καὶ δόρπον Ἀχαιοῖσιν τετυκέσθαι
ἐν φάει, αὐτὰρ ἔπειτα καὶ ἄλλως ἐψιάασθαι
μολπῇ καὶ φόρμιγγι· τὰ γάρ τ᾽ ἀναθήματα δαιτός.

[Now is the hour for a meal to be prepared for the Achaeans
in the light, but then to make merry in other ways
with singing and the lyre; for these are the ornaments of the feast.]

In the slaughter that ensues, Odysseus is the bard/avenger who serves
up this final feast/slaughter, providing the entertainment with his lyre/
bow. Appropriately, it is a feast in honor of Apollo, lord of the bow;
the anticipated sacrifice of a hecatomb (20.276–78) is comprised of the
108 suitors themselves.

These suitors, who have inverted the institution of hospitality, are pun-
ished in their own coin. Just as they have pelted a guest with implements
of hospitality, so they are pelted by a bard at a feast with a lyre, which
was, moreover, a guest-gift to Odysseus from Iphitus. Those who had
called the guest a "defiler of feasts" (δαιτῶν ἀπολυμαντῆρα 17.220; cf.
17.377) now themselves defile the feast with their spilt blood: Antinous,
who is appropriately shot in the throat while drinking wine, drops his cup,
kicks the table away with his foot, and spills the food on the ground, thus
defiling the bread and meat (22.8–21); Eurymachus' death is similarly
described (22.81–88). Just as the suitors have "destroyed" Odysseus' live-
lihood "without compensation" (νήποινον ὀλέσθαι 1.377 = 2.142) so they
are "destroyed without compensation" (νήποινοι ὄλοισθε 1.380 = 2.145).
These are truly the "acts of requital" (παλίντιτα ἔργα 1.379 = 2.144) for
which Telemachus so earnestly prayed to Zeus.

Odysseus' Return as a Theoxeny

Some readers of the *Odyssey* have reacted with distaste at what they
perceive to be an overly severe punishment exacted on the suitors by an

overly vindictive Odysseus.[25] I believe this results from overemphasis on Odysseus' role as a human avenger seeking retribution for a personal affront, and from failure to acknowledge his role as a guardian of society and an instrument of divine justice dispensing rewards on those who prove loyal and hospitable and punishment on those who have subverted the basic institutions that define civilization: marriage, inheritance, property rights, the agora, sacrifice, suppliancy, and, most pertinent here, *xenia.*

The denouement of the *Odyssey* takes on the form of a theoxeny, in which a disguised god comes to the homes of mortals in order to test their hospitality. Some, usually the poor and humble, treat the god well and are rewarded. Others, usually the rich and powerful, treat him ill and are punished. This universal folktale motif[26] is well attested in Greek and Roman myth.

The most well-known occurrence of this type of theoxeny is the tale of Baucis and Philemon as told by Ovid (*Met.* 8.611–724)—a tale that surely had Greek antecedents.[27] In Ovid's version, Jupiter and Mercury, disguised as mortals and having been denied a proper reception at thousands of homes, are finally received at the humble cottage of Baucis and Philemon, a morally upright, though poor, old couple. As a reward for their generous, albeit humble, hospitality, they are made priests of Apollo and granted a favor by the gods; their neighbors, who had rejected the gods, are destroyed in a flood. In an identical type of theoxeny, also told by Ovid (*Met.* 1.211–41) but with certain Greek antecedents,[28] Jupiter, disguised as a mortal, comes to earth in order to test men. Lycaon abuses his guest, setting human flesh before him to eat and planning to kill him as he sleeps. He is punished by being

---

25. Whitman (1958, 305–8) sees the "massacre" of the suitors as based on "the creed of the primitive clan" and is troubled by the "orgy of blood vengeance" that "peers through the moral scheme." Levy (1963) attributes the slaughter to the influence of a folktale from Redfield's "little tradition"—R. Redfield 1956, 70—in which unjust guests (here the suitors) outstay their welcome and impoverish their host. Levy believes that in the context of this "little tradition" a massacre would be sufficiently motivated and justified, however anomalous it seems alongside the courtly code of the Homeric warrior.

26. Thompson 1955–58, K1811, Q.1.1, Q45.

27. On both the Greek and Near Eastern antecedents of the tale of Baucis and Philemon, see Malten 1939; Fontenrose 1945; Hollis [1970] 1985.

28. Both Apollodorus (3.8.1–2) and Eratosthenes (*Catasterismi* 8) indicate that the tale of Lycaon is at least as old as Hesiod. For an exhaustive list of citations of the tale, see Fontenrose 1945, 98n.17.

turned into a wolf. Two less well-known occurrences are the tales of Macello, who entertains Zeus and Apollo and is rewarded by being spared while all her countrymen are destroyed (Nonnus *Dionysiaca* 18.35; scholia to Ovid *Ibis* 475; Servius on *Aeneid* 6.618), and of Hyrieus, a humble old man who to the best of his limited ability entertains Jupiter, Neptune, and Mercury while they are traveling incognito, and who is consequently rewarded (Ovid *Fasti* 5.495–536).

The tale of Demeter's reception by Metaneira and her daughters, as told in the *Hymn to Demeter* (98–281), is similar. Demeter does not come specifically to make a test of mortals, but she does come in disguise, and she is granted hospitality. For their kind reception, her hosts are rewarded both by her services as a nurse and by the institution of the Eleusinian rites. There is also some element of testing involved in the tale, since Metaneira can be said to fail by doubting the goddess and pulling her son out of the fire.

A related type of theoxeny is that of a divinity who, though not specifically coming to test hospitality, seeks a mortal's reception or acceptance of his rites. The wanderings of Dionysus chronicle a long series of mortals who either accept the god and are rewarded or reject him and are punished: Lycurgus, Oeneus, Pentheus, Amphictyon, Erigone, Pegasus, Brongos, Eleuther, Falernus, Semachus, Staphylos.[29]

Famous heroes too participate in some aspects of theoxeny. Theseus is hospitably received by Hecale, a poor, old woman, when he takes refuge in her hut during a storm; in return, he institutes the Hecalesian festival in her honor (Callimachus *Hecale*; Plutarch *Life of Theseus* 14). Heracles is hospitably received in the hut of the old man Molorchus, for which Molorchus receives a gift of a mule (Callimachus *Aetia* frs. 54–59).

The denouement of the *Odyssey* follows a similar pattern, taking on the form of a theoxeny. Odysseus, who is in many respects like a god, takes on the disguise of a beggar and visits first the hut of Eumaeus then his palace in Ithaca, in order to "make a test" of the inhabitants (πειράω 14.459–61; 15.304–6; 16.304–20; 17.360–64). Like Baucis and Philemon, Eumaeus, though poor, offers generous hospitality to the guest in his hut; in return, Odysseus pronounces a blessing on him (14.53–54) and later promises to reward him with a wife, property, and status equal

---

29. For an exhaustive list, with citations, of theoxenies of various types—gods in the service of mortals, gods in exile, gods on quests, gods on tours of inspection—see Burnett 1970, 24–25n.8.

to Telemachus' (21.214–16). The suitors, like Baucis' and Philemon's countrymen, abuse the guest and consequently suffer righteous, even divine, punishment.

Telemachus is the first to mistake Odysseus for a god. Odysseus' revelation of himself to his son is presented in the form of a divine epiphany. Athena supernaturally transforms him so that he is younger and stouter to look at, and quite naturally, Telemachus is struck with awe at his change in appearance (16.178–79):

θάμβησε δέ μιν φίλος υἱός,
ταρβήσας δ᾽ ἑτέρωσε βάλ᾽ ὄμματα μὴ θεὸς εἴη.

[His son marveled at him
and cast his eyes in the other direction, for fear that he was a god.]

Telemachus' reaction here is remarkably similar to Anchises' reaction at the epiphany of Aphrodite (*H.Aphr.* 182):

τάρβησέν τε καὶ ὄσσε παρακλιδὸν ἔτραπεν ἄλλῃ.

[He feared and turned his eyes aside in another direction.]

Just as Anchises recognizes Aphrodite as a god and pleads for mercy (*H.Aphr.* 185–90), so Telemachus mistakes Odysseus for a god and pleads for mercy (16.183–85):

ἦ μάλα τις θεός ἐσσι, τοὶ οὐρανὸν εὐρὺν ἔχουσιν·
ἀλλ᾽ ἴληθ᾽, ἵνα τοι κεχαρισμένα δώομεν ἱρὰ
ἠδὲ χρύσεα δῶρα, τετυγμένα· φείδεο δ᾽ ἡμέων.

[Surely you are one of the gods who possess the broad heaven.
But be gracious, in order that we may offer to you pleasing sacrifices
and well-wrought, golden gifts. And spare us.]

Aphrodite denies that she is a god upon her arrival at Anchises' hut (*H.Aphr.* 109–10):

οὔ τίς τοι θεός εἰμι· τί μ᾽ ἀθανάτῃσιν ἐΐσκεις;
ἀλλὰ καταθνητή γε, . . .

[I am not a god. Why do you liken me to the immortals?
But I am a mortal, . . .]

And Odysseus, in very similar language, denies his divinity (16.187–88):

οὔ τίς τοι θεός εἰμι· τί μ᾽ ἀθανάτοισιν ἐΐσκεις;
ἀλλὰ πατὴρ τεός εἰμι.

[I am not a god. Why do you liken me to the immortals?
But I am your father.]

The supernatural transformation of Odysseus and the awe that it inspires in Telemachus are elements naturally associated more with a divine epiphany than with a human recognition scene.[30] Seen in the context of a theoxeny, Telemachus' considerable fear at the transformation of the stranger takes on a new light. He realizes that he has not been able to provide this "disguised god" with proper hospitality (16.70–72) and so fears divine punishment, hence his plea to spare him (φείδεο δ᾽ ἡμέων 16.185).[31]

The suitors too raise the possibility that the beggar may be a disguised god who has come to test their conduct. In response to Antinous' pelting of the beggar, the other suitors admonish him (17.485–87):

καί τε θεοὶ ξείνοισιν ἐοικότες ἀλλοδαποῖσι,
παντοῖοι τελέθοντες, ἐπιστρωφῶσι πόληας,
ἀνθρώπων ὕβριν τε καὶ εὐνομίην ἐφορῶντες.

[Even the gods, likening themselves to guests from abroad,
taking on all forms, frequent the cities,
observing both the violence and the orderliness of men.]

To their doom, the suitors do not heed their own warning. When the "disguised god" finally does reveal himself by displaying his extraordinary power to string the bow, he casts off his disguise, and just as Demeter's partial epiphany at the threshold (οὐδόν *H.Dem.* 188) of

---

30. For a list of the typical elements of divine epiphanies, see Richardson 1974, 208. For a comparison of Demeter's epiphany in the Homeric Hymn to Odysseus' "epiphany" to Nausicaa in Phaeacia and to Telemachus in Ithaca, see Sowa 1984, 250–61.

31. So Kearns 1982, 5–6.

Celeos' palace causes "pale fear" to "seize" Metaneira (χλωρὸν δέος εἷλεν H.Dem. 190), so Odysseus' "epiphany" at the threshold (οὐδόν 22.2) of his own palace causes "pale fear" to "seize" the suitors (χλωρὸν δέος εἷλε 22.42). Like a god angered at abusive treatment, he dispenses appropriate punishment.

What, then, is the cumulative effect of Odysseus' return home taking on the form of a theoxeny? It places Odysseus' actions against the suitors on an entirely different moral plane. In this "theoxeny," Odysseus is not presented simply as a vindictive hero wasting the lives of his countrymen in order to reciprocate for a personal affront. The denouement of the *Odyssey* is not primarily concerned with revenge; it is concerned with justice and the restoration of the basic institutions of civilized society. Odysseus, as an instrument of divine justice, has the divine apparatus behind him. Throughout the epic, a series of omens and portents favor, indeed demand, the slaughter of the suitors: bird omens (2.146–76; 15.160–78, 525–34, cf. 17.152–61; 20.242–46), Zeus' thunder (20.98–121; 21.413–15); Penelope's dream (19.535–58); the suitors' hysteria (20.345–57); even Telemachus' sneeze (7.540–47). Among the gods, Athena, who is practically Odysseus' alter ego, has devised slaughter for the suitors from the beginning; she conspires regularly with Odysseus in order to accomplish it and actively assists in the fighting.[32] Zeus too clearly supports Odysseus' slaughter of the suitors,[33] as do the gods generally (1.253–69; 22.413–16; 23.63–67). Even the suitors realize in retrospect that their destruction was the work of the gods (24.164, 182, 443–49).

The suitors' crimes, then, are not mere personal abuses; they are crimes against the institutions of civilized society and, by extension, against the gods who watch over these institutions. In turn, Odysseus' response to the suitors' crimes is not that of a vindictive hero reciprocating for a personal affront but that of a morally upright king, who, as an instrument of divine justice, purges wickedness, reasserts moral integrity, and reestablishes those institutions that keep society functional. Unlike a triumphant Iliadic warrior, Odysseus refuses to exult over the fallen bodies of the suitors; instead he remarks impassively that it was the gods who subdued them for their wickedness (22.411–16). This is a

---

32. See 1.294–96; 2.281–84; 5.23–24; 13.303, 372–81, 386–96; 16.168–71, 233–34, 260–69, 282, 298; 18.346–48; 19.2, 33–53; 20.42, 284–86, 393–94; 22.256, 297–301; 24.479–80.

33. See 1.378–80 = 2.143–45; 16.260–69; 17.50–51, 59–60; 20.42, 98–121; 21.413–15; 24.164.

sentiment consistent with the overall view of justice in the *Odyssey.* The poet proclaims in his prologue (1.7), and Zeus reiterates shortly thereafter (1.32–34), that the wickedness of men is the cause of their destruction.

Chapter 9

Hospitality Scenes and the Architecture of the *Odyssey*

τί πρῶτόν τοι ἔπειτα, τί δ' ὑστάτιον καταλέξω;

[What, then, shall I narrate first, and what last?]
—(*Od.* 9.14)

The oral-formulaic theory of Parry and Lord has provided a clear picture of the dynamics of extemporaneous verse composition on the level of the shorter formulaic units. I have often wondered, though, how an oral poet, when performing a large-scale epic of the size of an *Iliad* or *Odyssey*, would, on a very practical level, go about arranging and structuring the larger units of his epic, the major scenes and large-scale narrative patterns, and, after having devised a satisfactory arrangement, how he would remember that arrangement accurately in subsequent performances.

The text of Homer itself suggests that the poet placed the utmost importance on the arrangement of his narrative: "What, then, shall I narrate first, and what last?" (τί πρῶτόν τοι ἔπειτα, τί δ' ὑστάτιον καταλέξω; 9.14; cf. *Il.* 5.703-4; 11.299-300; 16.692-93) asks Odysseus as a prologue to the tale of his adventures. The arrangement of the narrative is of such tantamount importance that the poet of the *Odyssey* specifically invokes the Muse for direction in his prologue: "From some point, goddess, daughter of Zeus, tell it also to us" (τῶν ἁμόθεν γε, θεά, θύγατερ Διός, εἰπὲ καὶ ἡμῖν 1.10). Indeed much of the special force of the *Odyssey* lies in Homer's arrangement of his narrative, beginning as he does almost at the end of the tale chronologically, and then filling in the background through the technique of flashback (i.e., *hysteron-proteron Homericos*).

The invocation to the Muse in the prologue of the *Odyssey* (1.10) is particularly notable because the poet seems to be placing his ability to arrange the larger narrative units of his epic in the same category

189

as his ability to compose individual verses and recall individual scenes. Both require divine assistance. Just as he must invoke the divinities in order to remember the catalogue of Achaean ships (*Il.* 2.484–93), so he must invoke the divinities in order to remember the arrangement of the narrative units of his entire epic. The poet is drawing on the same source for inspiration, to him the divine Muse, to our more analytic and less mythopoeic minds the reservoir of inherited formulae, type-scenes, and narrative patterns that facilitate the poet's composition of epic verse.

I suggest that Homer viewed the overall structures of his epics as sequences of traditional themes or type-scenes, and that during his performance of a large-scale epic like the *Iliad* or the *Odyssey* he was able to remember, even over a performance of several days, where he should start, where he should end, and where the various directions of his tale should turn, by recalling a sequence, perhaps a memorized sequence, of these traditional themes. Homer himself refers to the course of a song as an οἴμη (*Od.* 8.74, 481; 22.347), a word very early associated with οἶμος, the word for "path" (cf. *H.Herm.* 451). If the course of the song is a path, the direction markers along this path, in a practical sense, are these traditional themes or type-scenes. Like signposts along a road, they guide the poet through the course of his narrative as he composes, and they guide and inform the audience as it listens.

This is apparently the case in the Serbo-Croatian oral tradition. Aspiring *guslari* concentrate on the building of themes in the earliest period of their training, and their ability to create larger epic songs depends largely on their ability to string together a sequence of traditional themes: the gathering of an army, the numbering of wedding guests, the journey abroad and arrival home, and so on. Even the most experienced singer learns his songs by noting the sequence of themes as he listens to the songs of others. In one notorious case, the celebrated singer Avdo Medjedović, after listening to a song unfamiliar to him by Mumin Vlahovljak, was asked if he could then sing the song himself. Though Avdo elaborated the song to nearly three times its original length, he followed Mumin's original sequence of themes: assembly, arrival of messenger, delivery of letter, and so on. The *guslari,* it appears, think of their songs in terms of their constituent themes or type-scenes and how they are arranged.[1]

By far the most pervasive type-scene in the *Odyssey* is the hospitality

---

1. On the Serbo-Croatian analogue, see Lord 1960, 68–98, 223–24; Lord 1951, 71–80.

scene—the description of the events that take place between the time of a visitor's arrival and his departure. Such hospitality scenes make up a large part of the narrative of the *Odyssey,* since the tales of a young traveler on a quest for information and of a warrior wandering homeward from abroad are naturally conducive to this theme. In a practical sense, then, the *Odyssey* may be regarded as a sequence of hospitality scenes. In the preceding chapters, I have concentrated on the individual type-scenes of hospitality with a view to their conventional elements, that is, on how each scene functions diachronically against the backdrop of its inherited conventions. But this is only half the picture. These scenes are not simply independent allomorphs of a commonly inherited tradition; one must also focus on how these type-scenes of hospitality relate to one another synchronically, interacting with, anticipating and recalling, and variously informing one another within this individual epic. These type-scenes form the architectonic structure of the epic whole; they are the signposts that guide the poet and his audience through the lengthy narrative. The poet remembered the οἴμη, the "course," of his song by recalling the sequence of hospitality scenes; the audience was enabled to listen more comfortably and informatively through its familiarity with these traditional type-scenes.

More specifically, Homer may have thought of the following sequence of hospitality scenes as the οἴμη, the "course," of his *Odyssey*:

1. Athena-Mentes in Ithaca (1.103–324)
  2. Telemachus in Pylos (3.4–485)
    3. Telemachus in Pherae—a synoptic scene (3.487–94)
      4. Telemachus in Sparta (4.1–624)
        5. Odysseus and the Phaeacians (5.388–8.586)
          6. Odysseus' Adventures—an embedded flashback (9.1–12.453)
        5. Odysseus and the Phaeacians (13.1–187)
      7. Odysseus and Eumaeus (13.221–14.533, etc.)
      4. Telemachus in Sparta (15.1–184)
    3. Telemachus in Pherae—a repeated synoptic scene (15.185–92)
  2. Telemachus in Pylos—an aborted scene (15.193–214)
1. Odysseus in Ithaca (17.204–23.348)

Many kinds of interaction between these scenes present themselves. Of the first four major scenes of hospitality, each successive scene is more and more fully developed, rising in a crescendo from the relatively simple reception of Athena-Mentes in Ithaca, to the increasingly elaborate receptions of Telemachus in Pylos and Sparta, to the epic's central scene of Odysseus' reception among the Phaeacians, which is the longest and includes the entire spectrum of conventional elements. From a wider perspective, these first four scenes of the epic function together as paradigms of proper hospitality, preparing the way for the later reversals of proper hospitality by Polyphemus, the Laestrygonians, Circe, and various other uncivilized characters in the tales of Odysseus. By means of their narratological embedding within the Phaeacian episode, these tales of perverted hospitality function as a foil to the description of the Phaeacians' civilized and highly proper hospitality. In turn, the scene of Eumaeus' humble, but proper, hospitality functions as a foil both to the lavish hospitality of the Phaeacians that precedes and to the total inversion of hospitality by the suitors that follows. From an even wider perspective, the scenes of hospitality that frame the entire epic, Athena-Mentes' visit to Ithaca and Odysseus' return home to Ithaca, appear to respond to each other, the former being a sort of preview of the latter. Both scenes share in the motif of the theoxeny, in which a god in disguise visits the houses of mortals to test their hospitality.

From the shortest and apparently most insignificant episode to the largest and most fully elaborated scene, Homer has arranged his type-scenes of hospitality in all their variations so that they interact with and inform one another, much as a composer of a symphony arranges variations on a common musical theme. This interaction takes place on a number of levels: sometimes by the mere relative length of scenes, the longer and more fully elaborated scenes gaining emphasis and weight vis-à-vis the shorter and simpler ones; sometimes by the sequential arrangement of three or four scenes that, like a musical crescendo, build one on the other; sometimes by the repetition of details, episodes, and character types in two scenes, which creates a thematic association between them, that is, by using a "doublet"; sometimes by responsive alternation, as two antithetical scenes are placed, like foils, in antiphonal juxtaposition with each other. This interplay between individual scenes within the epic whole works throughout to produce the harmonious symphony of Homer's *Odyssey*.

Elaboration

The simplest kind of interaction between type-scenes is their relative length, considered entirely apart from their content. A short, synoptic, bare-bones type-scene carries relatively little narrative weight compared to a fully developed and elaborated scene. The scene of Paris' arming in the *Iliad,* for example, is short and perfunctory, containing just the skeleton of the arming type-scene, and thereby suggesting Paris' relative unimportance as a warrior on the battlefield. This is in stark contrast to the fully developed arming scenes of Agamemnon and Achilles, which are elaborated with extended descriptions of the armor; the scene of Achilles is even ornamented with a simile. Such elaboration slows down the pace of the narrative, adds weight to the scene, and signals the advent of a major episode on the battlefield.[2]

With regard to hospitality scenes, who but the most meticulous Homerist will recall that in the *Odyssey* Telemachus and Pisistratus receive hospitality from Diocles in Pherae twice (3.488–90; 15.186–88)? This synoptic hospitality scene of only three verses carries little narrative weight compared to the more fully developed hospitality scenes that frame it—the scenes of Nestor's hospitality in Pylos and Menelaus' in Sparta, both of which gain emphasis by their relative length. Conversely, the short synoptic scenes can be said to borrow details from the fuller scenes; the audience fills in the details from its experience with fuller scenes, so that, for example, the skeletal description of Diocles' hospitality in Pherae still suggests the entire ritual of hospitality.

Crescendo

The relative elaboration of a number of type-scenes in a sequence creates a more complex and aesthetically pleasing interaction. If one considers the sequence of the first four major hospitality scenes of the *Odyssey*— Athena-Mentes in Ithaca, Telemachus in Pylos, Telemachus in Sparta, and Odysseus among the Phaeacians in Scheria—three distinct patterns emerge.

First, in each succeeding scene, the guest arrives progressively later during the activities of a feast. When Athena-Mentes arrives in Ithaca, preliminary preparations are under way for a feast—servants are mixing wine with water, sponging off tables, and cutting up meat (1.109–12). When Telemachus arrives in Pylos, men are roasting and skewering meat in preparation for an imminent feast (3.32–33). When Telemachus arrives

---

2. *Il.* 3.328–38 (Paris); 11.15–46 (Agamemnon); 19.364–91 (Achilles); cf. Patroclus' arming at 16.130–44. The seminal article on this sequence of arming scenes is Armstrong 1958; see also Arend 1933, 92–97; Calhoun 1933, 11–12; Lord 1960, 89–91; Edwards 1987a, 72–74.

in Sparta, a feast is already under way, with a singer and dancers providing entertainment (4.15–19). And when Odysseus arrives in Scheria, a feast has just ended, and libations are being poured before bedtime (7.136–38).[3]

Second, each succeeding scene extends the description of the ritual of hospitality closer to its proper conclusion. In Ithaca, only the feasting and subsequent entertainment by the bard are described (1.130–55). In Pylos, the accommodations for the night and the bath are included (3.395–403, 464–68). In Sparta, the scene is extended to include farewell speeches, libations, omen, and gift giving (15.68–181).[4] And in Scheria, the ritual of hospitality is extended to its proper conclusion by the Phaeacians' provision of conveyance (πομπή) to their guest's next destination (13.4–125).

Third, the hospitality scene in Scheria, the last of the four, is in many ways a conflation and elaboration of the two preceding scenes in Pylos and Sparta. It presents a richer ornamentation of conventional elements, even combining specific details of the two preceding scenes.[5]

Telemachus arrives at Pylos on the *beach* in the *morning*. He arrives at Sparta at the *palace* in the *evening*. Odysseus arrives in Scheria and first meets Nausicaa on the *beach* in the *morning*, then he meets her parents at the *palace* in the *evening*.

On the *beach* at Pylos, Telemachus is greeted *promptly* by Pisistratus, *the king's and host's son*. At the *palace* in Sparta, the attendant Eteoneus *initially hesitates* to admit Telemachus, until Menelaus *admonishes* him to offer hospitality. On the *beach* in Scheria, Odysseus is greeted *promptly* by Nausicaa, *the king's and host's daughter*, but later at the *palace*, Alcinous and Arete *initially hesitate*, sitting in silence while Odysseus waits in the ashes, until the old hero Echeneus *admonishes* Alcinous to raise up his guest and offer hospitality.

In Pylos, Telemachus receives a bath from Nestor's youngest daughter, but not until *the day after arrival*. In Sparta, the maids bathe Telemachus

---

3. The regular progression in these four scenes is observed by Shelmerdine (1969), who admires Homer's control over such a long stretch of narrative.

4. But it should be noted that in the structure of the *Odyssey* as we have it the hospitality scene in Sparta is abruptly curtailed at the end of book 4 and left unfinished until the beginning of book 15 (i.e., after the scene in Scheria is over).

5. Some of the following details have been noticed and articulately described in A. Thornton's comparison of the themes in these three scenes of hospitality (1970, 38–46).

immediately upon arrival. In Scheria, Nausicaa's maids bathe Odysseus *immediately upon arrival* in the river; then, on *the day after arrival,* he receives another bath in the palace.

The description of Nestor's palace is dispensed with cursorily in just two verses (3.387–88). The description of Menelaus' palace is fuller; it is even ornamented by a simile, and a special point is made of the striking impression it makes on the visitors (4.43–47, 71–75). The description of Alcinous' palace uses some of the same formulaic diction (cf. 4.45–46 and 7.84–85; 4.47 and 7.134), it too is ornamented by a simile, and again the impression it makes on the visitors is emphasized. But it is even more fully ornamented by an account of the bronze walls, golden doors, and silver door posts, the gold and silver dogs crafted by Hephaestus, the fine tapestries decorating the hall, and even the gardens outside the courtyard (7.84–132).

In Pylos, the question of the guest's identity is simple and straightforward: Nestor asks his guest who he is, where he is from, and what his business is; in turn, Telemachus offers an immediate and clear reply (3.69–101). In Sparta, the revelation of the guest's identity, his *anagnorisis,* is more slowly worked out. Menelaus inadvertently makes mention of Telemachus' father, causing him to weep. This raises Menelaus' suspicions. Helen's suspicions are further raised by the boy's similarity in appearance to his father. Finally Pisistratus, not Telemachus, confirms their suspicions about Telemachus' identity (4.60–157). Among the Phaeacians, this theme of delayed *anagnorisis* is worked out even more fully. Odysseus remains incognito until the evening of his second day in Scheria, when Alcinous observes him weeping at the mention of Odysseus—just as in Sparta Menelaus had observed Telemachus weeping at the mention of Odysseus—and questions him openly about his identity (cf. 4.113–16 and 8.521–31); in turn, Odysseus' response is equally weighty, comprising the entire Apologoi (books 9–12).

The bedding type-scene in Scheria is longer than those in Pylos and Sparta, and it includes elements in common with each of the two previous scenes. As in Sparta, the mistress of the house orders the servants to make the bed (7.335; 4.296), and the elaborate preparation of the bedding is described by the same four-verse block of formulae (7.336–39 = 4.297–300). But the scene in Scheria also contains verbal echoes of the scene in Pylos: the bed on the portico is described by the same formulaic verse (7.345 = 3.399), and the descriptions of the bedding down of the master and mistress of the house are very similar (7.346–47 ≈ 3.402–3). Unique to the scene in Scheria is the rather formal announcement to the guest that his bed is ready (7.342).

The ritual of gift giving is conspicuously absent in Pylos. Presumably Nestor, proper host that he is, would have given guest-gifts to Telemachus had he not bypassed Pylos on his way home. Guest-gifts play a larger role in the hospitality scene in Sparta, where every formality is observed upon Telemachus' departure: Menelaus offers a libation cup, Megapenthes a krater, and Helen a precious peplos of her own weaving (15.99–129). Among the Phaeacians, gift giving is a passion. The ritual is described in great detail: the collection of mantles, tunics, and gold from the twelve kings of the district; Euryalus' additional offer of a silver-studded sword and ivory sheath; Alcinous' individual contribution of a mantle, a tunic, and a golden cup; the depositing of these guest-gifts at the feet of Arete, who stores them in a chest that Odysseus ties securely with a complicated knot; the offer, elicited by Odysseus' storytelling, of additional gifts of bronze tripods and bowls from each king of the district; the loading of these gifts onto the ship; and their safe conveyance to Ithaca (8.389–448; 11.336–61; 13.7–22, 122–38).

The first four major scenes of hospitality in the *Odyssey,* then, form a succession of increasingly full descriptions that creates an artistic effect much like that of a rising musical crescendo, with each movement more elaborate and extended than the previous one. This appears to be a fundamental feature of oral poetry, and it may have functioned somehow as a compositional aid to the oral poet, but at the same time it produces a thematically meaningful and aesthetically pleasing interaction between type-scenes that is a testimony to Homer's finely ordered design and to his precise control over long stretches of his narrative. It is analogous to the sequence of the four major arming type-scenes in the *Iliad*: Paris (3.328–38), Agamemnon (11.15–46), Patroclus (16.130–44), and Achilles (19.364–91)—the first scene, presenting the arming type-scene in its simplest form, functioning as a sort of archetype or preview of the more fully elaborated scenes to follow. It is also analogous, though on a much larger scale, to what has been called the "anticipatory scene" or "anticipatory doublet," a regular stylistic feature in Homer, in which an action or motif is presented briefly upon its first appearance, then returned to later for fuller development.[6]

---

6. Fenik 1968, 86, 213–15; Fenik 1974, 100–104; cf. Edwards 1991, 19–23.

Doublets

Repetition—of formulaic diction, minor details, character types, episodes, narrative patterns, and even major themes—is perhaps the most idiosyncratic stylistic feature of Homeric poetry. Surely this stylistic feature is a result of its oral background. Yet it serves not only the practical needs of an extemporaneously composing oral bard but the aesthetic purposes of a poet striving to develop allusion, parody, foreshadowing, and various other thematic associations, and at the same time trying to build a pleasing symmetry and an ordered narrative structure. Such repetition pervades the highly conventional scenes of hospitality in the *Odyssey,* and it often calls to mind associations between scenes that are highly significant for the thematic structure of the epic whole.

Homer has crafted his narrative in such a way that Telemachus is enjoying the hospitality of Menelaus and Helen in Sparta at the same time that Odysseus is enjoying the hospitality of Alcinous and Arete in Scheria. The two scenes form a thematic doublet, sharing many specific details and larger themes. In both scenes, a visitor arrives incognito at a palace where a feast is taking place. Instead of the spontaneous greeting that visitors are accustomed to receiving, the hosts initially hesitate to grant hospitality (4.22–29; 7.153–54); for this they are quickly reprimanded (4.30–36; 7.155–66), and thereafter the guests are properly received (4.37–68; 7.167–84). In both scenes, the visitors are awestruck at the splendor of the palace (4.43–47, 71–75; 7.81–135); Homer even uses the same simile to describe this splendor (4.45–46 ≈ 7.84–85). In both scenes, a powerful queen plays a central role as the hostess on whose good graces the visitor depends. In both scenes, the telling of the returns (νόστοι) of various heroes from Troy plays a significant role. In both scenes, the *anagnorisis* of the visitor is slowly worked out, creating rich dramatic irony. Just as Telemachus weeps and covers his eyes with his purple cloak at Menelaus' mention of his father (4.113–16), so Odysseus weeps and covers his eyes with his purple cloak when he hears his own troubles recounted by Demodocus (8.83–92, 521–31). Just as Menelaus' observation of Telemachus' weeping leads him to suspect his guest's identity (4.116–19, 147–54), so Alcinous' observation of Odysseus' weeping causes him to inquire into his guest's identity (8.93–95, 532–86). By drawing these many similarities in detail and theme, Homer has artistically linked this pair of scenes, creating a sympathetic harmony between father and son, as they experience similar treatment at the hands of their respective hosts.[7]

Odysseus' experience among the Phaeacians is in many ways a preview, an anticipatory doublet, of what is to follow upon his return home to Ithaca. The two scenes are linked thematically by many similarities in detail, character, and motif. In both scenes, a weary stranger awakens on the shore of a strange land (6.117–26; 13.187–216); this stranger is wrapped by Athena in a cloak of secrecy to avoid the danger posed by the local inhabitants, in Scheria by the cover of a mist (7.14–15, 30–31), in Ithaca by a disguise as a beggar (13.429–38; 16.454–59; 17.201–3). Athena sends a dream to the children of the ruling families—to Nausicaa in Scheria, to Telemachus in Sparta (6.13–40; 15.1–42)—both of whom are on the threshold of adulthood; Athena's instructions in these dreams result in their meeting the stranger. The stranger supplicates these children and in their presence is physically transformed by Athena (6.229–45; 16.172–85). They in turn give him clothing, fill him in on the situation at the palace, and then precede him into town (6.214, 303–15, 295–99; 16.79, 241–57; 17.1–25).

The most pervasive theme shared by the two scenes is that of suit and marriage. Nausicaa, like Penelope, is beset by suitors "many and noble" (πολέες τε καὶ ἐσθλοί 6.284; 22.204). The newly arrived stranger becomes a competitor in the suit and makes an unexpected show of strength—in the athletic contests of the Phaeacians, and in the trial of the bow among the suitors in Ithaca. Odysseus' boast to the Phaeacians that he is second to none in the bow, except perhaps Philoctetes, and that he would be first to strike his man in a crowd of enemies (8.215–28), is an omen of the trial of the bow and the subsequent slaughter of the suitors in Ithaca. The festivities of song and dance that follow the athletic contests in Scheria anticipate the wedding song and dance that follow the contest of the bow in Ithaca (8.250–67; 23.142–51): Odysseus, as the successful "suitor," presides over both these "wedding feasts" (8.469–98; 23.129–51); and the bard Demodocus sings a "wedding hymn" in Scheria about how Hephaestus, Aphrodite's legitimate husband, returns home unexpectedly to find his wife in bed with Ares (8.266–366), an artistic foreshadowing of Odysseus' unexpected return home to his beleaguered wife.[8]

Homer also draws a number of parallels between the treatment

---

7. For a more detailed comparison of these two scenes, see chapter 4.
8. For a more detailed comparison of these two scenes, see chapter 5.

Odysseus receives at the hands of Polyphemus the Cyclops and that which he receives at the hands of the suitors in Ithaca. Both groups blatantly disregard Zeus, the patron of guests and suppliants, by denying Odysseus the fundamental rights of guest and suppliant. Instead of welcoming their guest and offering him food, they try to strike him with objects (9.481-86, 537-42; 17.462-63; 18.394-97; 20.299-302) and to devour him—literally in the case of the Cyclops, figuratively in the case of the suitors, who are often said to be devouring his possessions. Both groups violate the rituals of hospitality by offering cynical and cruel guest-gifts: Polyphemus grants Odysseus the privilege of being devoured last (9.369-70); Ctesippus gives Odysseus a pelting with an ox-hoof (20.296-300). Both are in turn punished appropriately for their blatant violations of hospitality (22.285-91; 9.474-79). The vengeance Odysseus himself wreaks on both groups is full of irony in its poetic justice: he kills the suitors with a bow that was a guest-gift from Iphitus (21.31-41); to facilitate his blinding of the Cyclops he incapacitates him with some wine that was a guest-gift from Maron (9.196-211).

Thus the behavior of the suitors toward Odysseus and their consequent punishment by him echo Odysseus' experiences with the Cyclops. Odysseus himself associates the two when, in the midst of his suffering at the hands of the suitors, he reminds himself that he has endured worse things at the hands of the Cyclops (20.18-21):

τέτλαθι δή, κραδίη· καὶ κύντερον ἄλλο ποτ' ἔτλης,
ἤματι τῷ ὅτε μοι μένος ἄσχετος ἤσθιε Κύκλωψ
ἰφθίμους ἑτάρους· σὺ δ' ἐτόλμας, ὄφρα σε μῆτις
ἐξάγαγ' ἐξ ἄντροιο ὀϊόμενον θανέεσθαι.

[Endure, my heart! You once endured something even more
    shameful
on that day when the Cyclops, with irresistable fury, was
    devouring my
mighty companions. But you endured, until your wiliness
brought you, expecting to die, out of the cave.]

The parallels in formulaic diction and in specific details and motifs create a thematic association between the two scenes, thereby emphasizing the danger that still confronts Odysseus, even at home in the supposedly civilized human world, while at the same time reasserting that Odysseus is prepared by past experience for such dangers as those he will confront in Ithaca. This thematic association between the two scenes also accentuates the suitors' total lack of regard for both the secular and the religious dimensions of the ritual of hospitality, thereby placing them on the same level of civilization as the savage Cyclops.[9]

The first and last hospitality scenes of the *Odyssey* are the scenes of Athena's and Odysseus' arrivals in Ithaca; these two scenes, which frame the entire epic, form a doublet with overarching thematic associations. Most conspicuously, both scenes draw on the common folktale motif of the theoxeny, in which a god in disguise visits the home of mortals in order to make a test of their hospitality. The association of these two framing scenes of theoxeny places Odysseus' actions against the suitors within the realm of divine justice rather than human vengeance.

Athena, a divinity, arrives in Ithaca disguised as the mortal Mentes, on the most superficial level simply to deliver a message to Telemachus, but on a more complex and subliminal level to make a test of the hospitality of Telemachus and the suitors. This molding of the scene of Athena's visit into the framework of a theoxeny accentuates the contrast between Telemachus' proper and generous hospitality and the suitors' blatant disregard for the stranger standing at the door. This first hospitality scene of the *Odyssey* thereby serves as a preview in synoptic form of the last, anticipating the violations of hospitality that the suitors perpetrate against Odysseus upon his arrival home.

Odysseus' arrival too is molded into the framework of a theoxeny. He takes on the disguise of a beggar in order to "make a test" (πειράω 14.459–61; 15.304–6; 16.304–20; 17.360–64) of the inhabitants, visiting first the hut of the swineherd Eumaeus, where he is offered proper, albeit humble, accommodations, then the palace overrun by suitors, where he is violently abused. He is more than once mistaken for a god, first by Telemachus upon his sudden transformation in appearance (16.178–79):

θάμβησε δέ μιν φίλος υἱός,
ταρβήσας δ' ἑτέρωσε βάλ' ὄμματα μὴ θεὸς εἴη.

[His son marveled at him
and cast his eyes in the other direction, for fear that he was a god.]

---

9. For a more detailed comparison of these two scenes, see chapter 8.

The awestruck Telemachus fears divine anger and pleads for mercy (16.183–85):

ἦ μάλα τις θεός ἐσσι, τοὶ οὐρανὸν εὐρὺν ἔχουσιν·
ἀλλ᾽ ἵληθ᾽, ἵνα τοι κεχαρισμένα δώομεν ἱρὰ
ἠδὲ χρύσεα δῶρα, τετυγμένα· φείδεο δ᾽ ἡμέων.

[Surely you are one of the gods who possess the broad heaven.
But be gracious, in order that we may offer to you pleasing
    sacrifices
and well-wrought, golden gifts. And spare us.]

Later the suitors too raise the possibility that Odysseus may be a disguised god who has come to test their conduct. In response to Antinous' pelting of the beggar, they warn him (17.485–87):

καί τε θεοὶ ξείνοισιν ἐοικότες ἀλλοδαποῖσι,
παντοῖοι τελέθοντες, ἐπιστρωφῶσι πόληας,
ἀνθρώπων ὕβριν τε καὶ εὐνομίην ἐφορῶντες.

[Even the gods, likening themselves to guests from abroad,
taking on all forms, frequent the cities,
observing both the violence and the orderliness of men.]

But the suitors do not heed their own warning. When the "disguised god" finally reveals himself by displaying his extraordinary power to string the bow, casting off his disguise as in a divine epiphany, he begins to dispense appropriate punishment as the instrument of divine justice.[10]

Foils

Just as scenic doublets emphasize thematic correspondences, so scenic foils accentuate thematic differences. Among the scenes of hospitality in the *Odyssey,* such foils are often antithetically juxtaposed to accentuate this contrapuntal relationship.

Although the hospitality scenes in Pylos and Sparta have much in

---

10. For a more detailed analysis of these two scenes as theoxenies, see chapters 2 and 8.

common, their differences are accentuated by their juxtaposition in the narrative. Telemachus receives a proper and generous reception in both places, but while Nestor's hospitality, though relatively humble, is warm and intensely personal, Menelaus' hospitality, though extremely luxurious, lacks this personal warmth. Further, while Nestor's expression of hospitality is greatly influenced by his piety toward the gods, Menelaus' expression of hospitality is largely secular in tone.

Nestor's accommodations for his guests are humble in contrast to the luxury of Menelaus' palace in Sparta. In Sparta, heralds, servants, and handmaids attend to the guests; in Pylos, these duties fall to members of Nestor's own family. In Sparta, the preparation and consumption of lavish feasts are described at great length (4.52–68; 15.135–44); in Pylos, the descriptions of the serving of food are cursory (3.65–67, 470–73), yielding to the longer descriptions of sacrifice. In Sparta, Telemachus is provided a luxurious bed, the preparation of which is elaborately described (4.296–301); in Pylos, a very simple bed suffices (3.399). And in Sparta, Telemachus receives precious guest-gifts (4.613–19; 15.102–29); in Pylos, he receives nothing.

Yet what Nestor lacks in wealth and luxury he makes up for in warmth and personal affection. In Sparta, the guests are initially received rather hesitantly by a herald (4.22–36); in Pylos, they are greeted spontaneously by Nestor's own relatives and sons (3.31–42). In Sparta, the housemaids bathe the guests (4.48–50); in Pylos, Nestor's own youngest daughter Polycaste fulfills this duty (3.464–68). In Sparta, the servants perform the tasks of the feast (4.52–58; 15.92–98, 135–41); in Pylos, Nestor and his sons prepare the food and serve the wine (3.32–33, 390–94). Furthermore, in Sparta there is no one to correspond to Nestor's youngest son Pisistratus, who becomes Telemachus' bedmate, close companion, and personal guide (3.36–39, 400–401, 415–16, 481–85).

Nestor is exceptionally pious. Nowhere else in the *Odyssey* are so many sacrifices, libations, and prayers described, and in such elaborate detail (3.5–9, 40–64, 332–42, 380–84, 390–95, 418–63). These religious rituals characterize Nestor's expression of hospitality toward his guests. On a formal level, they complement, and in some instances actually replace, the conventional elements of the normal feasting scene. What feasting does occur in Pylos is always done in conjunction with sacrifice, what drinking with libation. This is a stark contrast to Sparta, where no sacrifices are performed, and where the overall tenor of the hospitality scene is much more secular.[11]

---

11. For a more detailed contrast between these two scenes, see chapters 3 and 4.

The embedding of Odysseus' tale of Polyphemus' perverted hospitality within Homer's larger tale of the Phaeacians' highly proper hospitality is also very striking. In their expressions of hospitality, and in many other ways, the Cyclopes and the Phaeacians are polar opposites: stubbornly asocial vs. intensely social; pastoral vs. urban; despisers of the gods vs. builders of temples to the gods; landlubbers vs. shipbuilders; brutal vs. sybaritic.[12] In general, the Phaeacians enjoy all the refinements of a highly cultured, civilized society, while the Cyclopes remain primitive and uncivilized. It should be no surprise, then, that in the very fundamental human institution of *xenia,* the Phaeacians indulgently practice every refinement, while Polyphemus brutally commits every perversion. These contrasts between the two groups are particularly acute in view of the Phaeacians former proximity to the Cyclopes and their actual genetic relationship: they used to be neighbors (6.2–6; cf. 7.205–6), and they are both offspring of Poseidon (7.56–68; 9.517–19, 526–29).[13] Their present contrasts, then, starkly illustrate the potential for societies to stray in opposite directions.

This polar opposition is especially pertinent to the theme of hospitality because Odysseus, the guest, is telling the tale of the Cyclops to the Phaeacians, his hosts. As is often the case in the tales of guests to their hosts, there is a didactic, or at least a protreptic, purpose involved.[14] In his tale of the Cyclops, Odysseus illustrates to the Phaeacians the consequences of perverted hospitality, thereby warning them not to treat him inhospitably. And in the various other tales of his Apologoi, primarily those of Circe and Calypso, Odysseus warns the Phaeacians not to go to the opposite extreme—not to obstruct his return home by being overly hospitable. By their sexual attractions, Calypso detained him for seven years, Circe for one. The potential for a similar detention in Scheria

---

12. On the contrasts between the Cyclopes and the Phaeacians, see Belmont 1962, 166–67; Segal 1962, 33; Kilb 1973, 88–89; Austin 1975, 143–49, 153–62; Vidal-Naquet 1981, 64; Clay 1983, 125–32; Mondi 1983, 24–28; Heubeck, in Heubeck and Hoekstra 1989, 9.106–15n.

13. Clay (1980) locates the Phaeacians' former home at Goat Island, just off the coast of the land of the Cyclopes. This is unprovable, of course, but if true would add a new dimension to Odysseus' story of the Phaeacians; his long description of the island would be a vivid portrayal of his hosts' former homeland, strikingly illustrating their once close connection to the Cyclopes.

14. Cf. Athena-Mentes' claim to Telemachus that she is a guest-friend of his father (1.187–88) and the disguised Odysseus' claim to Laertes that he is a guest-friend of Odysseus, having once entertained him and given him gifts in abundance (24.265–79). For the view that all Odysseus' lies are directed toward the securing of practical ends, see Most 1989a, 131–32.

has already been introduced in the equally attractive figure of Nausicaa, whom Alcinous wishes to give in marriage to the stranger. Odysseus' Apologoi, then, function rhetorically within the narrative situation as an exhortation to his Phaeacian hosts: "Do not be improper in your hospitality, like the Cyclops, but do not be overzealous either, like Circe and Calypso, and thereby deprive me of my return home."[15] It is a great irony that the Phaeacians, like the Cyclops, ultimately suffer for their expression of hospitality toward Odysseus. While Polyphemus is blinded for offering too little, the Phaeacians are punished by Poseidon for offering too much.

The scene of Odysseus' reception in Eumaeus' hut functions as a foil both to the scene that precedes, Odysseus among the Phaeacians, and to the scene that follows, Odysseus among the suitors. It contrasts with the scene of Odysseus' reception among the Phaeacians in the extreme simplicity of Eumaeus' accommodations vis-à-vis the Phaeacians' luxurious hospitality. But the contrast with the scene that follows, Odysseus' reception by the suitors in his own palace, is much more fully worked out, the kind hospitality enjoyed in Eumaeus' hut acting as a foil to the cruel inhospitality suffered in the palace, just as, in the first hospitality scene of the *Odyssey,* Telemachus' warm reception of Athena acts as a foil to the cold indifference shown her by the suitors.

The contrast between the behavior of Eumaeus and that of the suitors is very explicit. Eumaeus is kindly and hospitable in spite of his poverty; the suitors are hostile and greedy in spite of their wealth. Eumaeus is scrupulous, observing almost all the conventional rituals of proper hospitality; the suitors invert the conventions of hospitality either by disregarding them altogether or by turning them on their head. Eumaeus' piety is notable—he makes frequent reference to Zeus and offers sacrifices and libations to the gods; the suitors do not sacrifice at all, in spite of the frequency and length of their feasts. Eumaeus, as a loyal servant, is faithful to his social contract with his master Odysseus; although

---

15. This is essentially the conclusion of Most (1989b), who, following the structure of the Apologoi proposed by Niles (1978), in which the episodes are grouped in a symmetrical ring-composition around the Necuia, notes that Odysseus has located the paradigms of the two extremes of hospitality at the extremities of his stories—the Polyphemus tale at the beginning, a recapitulation of the Calypso tale at the end. J.M. Redfield (1983, 235–44) similarly divides the adventures of the Apologoi into cases of hypo- and hyperentertainment, observing that Odysseus crisscrosses back and forth between the two extremes. For some further contrasts on a dictional level between the hospitality of the Cyclops and that of the Phaeacians, see chapter 6.

Antinous' father was a suppliant of Odysseus, and although Eurymachus was nurtured by Odysseus as a child, these two, the most prominent of the suitors, repay him with offensive and hubristic behavior. In sum, while Eumaeus shows his guest proper and generous, albeit humble, hospitality and proves to be a model of piety, the suitors are either indifferent to or actually violent toward their guest, overstepping all the bounds of proper behavior. Their treatment of this guest has far-reaching consequences, since the motif of theoxeny is active in both scenes: as in Ovid's tale of Baucis and Philemon (*Met.* 8.611–724), the humble but generous host, Eumaeus, gets the reward, while those with the means to provide even extravagant hospitality, the suitors in the palace, prove inhospitable and are consequently punished.[16]

Hysteron-Proteron Homericos

The most elaborate foil of the *Odyssey,* one that greatly influences the narrative structure of the entire epic, is the placement of the Apologoi in relation to the sequence of hospitality scenes that frames them. This is a sequence of scenes that is particularly well crafted, showing a high degree of planning and careful arrangement over the entire breadth of the narrative. The scenes of proper hospitality—at Ithaca, Pylos, Sparta, and Scheria—are placed early in the epic, in books 1–8, so that they function as paradigms with which all the subsequent scenes of hospitality may be compared or contrasted. Deviations from, and perversions of, these paradigms are presented in the Apologoi, books 9–12—after all, for a parody, such as the Cyclopeia, to work, acquaintance with the established norm is prerequisite. Finally, this sequence of hospitality scenes culminates in the complete inversion of the norm at the end of the *Odyssey,* where the master comes to his own home as a guest and is treated inhospitably by the nominal masters of the house, who under normal circumstances would be the guests. The design of this sequence of scenes is particularly remarkable when one observes that it is only achieved by Homer's hysteron-proteron, the fact that the events of books 9–12, which happened chronologically *before* the events of books 1–8, are arranged narratologically *after* books 1–8.

Such control over the architectonics of an entire epic of the size of

---

16. For a more detailed analysis of the contrasts between these two scenes, see chapters 7 and 8.

the *Odyssey* is a quality often denied Homer by modern literary critics, who, perhaps swayed too much by his admittedly paratactic style, regard such elaborate, large-scale structuring as beyond the ability of a preliterate bard. I suggest that this is merely a modern conceit. In the intricate interplay of his hospitality scenes, around which arises the harmonious and well-balanced structure of the *Odyssey,* Homer clearly exhibits the kind of control over a monumental work that we moderns mistakenly attribute exclusively to the studied, self-conscious, literary texts with which we are perhaps too familiar.

Appendix: Schematic Synopses of Conventions of Hospitality

Athena-Mentes in Ithaca
(*Od.* 1.103–324)

I.	Maiden at the well/Youth on the road	
II.	Arrival at the destination	
III.	Description of the surroundings . . .	
	a. Of the residence	
	b. Of (the activities of) the person sought	1.114–17
	c. Of (the activities of) the others	1.106–12
IV.	Dog at the door	
V.	Waiting at the threshold	1.103–4
VI.	Supplication	
VII.	Reception . . .	
	a. Host catches sight of the visitor	1.113, 118
	b. Host hesitates to offer hospitality	
	c. Host rises from his seat	
	d. Host approaches the visitor	1.119–20
	e. Host attends to the visitor's horses	
	f. Host takes the visitor by the hand	1.121
	g. Host bids the visitor welcome	1.122–24
	h. Host takes the visitor's spear	1.121, 127–29
	i. Host leads the visitor in	1.125
VIII.	Seat	1.130–32, 145
IX.	Feast . . .	
	a. Preparation	1.136–43, 146–[48]

Telemachus in Pylos
(*Od.* 3.4–485; 15.193–214)

Telemachus in Sparta
(*Od.* 4.1–624; 15.1–184)

XX. Guest-gifts	4.589–619; 15.48–55, 75–76, 99–132 ([113–19])
XXI. Departure meal	15.76–79, 92–98, 133–43
XXII. Departure libation	15.147–50
XXIII. Farewell blessing	15.111–12, 128–29, 150–59
XXIV. Departure omen and interpretation	15.160–81
XXV. Escort to visitor's next destination	4.589; 15.64–74

Hermes and Calypso
(*Od.* 5.55–148)

I. Maiden at the well/Youth on the road	
II. Arrival at the destination	5.55–58
III. Description of the surroundings ...	
a. Of the residence	5.59–61, 63–76
b. Of (the activities of) the person sought	5.57–58, 61–62
c. Of (the activities of) the others	5.81–84
IV. Dog at the door	
V. Waiting at the threshold	5.75–76
VI. Supplication	
VII. Reception ...	
a. Host catches sight of the visitor	5.77–78
b. Host hesitates to offer hospitality	
c. Host rises from his seat	
d. Host approaches the visitor	
e. Host attends to the visitor's horses	
f. Host takes the visitor by the hand	
g. Host bids the visitor welcome	
h. Host takes the visitor's spear	
i. Host leads the visitor in	[5.91]
VIII. Seat	5.86
IX. Feast ...	
a. Preparation	5.92–93
b. Consumption	5.94
c. Conclusion	5.95
X. After-dinner drink	

Odysseus and the Phaeacians
(*Od.* 5.388–13.187)

XXII. Departure libation	13.50–56
XXIII. Farewell blessing	8.406–15, 460–68; 13.36–46, 56–62
XXIV. Departure omen and interpretation	
XXV. Escort to visitor's next destination	7.191–98, 226–27, 317–28; 8.30–38, 48–55, 555–71; 11.332, 352–53; 13.4–6, 47–52, 63–125; 16.227–30

Odysseus and Polyphemus
(*Od.* 9.105–564)

I. Maiden at the well/Youth on the road	
II. Arrival at the destination	9.181, 216
III. Description of the surroundings . . .	
a. Of the residence	9.182–86, 218–23
b. Of (the activities of) the person sought	9.187–92, 216–17
c. Of (the activities of) the others	9.188–89
IV. Dog at the door	
V. Waiting at the threshold	
VI. Supplication	9.266–71
VII. Reception . . .	
a. Host catches sight of the visitor	
b. Host hesitates to offer hospitality	
c. Host rises from his seat	
d. Host approaches the visitor	
e. Host attends to the visitor's horses	
f. Host takes the visitor by the hand	
g. Host bids the visitor welcome	
h. Host takes the visitor's spear	
i. Host leads the visitor in	
VIII. Seat	
IX. Feast . . .	
a. Preparation	9.308–11, 341–44
b. Consumption	9.288–93
c. Conclusion	9.296–97

X.	After-dinner drink	9.345-61
XI.	Identification ...	
	a. Host questions the visitor	9.251-55, 355-56
	b. Visitor reveals his identity	9.258-66, 364-67, 504-5
XII.	Exchange of information	9.272-86
XIII.	Entertainment	
XIV.	Visitor pronounces a blessing on the host	
XV.	Visitor shares in a libation or sacrifice	
XVI.	Visitor asks to be allowed to sleep	
XVII.	Bed	9.306, 436
XVIII.	Bath	
XIX.	Host detains the visitor	9.303-5, 313-14, 340, 417-19, 517
XX.	Guest-gifts	9.229, 266-68, 355-56, 364-70, 517
XXI.	Departure meal	
XXII.	Departure libation	9.458-60
XXIII.	Farewell blessing	9.522-35
XXIV.	Departure omen and interpretation	9.550-55
XXV.	Escort to visitor's next destination	9.349-50, 518

Odysseus and Aeolus
(*Od.* 10.1-76)

I.	Maiden at the well/Youth on the road	
II.	Arrival at the destination	10.1, 13, 60
III.	Description of the surroundings ...	
	a. Of the residence	10.3-4
	b.-c. Of (the activities of) the person sought	10.5-12, 60-61
	Of (the activities of) the others	
IV.	Dog at the door	
V.	Waiting at the threshold	10.62-63
VI.	Supplication	
VII.	Reception ...	
	a. Host catches sight of the visitor	

b. Host hesitates to offer hospitality
c. Host rises from his seat
d. Host approaches the visitor
e. Host attends to the visitor's horses
f. Host takes the visitor by the hand
g. Host bids the visitor welcome
h. Host takes the visitor's spear
i. Host leads the visitor in

VIII. Seat
IX. Feast . . .
    a. Preparation
    b. Consumption
    c. Conclusion
X. After-dinner drink
XI. Identification . . .
    a. Host questions the visitor
    b. Visitor reveals his identity

XII. Exchange of information	10.14–16
XIII. Entertainment	10.14–16
XIV. Visitor pronounces a blessing on the host	
XV. Visitor shares in a libation or sacrifice	
XVI. Visitor asks to be allowed to sleep	
XVII. Bed	
XVIII. Bath	
XIX. Host detains the visitor	10.14–16
XX. Guest-gifts	10.19–20, 35–45
XXI. Departure meal	
XXII. Departure libation	
XXIII. Farewell blessing	
XXIV. Departure omen and interpretation	
XXV. Escort to visitor's next destination	10.17–26, 72–76

Odysseus and the Laestrygonians
(*Od.* 10.80–132)

I. Maiden at the well/Youth on the road	10.103–11
II. Arrival at the destination	10.81–82, 87, 112

III. Description of the surroundings...
    a. Of the residence   10.81–99
    b. Of (the activities of) the person sought   10.112–13
    c. Of (the activities of) the others
IV. Dog at the door
 V. Waiting at the threshold
VI. Supplication
VII. Reception...
    a. Host catches sight of the visitor
    b. Host hesitates to offer hospitality
    c. Host rises from his seat
    d. Host approaches the visitor
    e. Host attends to the visitor's horses
    f. Host takes the visitor by the hand
    g. Host bids the visitor welcome
    h. Host takes the visitor's spear
    i. Host leads the visitor in
VIII. Seat
IX. Feast...
    a. Preparation   10.116
    b. Consumption
    c. Conclusion
 X. After-dinner drink
XI. Identification...
    a. Host questions the visitor
    b. Visitor reveals his identity
XII. Exchange of information
XIII. Entertainment
XIV. Visitor pronounces a blessing on the host
XV. Visitor shares in a libation or sacrifice
XVI. Visitor asks to be allowed to sleep
XVII. Bed
XVIII. Bath
XIX. Host detains the visitor
XX. Guest-gifts
XXI. Departure meal
XXII. Departure libation
XXIII. Farewell blessing

XXIV. Departure omen and interpretation
XXV. Escort to visitor's next destination

Odysseus and Circe
(*Od.* 10.133–11.12; 12.1–152)

I. Maiden at the well/Youth on the road	10.274–306
II. Arrival at the destination	10.135, 210, 308–9; 12.2–3
III. Description of the surroundings ...	
a. Of the residence	10.194–97, 210–19; 12.3–4
b. Of (the activities of) the person sought	10.135–39, 221–23
c. Of (the activities of) the others	
IV. Dog at the door	10.212–19
V. Waiting at the threshold	10.220, 310–11
VI. Supplication	
VII. Reception ...	
a. Host catches sight of the visitor	
b. Host hesitates to offer hospitality	
c. Host rises from his seat	
d. Host approaches the visitor	10.230, 312
e. Host attends to the visitor's horses	
f. Host takes the visitor by the hand	
g. Host bids the visitor welcome	
h. Host takes the visitor's spear	
i. Host leads the visitor in	10.231, 233, 313–14
VIII. Seat	10.233, 314–[15], 366–67
IX. Feast ...	
a. Preparation	10.234–36, 316–17, 352–57, [368–72]; 12.18–19, 23–24
b. Consumption	10.375–76, 452, 460, 467–68, [476–77]; 12.29–30

Odysseus and Eumaeus
(*Od.* 13.221–14.533; 15.301–494; 16.452–17.25; 17.182–203)

Telemachus and Eumaeus
(*Od.* 15.555–16.155)

XII. Exchange of information	16.30–39, 90–153
XIII. Entertainment	
XIV. Visitor pronounces a blessing on the host	
XV. Visitor shares in a libation or sacrifice	
XVI. Visitor asks to be allowed to sleep	
XVII. Bed	
XVIII. Bath	
XIX. Host detains the visitor	16.82
XX. Guest-gifts	16.79–80, 83–84
XXI. Departure meal	
XXII. Departure libation	
XXIII. Farewell blessing	
XXIV. Departure omen and interpretation	
XXV. Escort to visitor's next destination	16.81

Odysseus' Homecoming
(*Od.* 17.204–23.348)

I. Maiden at the well/Youth on the road	17.204–53
II. Arrival at the destination	17.260–61, 336
III. Description of the surroundings . . .	
a. Of the residence	17.263–68
b.–c. Of (the activities of) the person sought	17.261–63, 269–71
Of (the activities of) the others	
IV. Dog at the door	17.291–327
V. Waiting at the threshold	17.261, 339–41
VI. Supplication	
VII. Reception . . .	
a. Host catches sight of the visitor	
b. Host hesitates to offer hospitality	
c. Host rises from his seat	
d. Host approaches the visitor	
e. Host attends to the visitor's horses	
f. Host takes the visitor by the hand	
g. Host bids the visitor welcome	
h. Host takes the visitor's spear	
i. Host leads the visitor in	

The Embassy to Achilles
(*Il.* 9.185–668)

Nestor and Odysseus in Phthia
(*Il.* 11.769–82)

f. Host takes the visitor by the hand	11.778
g. Host bids the visitor welcome	
h. Host takes the visitor's spear	
i. Host leads the visitor in	11.778
VIII. Seat	11.778
IX. Feast...	
a. Preparation	11.779
b. Consumption	
c. Conclusion	11.780
X. After-dinner drink	
XI. Identification...	
a. Host questions the visitor	
b. Visitor reveals his identity	
XII. Exchange of information	11.781–82
XIII. Entertainment	
XIV. Visitor pronounces a blessing on the host	
XV. Visitor shares in a libation or sacrifice	
XVI. Visitor asks to be allowed to sleep	
XVII. Bed	
XVIII. Bath	
XIX. Host detains the visitor	
XX. Guest-gifts	
XXI. Departure meal	
XXII. Departure libation	
XXIII. Farewell blessing	
XXIV. Departure omen and interpretation	
XXV. Escort to visitor's next destination	

Thetis and Hephaestus
(*Il.* 18.369–19.3)

I. Maiden at the well/Youth on the road	
II. Arrival at the destination	18.369, [381]
III. Description of the surroundings...	
a. Of the residence	18.370–71
b. Of (the activities of) the person sought	18.372–80
c. Of (the activities of) the others	18.373–79
IV. Dog at the door	
V. Waiting at the threshold	

Priam and Achilles
(*Il.* 24.334–694)

Demeter in the Home of Celeos
(*H.Dem.* 98–230)

Aphrodite and Anchises
(*H.Aphr.* 68–291)

References

Abbreviations are those of *L'Année philologique,* with the exceptions of *CP* for *CPh, TAPA* for *TAPhA, AJP* for *AJPh,* and *HSCP* for *HSPh.*

Allen, T.W. 1912. *Homeri Opera, Tomus V, "Hymnos" "Cyclum" "Fragmenta" "Margiten" "Batrachomyomachiam" "Vitas" Continens.* Oxford.
———. 1917-19. *Homeri Opera, Tomi III-IV, "Odysseae" Libros Continentes.* 2d ed. Oxford.
———. [1924] 1969. *Homer: The Origins and the Transmission.* Oxford.
Allen, T.W. and D.B. Monro. 1920. *Homeri Opera, Tomi I-II, "Iliadis" Libros Continentes.* 3d ed. Oxford.
Alter, R. 1981. *The Art of Biblical Narrative.* New York.
Andersen, Ø. 1977. "Odysseus and the Wooden Horse." *SO* 52:5-18.
Anderson, W.S. 1958. "Calypso and Elysium." *CJ* 54:2-11.
Apthorp, M.J. 1980a. *The Manuscript Evidence for Interpolation in Homer.* Heidelberg.
———. 1980b. "The Obstacles to Telemachus' Return." *CQ* 30:1-22.
Arend, W. 1933. *Die typischen Scenen bei Homer.* Berlin.
Armstrong, J.I. 1958. "The Arming Motif in the *Iliad.*" *AJP* 79:337-54.
Austin, N. 1969. "Telemachos Polymechanos." *California Studies in Classical Antiquity* 2:45-63.
———. 1972. "Name Magic in the *Odyssey.*" *California Studies in Classical Antiquity* 5:1-19.
———. 1975. *Archery at the Dark of the Moon.* Berkeley.
Bader, F. 1976. "L'art de la fugue dans l'*Odyssée.*" *REG* 89:18-39.
Barck, C. 1971. "Menelaos bei Homer." *WS* 5:5-28.
Bassett, S.E. 1938. *The Poetry of Homer.* Berkeley.
Beck, W. 1991. "Dogs, Dwellings, and Masters: Ensemble and Symbol in the *Odyssey.*" *Hermes* 119:158-67.
Belmont, D. 1962. *Early Greek Guest-Friendship and Its Role in Homer's "Odyssey."* Ph.D. diss., Princeton.
———. 1967. "Telemachus and Nausicaa: A Study of Youth." *CJ* 63:1-9.
Benveniste, E. 1969. *Le vocabulaire des institutions indo-européennes.* Paris.

233

Bérard, V. 1930. *La résurrection d'Homère: Au temps des héros: Le drame épique.* Paris.

Bergren, A.L.T. 1981. "Helen's 'Good Drug': *Odyssey* IV 1–305." In *Contemporary Literary Hermeneutics and Interpretation of Classical Texts,* ed. S. Kresic, 201–14. Ottawa.

Bethe, E. 1922. *Homer II.* Leipzig.

Block, E. 1982. "The Narrator Speaks: Apostrophe in Homer and Vergil." *TAPA* 112:7–22.

———. 1985. "Clothing Makes the Man: A Pattern in the *Odyssey.*" *TAPA* 115:1–11.

Bolling, G.M. [1925] 1968. *The External Evidence for Interpolation in Homer.* Oxford.

Bremmer, J. 1980. "Gelon's Wife and the Carthaginian Ambassadors." *Mnemosyne* 33:366–68.

Brown, C. 1966. "Odysseus and Polyphemus: The Name and the Curse." *Comparative Literature* 18:193–202.

Buck, C.D. [1955] 1973. *The Greek Dialects.* Chicago.

Burnett, A.P. 1970. "Pentheus and Dionysus: Host and Guest." *CP* 65:15–29.

Calhoun, G.M. 1933. "Homeric Repetitions." *University of California Publications in Classical Philology* 12:1–26.

Cauer, P. 1909. *Grundfragen der Homerkritik.* Leipzig.

Chantraine, P. 1973. *Grammaire homérique: Tome I: Phonétique et morphologie.* 2d ed. Paris.

Clarke, H.C. 1963. "Telemachus and the Telemacheia." *AJP* 84:129–45.

Clay, J.S. 1980. "Goat Island: *Od.* 9.116–141." *CQ* 74:261–64.

———. 1983. *The Wrath of Athena.* Princeton.

Coldstream, J.N. 1983. "Gift Exchange in the Eighth Century B.C." In *The Greek Renaissance of the Eighth Century B.C.: Tradition and Innovation,* ed. R. Hägg, 201–7. Stockholm.

Cook, A.B. 1925. *Zeus II pt. 2.* Cambridge.

Coote, M.P. 1981. "Lying in Passages." *Canadian-American Slavic Studies* 15 (1): 5–23.

Crane, G. 1988. *Calypso: Backgrounds and Conventions of the "Odyssey."* Beiträge zur klassischen Philologie 191. Frankfurt am Main.

Dawkins, R.M. 1955. *More Greek Folktales.* Oxford.

Delebecque, E. 1958. *Télémaque et la structure de "l'Odyssée."* Aix-en-Provence.

De Vries, G.J. 1977. "Phaeacian Manners." *Mnemosyne* 30 (2): 113–21.

Dindorf, G. 1855. *Scholia Graeca in Homeri "Odysseam."* Oxford.

Donlan, W. 1982a. "The Politics of Generosity in Homer." *Helios* 9 (2): 1–15.

———. 1982b. "Reciprocities in Homer." *CW* 75 (3): 137–75.

Dupont-Roc, R., and A. Le Boulluec. 1976. "Le charme du récit." In *Écriture et Théorie Poétiques,* 30–39. Paris.

Edwards, M.W. 1975. "Type-Scenes and Homeric Hospitality." *TAPA* 105: 51–72.

———. 1980. "Convention and Individuality in *Iliad* 1." *HSCP* 84:1–28.

———. 1987a. *Homer: Poet of the "Iliad."* Baltimore.

———. 1987b. "*Topos* and Transformation in Homer." In *Homer: Beyond Oral Poetry,* ed. J.M. Bremer, I.J.F. De Jong, and J. Kalff, 47–60. Amsterdam.

———. 1991. *The "Iliad": A Commentary,* ed. G.S. Kirk. Vol. 5. Cambridge.

Eisenberger, H. 1973. *Studien zur "Odyssee."* Wiesbaden.

Erbse, H. 1972. *Beiträge zum Verständnis der "Odyssee."* Berlin.

Fenik, B. 1968. *Typical Battle Scenes in the "Iliad."* Hermes Einzelschriften 21. Wiesbaden.

———. 1974. *Studies in the "Odyssey."* Hermes Einzelschriften 30. Wiesbaden.

Finley, M. 1955. "Marriage, Sale and Gift in the Homeric World." *RIDA,* 3d ser., 2:167–94.

———. [1965] 1978. *World of Odysseus.* New York.

Focke, F. 1943. *Die "Odyssee."* Stuttgart.

Foley, J.M. 1986. "Tradition and the Collective Talent: Oral Epic, Textual Meaning, and Receptionalist Theory." *Cultural Anthropology* 1:203–22.

———. 1987. "Reading the Oral Traditional Text: Aesthetics of Creation and Response." In *Comparative Research on Oral Tradition: A Memorial for Milman Parry,* ed. J.M. Foley, 185–212. Columbus, Ohio.

———. 1988. *The Theory of Oral Composition: History and Methodology.* Bloomington.

———. 1990. *Traditional Oral Epic: The "Odyssey," "Beowulf," and the Serbo-Croatian Return Song.* Berkeley.

Fontenrose, J. 1945. "Philemon, Lot, and Lycaon." *University of California Publications in Classical Philology* 13:93–119.

Frame, D. 1978. *The Myth of Return in Early Greek Epic.* New Haven.

Fränkel, H. [1931] 1960. "Die Zeitauffassung in der frühgriechischen Literatur." In Fränkel, *Wege und Formen frühgriechischen Denkens,* 1–22. Munich.

Frazer, J.G., ed. 1921. *Apollodorus: The Library.* London.

Frazer, R.M. 1971. "The Κλισμός of Achilles, *Iliad* 24.596–98." *GRBS* 12: 295–301.

Germain, G. 1954. *Genèse de "l'Odyssée."* Paris.

Glenn, J. 1971. "The Polyphemus Folktale and Homer's Kyklopeia." *TAPA* 102:133–81.

Gould, J.P. 1973. "Hiketeia." *JHS* 93:74–103.

Grenfell, B.P., and A.S. Hunt. 1901. *The Amherst Papyri.* Vol. 2. London.

Griffin, J. 1977. "The Epic Cycle and the Uniqueness of Homer." *JHS* 97: 39–53.

Grimm, W. 1857. "Die Sage von Polyphem." *Abhandlungen der Königl. Akad. der Wiss. zu Berlin,* 1–30.

Gunn, D. 1970. "Narrative Inconsistency and the Oral Dictated Text in the Homeric Epic." *AJP* 91:192–203.

Hackman, O. 1904. *Die Polyphemsage in der Volksüberlieferung.* Helsinki.

Hainsworth, J.B. 1969. "Homer." *Greece and Rome: New Surveys no. 3.* Oxford.

Hellwig, B. 1964. *Raum und Zeit im homerischen Epos.* Hildesheim.

Heubeck, A. 1954. *Der "Odyssee"-Dichter und die "Ilias."* Erlangen.

Heubeck, A., and A. Hoekstra. 1989. *A Commentary on Homer's "Odyssey."* Vol. 2. Oxford.

Heubeck, A., S. West, and J.B. Hainsworth. 1988. *A Commentary on Homer's "Odyssey."* Vol. 1. Oxford.

Hirvonen, K. 1968. *Matriarchal Survivals and Certain Trends in Homer's Female Characters.* Helsinki.

Hoekstra, A. 1965. *Homeric Modifications of Formulaic Prototypes.* Amsterdam.

Hollis, A.S. [1970] 1985. *Ovid, "Metamorphoses," Book VIII.* Oxford.

Hölscher, U. 1939. *Untersuchungen zur Form der "Odyssee."* Hermes Einzelschriften 6. Berlin.

Hooker, J.T. 1989. "Gifts in Homer." *BICS* 36:79–90.

Houston, G.W. 1975. "Θρόνος, Δίφρος, and Odysseus' Change from Beggar to Avenger." *CP* 70:212–14.

Hunt, A.S. 1911. *Catalogue of the Greek Papyri in the John Rylands Library.* Vol. 1. Manchester.

Jaeger, W. 1945. *Paideia: Volume I.* 2d ed. Trans. G. Highet. Oxford.

Janko, R. 1982. *Homer, Hesiod and the Hymns.* Cambridge.

———. 1992. *The "Iliad": A Commentary,* ed. G.S. Kirk. Vol. 4. Cambridge.

Jones, P.V. 1989. "*Odyssey* 6.209–23: The Instructions to Bathe." *Mnemosyne* 42:349–64.

Kakridis, H. 1963. *La notion de l'amitié et de l'hospitalité chez Homère.* Thessaloniki.

Kakridis, J.T. 1971. "Problems of the Homeric Helen." In Kakridis, *Homer Revisited,* 25–53. Lund.

———. 1975. "Griechische Mahlzeits- und Gastlichkeitsbräuche." In *Dialogus. Für Harald Patzer zum 65. Geburtstag von seinen Freunden und Schülern,* ed. J. Cobet, R. Leimbach, and A.B. Neschke-Hentschke, 13–21. Wiesbaden.

Kearns, E. 1982. "The Return of Odysseus: A Homeric Theoxeny." *CQ* 76:2–8.

Kilb, H. 1973. *Strukturen epischen Gestaltens im 7. und 23. Gesang der "Odyssee."* Munich.

Kirchhoff, A. 1879. *Die homerische "Odyssee."* Berlin.

Kirk, G.S. 1962. *The Songs of Homer.* Cambridge.

———. 1985. *The "Iliad": A Commentary,* ed. G.S. Kirk. Vol. 1. Cambridge.

Klingner, F. [1944] 1964. "Über die vier ersten Bücher der *Odyssee.*" In Klingner, *Studien zur griechischen und römischen Literatur,* 39–79. Zürich.

Krischer, T. 1985. "Phäaken und *Odyssee.*" *Hermes* 113:9–21.

Kullmann, W. 1960. *Die Quellen der "Ilias."* Wiesbaden.

Lang, M. 1969. "Homer and Oral Techniques." *Hesperia* 38:159–68.

Laser, S. 1968. *Hausrat.* In Archaeologia Homerica: Die Denkmäler und das frühgriechische Epos. II Kap. P, ed. F. Matz and H.G. Buchholz. Göttingen.

Leeuwen, J. van. 1911. "Homerica." *Mnemosyne* 39:19–30.

Levine, D. 1984. "Odysseus' Smiles: *Odyssey* 20.301, 22.371, 23.111." *TAPA* 114:1–9.

Levy, H. 1963. "The Odyssean Suitors and the Host-Guest Relationship." *TAPA* 94:145–53.

Lord, A.B. 1951. "Composition by Theme in Homer and Southslavic Epos." *TAPA* 82:71–80.

———. 1960. *The Singer of Tales.* Cambridge, Mass.

Ludwich, A. 1888–90. *Scholia in Homeri "Odysseae" A 1–309 Auctiora et Emendatiora.* Königsberg.

Malten, L. 1939. "Motivgeschichtliche Untersuchungen zur Sagenforschung." *Hermes* 74:176–206.

Matthews, V.J. 1980. "Metrical Reasons for Apostrophe in Homer." *Liverpool Classical Monthly* 5:93–99.

Mauss, M. 1924. *Le don, forme primitive de l'échange.* L'Année Sociologique. Paris.

Merkelbach, R. 1951. *Untersuchungen zur "Odyssee."* Munich.

Meuli, K. 1921. *"Odyssee" und "Argonautika."* Berlin.

Millar, C.M.H., and J.W.S. Carmichael. 1954. "The Growth of Telemachus." *Greece & Rome* 1:58–64.

Mondi, R. 1983. "The Homeric Cyclopes: Folktale, Tradition, and Theme." *TAPA* 113:17–38.

Monro, D.B. 1901. *Homer's "Odyssey": Books XIII to XXIV.* Oxford.

Most, G. 1989a. "The Stranger's Stratagem: Self-Disclosure and Self-Sufficiency in Greek Culture." *JHS* 109:114–33.

———. 1989b. "The Structure and Function of Odysseus' *Apologoi.*" *TAPA* 119:15–30.

Mühll, P. von der. 1940. "Odyssee." *RE,* supplementband, 7:696–768.

Murnaghan, S. 1987. *Disguise and Recognition in the "Odyssey."* Princeton.

Nagy, J. 1981. "The Deceptive Gift in Greek Mythology." *Arethusa* 14 (2): 191–204.

Nestle, W. 1942. "Odysseeinterpretationen." *Hermes* 77:46–77.

Niles, J.D. 1978. "Patterning in the Wanderings of Odysseus." *Ramus* 7:46–60.

Olson, S.D. 1989. "The Stories of Helen and Menelaus." *AJP* 110:387–94.

Page, D.L. 1955. *The Homeric "Odyssey."* Oxford.

Parry, A.M., ed. 1971. *The Making of Homeric Verse: The Collected Papers of Milman Parry.* Oxford.

———. 1972. "Language and Characterization in Homer." *HSCP* 76:1–22.

Paton, W.R. 1912. "Book VIII of the *Odyssey.*" *CR* 26:215–16.

Pitt-Rivers, J. [1967] 1977a. "The Law of Hospitality." In Pitt-Rivers, *The Fate of Shechem,* 94–112. Cambridge. Originally published in "La loi de l'hospitalité." *Les Temps Modernes* 22 (4): no. 253 (June 1967).

———. [1970] 1977b. "Women and Sanctuary in the Mediterranean." In Pitt-Rivers, *The Fate of Shechem,* 113–25. Cambridge. Originally published in *Studies in General Anthropology,* Vol. 2, ed. D. Bidney, D. Hymes, P.E. de J. de Jong, and E.R. Leach, 862–75 (Paris, 1970).

Podlecki, A.J. 1961. "Guest-Gifts and Nobodies in *Odyssey* 9." *Phoenix* 15: 125–33.

Poestion, J.C. 1886. *Lappländische Märchen.* Vienna.

Powell, B.B. 1977. *Composition by Theme in the "Odyssey."* Beiträge zur klassischen Philologie 81. Meisenheim am Glan.

Propp, V.J., and B.N. Putilov, eds. 1958. *Byliny.* Vol. I. Moscow.

Redfield, J.M. 1983. "The Economic Man." In *Approaches to Homer,* ed. C.A. Rubino and C.W. Shelmerdine, 218–47. Austin.

Redfield, R. 1956. *Peasant Society and Culture*. Chicago.

Reece, S. 1988. "Homeric Influence in Stesichorus' *Nostoi*." *BASP* 25:1–8.

Reinhardt, K. 1948. *Von Werken und Formen*. Godesberg.

Richardson, N.J. 1974. *The Homeric "Hymn to Demeter*." Oxford.

———. 1983. "Recognition Scenes in the *Odyssey*." *Papers of the Liverpool Latin Seminar* 4:223–25.

Röhrich, L. 1962. "Die mittelalterlichen Redaktionen des Polyphem-Märchens (AT 1137) und ihr Verhältnis zur ausserhomerischen Tradition." *Fabula* 5:48–71.

Rose, G.P. 1967. "The Quest of Telemachus." *TAPA* 98:391–98.

———. 1969a. *The Song of Ares and Aphrodite: Recurrent Motifs in Homer's "Odyssey*." Ph.D. diss., University of California, Berkeley.

———. 1969b. "The Unfriendly Phaeacians." *TAPA* 100:387–406.

———. 1971. "*Odyssey* 15.143–82: A Narrative Inconsistency?" *TAPA* 102: 509–14.

———. 1979. "Odysseus' Barking Heart." *TAPA* 109:215–30.

Rothe, C. 1914. *Die "Odyssee" als Dichtung*. Paderborn.

Russo, J. 1985. *Omero, "Odissea," libri xvii–xx*. Rome.

Rüter, K. 1969. *Odysseeinterpretationen*. Hypomnemata 19. Göttingen.

Saïd, S. 1979. "Les crimes des prétendants, la maison d'Ulysse et les festins de l'*Odyssée*." *Études de Littérature Ancienne*, 9–49. Paris.

Saussure, F. de. 1959. *Course in General Linguistics*. Trans. Wade Baskin. New York.

Schadewaldt, W. 1959. "Kleiderdinge: Zur Analyse der *Odyssee*." *Hermes* 87: 13–26.

———. 1965. *Von Homers Welt und Werk*. 4th ed. Stuttgart.

Schein, S.L. 1970. "Odysseus and Polyphemus in the *Odyssey*." *GRBS* 11:73–83.

Schmiel, R. 1972. "Telemachus in Sparta." *TAPA* 103:463–72.

Schwartz, E. 1924. *Die "Odyssee*." Munich.

Scott, J.A. 1917. "The Journey Made by Telemachus and Its Influence on the Action of the *Odyssey*." *CJ* 13:420–28.

———. [1921] 1965. *The Unity of Homer*. Berkeley. Reprint New York.

Scott, W.C. 1971. "A Repeated Episode at *Odyssey* 1.125–48." *TAPA* 102: 541–51.

Segal, C. 1962. "The Phaeacians and the Symbolism of Odysseus' Return." *Arion* 1 (4): 17–64.

———. 1967. "Transition and Ritual in Odysseus' Return." *La Parola del Passato* 40:331–42.

Seitz, E. 1950. *Die Stellung der "Telemachie" im Aufbau der "Odyssee*." Ph.D. diss., Marburg.

Shelmerdine, C. 1969. "The Pattern of Guest Welcome in the *Odyssey*." *CJ* 65:124.

Shewan, A. 1926. "Telemachus in Sparta." *CJ* 22:31–37.

Shipp, G.P. 1972. *Studies in the Language of Homer*. 2d ed. Cambridge.

Sowa, C. 1984. *Traditional Themes and the Homeric Hymns*. Chicago.

Stallbaum, G. [1825–30] 1960. *Eustathii Commentaria ad "Iliadem" et "Odysseam."* Leipzig. Reprint Hildesheim.

Stanford, W.B. 1939. *Ambiguity in Greek Literature.* Oxford.

———. 1958–59. *The "Odyssey" of Homer.* 2d ed. London.

Stewart, D. 1976. *The Disguised Guest.* Lewisburg.

Stummer, A. 1886. *Über den Artikel bei Homer.* Schweinfurt.

Thompson, S. 1955–58. *Motif Index of Folk Literature.* Copenhagen.

Thornton, A. 1970. *People and Themes in Homer's "Odyssey."* London.

Valavánis, I.G. 1884. "Tepekózis." *Astír tou Pontou* 1:135

Valk, M. van der. 1949. *Textual Criticism of the "Odyssey."* Leiden.

———. 1964. *Researches on the Text and Scholia of the "Iliad."* Vol. 2. Leiden.

Vernant, J.P. 1977. "Sacrifice et alimentation humaine. A propos du Prométhée d'Hésiode." *Annali della Scuola Normale Superiore di Pisa* (Classe di Lettere e Filosofia, 3.7.3).

Vidal-Naquet, P. 1970. "Valeurs religieuses et mythiques de la terre et du sacrifice dans l'*Odyssée.*" *Annales (ESC)* 25:1278–97.

———. 1981. *Le chasseur noir: Formes de pensées et formes de société dans le monde grec.* Paris.

West, M.L. 1988. "The Rise of Greek Epic." *JHS* 108:151–72.

West, S. 1967. *The Ptolemaic Papyri of Homer.* Cologne.

Whitman, C. 1958. *Homer and the Heroic Tradition.* Cambridge, Mass.

Wilamowitz-Moellendorff, U. von. 1884. *Homerische Untersuchungen.* Berlin.

Williams, F. 1986. "Odysseus' Homecoming as a Parody of Homeric Formal Welcomes." *CW* 79 (6): 395–97.

Woodhouse, W.J. 1930. *The Composition of Homer's "Odyssey."* Oxford.

Yamagata, N. 1989. "The Apostrophe in Homer as Part of the Oral Technique." *BICS* 36:91–103.

Zielinski, T. 1899–1901. "Die Behandlung gleichzeitiger Ereignisse im antiken Epos." *Philologus,* supplementband, 8:407–49.

General Index

Index Locorum